Documentum 6.5 Content Management Foundations

EMC Proven Professional Certification Exam E20-120 Study Guide

Master Documentum Fundamentals and Ace the E20-120 Exam

Pawan Kumar

BIRMINGHAM - MUMBAI

Documentum 6.5 Content Management Foundations
EMC Proven Professional Certification Exam E20-120 Study Guide

Copyright © 2010 Packt Publishing

First published: June 2010

Production Reference: 1250510

Published by Packt Publishing Ltd.
32 Lincoln Road
Olton
Birmingham, B27 6PA, UK.

ISBN 978-1-849680-22-6

www.packtpub.com

Cover Image by Tina Negus (tina_manthorpe@sky.com)

Credits

Author
Pawan Kumar

Reviewers
Robin East

Johnny Gee

Ajith Prabhakar

Acquisition Editor
Douglas Paterson

Development Editor
Dhiraj Chandiramani

Technical Editor
Tariq Rakhange

Indexer
Rekha Nair

Editorial Team Leader
Mithun Sehgal

Project Team Leader
Lata Basantani

Project Coordinator
Joel Goveya

Proofreader
Aaron Nash

Graphics
Geetanjali Sawant

Production Coordinator
Melwyn D'sa

Cover Work
Melwyn D'sa

About the Author

Pawan Kumar is a Technical Architect specializing in content management, particularly on the EMC Documentum platform. His expertise spans solution architecture, document management, system integration, web content management, business process management, imaging and input management, and custom application development. He is intimately familiar with effective processes and tools for achieving business objectives through Documentum-based solutions. He has also created two products for the Documentum platform.

Pawan has been architecting, designing, and developing enterprise applications for over ten years. He has developed software systems for financial services, healthcare, pharmaceutical, logistics, energy services, and retail industries. He is the author of *Documentum Content Management Foundations: EMC Proven Professional Certification Exam E20-120 Study Guide*, which was written for Documentum version 5.3.

Pawan earned his M.S. in Computer Science from the University of North Carolina at Chapel Hill and his B.S. in Electrical Engineering from the Indian Institute of Technology, New Delhi (India).

As a Principal at **doQuent** (http://doquent.com), Pawan has been helping clients succeed for the last three years via consulting and training services. He also serves as Director of Management Services (Technology) at Prax|Sage Inc. He has also been giving back to the community in various ways. He founded the free online Documentum community—*dm_cram* (http://dmcram.org), which is a test preparation resource for Documentum exams and has helped over 3,500 community members since its launch. He shares technical tips and his experiences via his blog—**Content Management etc**. (http://doquent.wordpress.com). He has also been contributing to various online Documentum forums. He can be reached at pk@doquent.com.

Acknowledgement

I dedicate this book to my parents.

This book would not have been possible without the unrelenting support of my wife. Working on this book also kept me away from my kids who persistently sought my attention.

I am immensely indebted to the technical reviewers—Johnny Gee, Robin East, and Ajith P. Menon, for the quality of the contents of this book. They provided painstakingly detailed feedback which helped improve the accuracy and suitability of the text. Johnny, Robin, and Ajith are well known in the Documentum community through their blogs and contributions to Documentum forums.

The entire PACKT team working on this book has once again made the experience a thoroughly pleasant one. I would like to thank Joel Goveya, Lata Basantani, Dhiraj Chandiramani, and everyone else who worked on this book behind the scenes.

I thank Scott Evans and his team at Family Mortgage of Georgia for sharing their loan origination and approval processes with me. The example business scenario in the book would have been simplistic without their contribution.

I thank Laura DelBueno for continuously challenging me to improve and for providing a pleasant work environment during my core work day.

I thank my friends who have been exceptionally patient and understanding while I worked on this book. I particularly thank Sumitra Tyagi, Manmohan Singh, Saket Kumar, and Rohit Bhagat for their support and encouragement while I worked on this book.

Finally, I thank the members of *dm_cram* (http://dmcram.org), who provided a constant stream of feedback on the first book and confirmed the need for this one.

About the Reviewers

Robin East has worked with Documentum since 1999 covering the evolution of Documentum from EDMS98 through Documentum 6.5. He has worked on numerous Documentum-related projects, mainly in the Banking, Telecommunications and Government sectors, performing all manner of roles from Developer to Technical Consultant to Development Manager.

He specializes in Documentum system performance tuning and is recognized as a world-wide expert in tuning Documentum on Oracle. His biggest tuning success so far is to improve the display of a properties screen that would have taken several days to display; some judicious re-writing of DQL provided the required sub-second performance.

He also maintains a popular Documentum internals and tuning blog, **Inside Documentum** (`http://robineast.wordpress.com`), and founded the Documentum performance tuning consultancy Xense (`http://www.xense.co.uk`). Xense sells the Documentum performance tuning tools Xense Profiler and Xense Profiler for DFC.

Johnny Gee is the Chief Technology Officer at Beach Street Consulting, Inc. In that role, he is responsible for architecting solutions for multiple clients across various industries and building **Content Enabled Vertical Applications (CEVA)** on the Documentum platform. He has over 12 years of experience in ECM system design and implementation, with a proven record of successful Documentum project implementations.

In addition to earning his undergraduate degree in Aerospace Engineering from the University of Maryland, Johnny achieved two graduate degrees; one in Aerospace Engineering from Georgia Institute of Technology, and another in Information Systems Technology from George Washington University.

Johnny is an EMC Proven Professional Specialist in Application Development in Content Management and helped co-author EMC Documentum Server Programming certification exam. He holds the position of top contributor to the EMC Support Forums and is one of twenty EMC Community Experts worldwide. He has been invited on multiple occasions to the EMC Software Developer Conference and has spoken at EMC World. He also has a blog dedicated to designing Documentum solutions.

Ajith Prabhakar is a lawyer turned software expert. He has over 10 years of experience in the IT industry. His Documentum career started when he joined the EMC Documentum Engineering team in 2004. He was actively involved in the development and feature enhancements of Documentum Business Process Services (currently known as Documentum Process Integrator). Eventually he moved out of EMC and got into Documentum customization and consulting. During this consulting period he worked with many Fortune 500 companies on various projects.

He is also known for his blog **A Beginners guide to Documentum** (www.ajithp.com). He is also a part of EMC Documentum Community and has been featured as a Community Expert by EMC Developer community.

He is married to Usha and they have a daughter Aditi. He spends his spare time experimenting with photography and playing with his sweet little daughter Aditi.

Table of Contents

Part 2 – Security

Part 3 – User Interface

Part 4 – Application Development

Part 5 – Advanced Concepts

The Appendices are available for free at http://www.packtpub.com/
sites/default/files/0226EN_Appendices.zip.

The Practice Tests are available for free at http://www.packtpub.com/
sites/default/files/0226EN_Practice tests.zip.

Preface

Two years ago, I wrote *Documentum Content Management Foundations* to help readers prepare for the E20-120 (EMC Documentum Content Management Foundations) exam. A secondary goal of the book was to provide a gentle introduction to Documentum for new-comers. The key challenge in meeting this goal was to present a large number of concepts, some of them quite complex, in an easy-to-understand form. The book included a significant number of practice questions to support test preparation. The questions were designed to test comprehension and the application of concepts. After the book was released, I used the online community *dm_cram* (`http://dmcram.org`) to provide additional test preparation resources and to connect with the readers directly. Direct interaction with the readers and similarly interested community members has provided me with an extremely enriching experience.

Over the last two years, I learned much about readers' likes, dislikes, and wishes. I also gathered the opinions of some Documentum experts about the book. I also discovered what I would like to do differently if I had to do it all over again. For example, I wished that the book had more details on certain topics. Two major Documentum versions were released during this time and I have received an increasing number of queries from the readers about a new book for versions 6.x. With all the accumulated ideas and this new demand, the time was ripe for a new book.

That brings us to this book and readers familiar with the first one must have already noticed the eye-popping weight gain. It is no longer the featherweight that you could run through in a couple of days to take the exam. However, the added benefits should far outweigh the few extra ounces and keep the book relevant for reference in everyday Documentum development. This book is based on version 6.5 SP2 yet it preserves some content specific to version 5.3 to satisfy the exam syllabus. It provides more depth in discussion supported by a large number of illustrations. It uses one example business scenario to connect various concepts discussed throughout the book. There are over 120 new practice questions. Finally, the three stellar technical reviewers for this book have a long history of helping the Documentum community. Hopefully, their diverse and insightful perspectives have rounded out this book into a valuable resource for Documentum professionals.

EMC Documentum is the leading **enterprise content management (ECM)** platform. EMC Proven Professional certification is an exam-based certification program, that introduced Content Management certifications in 2007. The core exam for these certifications is the **Content Management Foundations Associate-level Exam**, whose exam code is E20-120.

This book is a complete study guide and includes study material and practice questions for test preparation. Even though this book focuses on test preparation, it strives to serve Documentum beginners and practitioners irrespective of their interest in the certification exam. It can also serve as a handy guide and quick reference to the technical fundamentals that is fully up to date for Documentum 6.5 SP2. Concepts are introduced in a logical order for beginners while practitioners can use it as a reference to jump to the desired concepts directly.

Enterprise Content Management (ECM)

Electronic content is common in everyday life today. Resumes, emails, spreadsheets, digital pictures, scanned documents or images, audio files, and video clips are some examples of electronic content that we use in our personal lives. Managing such electronic content often consists of saving them in appropriate folder structure and finding them by folder path or the search capability provided by the operating system of the computer.

Organizations often have a larger variety of content to manage, for example, letters, invoices, policies, standards, procedures, project plans, marketing collateral, product specifications, and reports. Their content management needs also go far beyond saving and searching files. Versioning, security, auditing, metadata management, reporting, and business process management are some such needs. Some organizations rely heavily on information workers for most of their business operations. For example, a mortgage lender uses loan application, several forms, and supporting documents to verify information in the application. These documents are used in various parts of the loan approval process.

The content management discipline brings the same rigor to managing *unstructured* content (for example, documents) that databases brought to structured data decades ago. Content management addresses various aspects of creating, manipulating, and accessing content including lifecycle and business process automation. Content lifecycle helps move content through various stages of its life, often starting with creation and ending with expiration and archiving. Automating business processes that manipulate content can bring efficiency to operations and can create a searchable record of events, actions, and performers involved in these processes.

ECM takes these content management aspects to enterprise scales (large number of users, high availability, distributed deployments, high performance, and so on) and enables integration with other systems, which can act as sources or consumers of managed content.

While ECM refers to management of electronic documents in general, several specialized forms of content management have evolved to meet specific needs in more effective ways. Some of these specialized forms are listed as follows:

- **Web Content Management (WCM)** is a popular form of content management. It provides rich features for managing web content. For example, web content authors can create content using simple user interfaces without knowing much about technology. Content can be routed to reviewers and approvers and once approved, can be automatically published to the target website.

- **Enterprise Records Management (ERM)** is another form of content management that creates and controls records in various forms that typically serve the legal needs of enterprises.

- **Collaborative Content Management (CCM)** enables participants in collaborative processes to work together as a team. The participants can create, share, and discuss common content items. CCM facilitates management of collaborative content such as discussion threads and voting results along with the usual electronic documents.

- **Compliance Management** enables organizations to comply with legal requirements and to prove their compliance with law. This is a popular application of ECM in highly regulated industries such as pharmaceuticals.

Each of these different forms of content management is implemented on the Documentum platform as a combination of applications and services.

EMC Documentum

Enterprises utilize content-enabled solutions to capture, organize, manage, store, retrieve, and archive content that is created or consumed during their day-to-day operation. When enterprises interact with other entities such as suppliers, consumers, and other businesses some content needs to even cross boundaries of organizations and systems. EMC Documentum provides a **unified content platform** with the capabilities needed for developing such content-enabled solutions.

At a high level, ECM needs can be categorized as capture, management, delivery, archival, and integration. Thus enterprises can focus on developing business logic rather than on content management infrastructure. **Capture** brings the content under the purview of the platform. It could have originated in various sources such as being manually created using desktop applications, digitized from paper sources, created from various devices such as cameras, or exported from other existing systems. **Delivery** consists of exporting a copy of the content and persisting to other media, including disks, publications, and websites. **Archival** consists of removing content from day-to-day management and putting it away in long-term storage. **Integration** involves exchange of content and interaction with processes. EMC Documentum provides capabilities in all of these categories.

Gartner research produces an annual report on the global ECM space. The 2009 report forecasts a compound annual growth at 9.5% through 2013 and shows EMC Documentum as a leader in this space. The magic quadrant from the Gartner report is shown in the following figure:

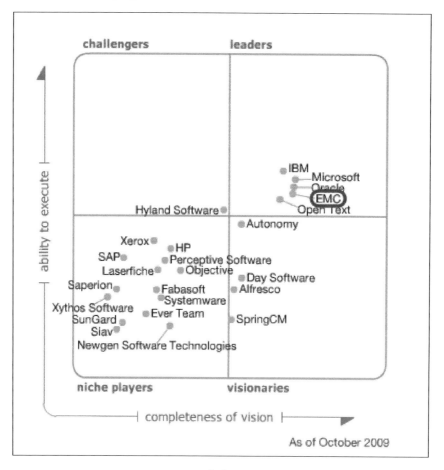

EMC certification

EMC Proven Professional certification is an exam-based certification program that introduced Content Management certifications in 2007. Associate-level certification can be achieved by passing the **Content Management Foundations (CMF) Associate-level Exam (E20-120)**. This exam tests knowledge about technical fundamentals of Documentum. It is also a requirement for all current Specialist-level certifications, whose additional requirements are outlined below:

Track	Exam code	Exam title
Application Developer (EMCApD)	E20-405	Content Management Server Programming
	E20-455	Content Management Web Application Programming
System Administration (EMCSyA)	E20-465	Content Management System Administration
Technology Architect (EMCTA)	E20-475	Content Management System Architecture
	E20-485	Content Management Application Architecture

Resources listed at the end of this chapter include a reference to the EMC web page which provides details about the complete certification program.

Why?

What is the value of possessing a certification? Should I take this certification exam? Such questions inevitably arise when one considers working towards any certification.

The answers to these questions are also inevitably specific to the individual asking the question. The answer depends on various factors including the industry, the supply and demand of skilled professionals in the space, the individual's demonstrable experience, and the employer's policies around certifications.

For EMC Documentum, demand far outweighs the supply of skilled professionals and this is reflected in the (average) compensation for EMC Documentum services relative to other areas like enterprise Java. As a result, it is a burden on the entity paying for these services to ensure that the services are well worth the costs. A certification provides an assurance of a baseline skill level for the professional providing these services. Therefore, possession of a certification makes the professional's services more marketable. However, bear in mind that possession of a certificate may not be valuable if it doesn't translate into demonstrable knowledge; see resources at the end of the chapter.

Along the same lines, a professional seeking to enter this space may have little specific experience to show and may find it hard to compete with people already working in this space. Possession of a certification may push the individual's credibility just high enough to provide an opening from where the professional can prove his or her worth.

Irrespective of your reason for taking a certification exam, it will take commitment (and money, currently US$200) to pass such an exam. Certification exams tend to be more academic than reflective of the real-life practice for the subject. Typically, these exams are based on a well-defined syllabus and tend to test the candidate's awareness or understanding of the concepts, though a smaller number of exams are oriented towards the application of the knowledge as well. Real-life practice typically utilizes a small section of the overall subject knowledge (the clichéd 80-20 term comes to mind) and additional knowledge of related areas to make effective use of the subject.

I recall crossing the fence over to the *certified* side with the Java Programmer certification exam about 10 years ago. The preparation experience was incredibly enriching as well as humbling as I systematically nailed my weak areas and worked on them to come out stronger each time. In the next section, I share this preparation approach that essentially ferrets out and eliminates one's weaknesses.

How?

Once you have decided to take the exam the focus shifts to the preparation approach. The following sections provide an effective approach and information for taking the first step.

Approach

Preparation for a professional certification typically competes with other individual responsibilities including work and family. As such, it often becomes an exercise in resource (time, effort, and money) allocation to maximize the results with minimal contention of conflicting demands. In order to make the most of the effort and resources being spent, one needs to prioritize the order in which the topics need attention and the amount of attention required by each topic.

There are probably several good approaches for exam preparation and their effectiveness varies for individuals due to differences in learning styles. However, I believe that the following high-level approach can be used to tune specific styles of preparation.

If you are familiar with the concept of **bottlenecks** (as in performance tuning) you will easily identify with this preparation approach. Even if this is a new concept for you it is not very difficult to grasp. It is also similar to what is known as the **theory of constraints,** where you systematically remove constraints to achieve higher performance relative to the goals. The key concept in the approach is to identify your weakest area (bottleneck or constraint) and spend time and resources on learning about it. Now repeat and move on to the next bottleneck. This won't be an exact science but you should be able to see tangible returns in terms of the new knowledge gained (and improving scores).

As may be obvious to the keen mind, the key step in this process is *identification of the bottleneck*. We need a good tool for identifying our weak areas so that we can focus our efforts and mock tests or practice tests fit this bill wonderfully. Of course, the quality of the questions will matter but if you have a large number of questions to practice with, you are very likely to see the benefits in a short period.

The other key aspect is *repetition* and that relates to how our memory works. Reading specific topics again, making notes, and trying the practice questions again are all different ways of ensuring that the concepts stick. Specifically, repeating practice tests can give you the assurance to build your confidence for the real exam.

This book attempts to provide a good set of over 400 questions to help you focus your learning. Each chapter provides content around the concepts to fill the gaps in your knowledge, but in my opinion the biggest value for the certification candidate is added by the rich set of practice questions. Take this approach as a general guideline and tweak your style to make the most out of this book.

Logistics

The E20-120 exam is administered by *Pearson Vue* (http://www.vue.com/emc). The exam currently costs US$200. Check for your local test center and review the exact details and policies.

Useful resources

This book offers an economical option that coherently presents the relevant information in one place along with a large number of practice questions. While this book strives to be the key preparation aid for E20-120, there are other valuable resources that can help you excel in this exam and carry on the learning process beyond it. Some of these resources are as follows:

- *dm_cram* (http://dmcram.org) is a free online community to support test preparation for Documentum exams and it offers practice tests, useful tips, and discussion forums.

- *EMC Powerlink* is the Documentum Support Site (http://powerlink. emc.com/) that provides access to support resources including product documentation and white papers.

- *Product documentation* is a good reference whenever you need to learn about a concept or clarify a doubt. It may be hard to read the documentation end to end like a book. The following product documents may be worthwhile to reference in your preparation—Content Server Fundamentals, Content Server Administration Guide, Content Server Object Reference, Content Server DQL Reference, Documentum Composer User Guide, Documentum Application Builder User Guide, User Guide/Help for Webtop, and Documentum Administrator.

- The number of documents and their level of detail make it challenging to use them efficiently and effectively as a study aid. One the other hand, Documentum developers must become conversant with the reference documentation for implementing Documentum solutions successfully. Therefore, it will be helpful to connect the topics in this book with the corresponding sections in the reference documentation.

- *EMC Documentum training* offers the *Technical Fundamentals of Documentum* (http://mylearn.emc.com/portals/home/ml.cfm?actionID=65&subje ctID=19676) course, which is recommended by EMC for preparing for this exam. EMC Documentum training is a great resource as well, though it is a relatively expensive option.

- *EMC Community Network* includes Documentum Developer Community (https://community.emc.com/community/edn/documentum), which provides frequent articles and downloads and has active discussion forums. It also provides free download of the Content Server Developer Edition. It can be very helpful if you don't otherwise have access to Documentum software.

- *documentum-users* (http://groups.yahoo.com/group/documentum-users/) has been a useful user group (Yahoo! Groups) where the Documentum community members ask questions and share their knowledge and expertise. Even if there is not much new content it may be a good place to search the archives.

- *dm_developer* (http://dmdeveloper.com/) is another online community where members ask questions and share their knowledge and expertise. It also features technical articles and case studies.

- *Contology Forum* (http://forums.contology.com/) is another discussion forum for Documentum community.

What this book covers

This book is organized in chapters loosely based on the structure of the recommended training for the CMF exam (http://mylearn.emc.com/portals/home/ml.cfm?actionID=65&subjectID=19676). The chapters are grouped together in parts to provide a logical grouping and order of topics as described below.

Part 1: **Fundamentals** (Chapters 1 - 4)

Chapter 1, ECM Basics introduces content management concepts. *Chapter 2, Working with Content* describes the process of creating and manipulating content. *Chapter 3, Objects and Types* lays the foundation of designing and using metadata. *Chapter 4, Architecture* describes the key components of the EMC Documentum platform and how they interact to provide content management capabilities.

Part 2: **Security** (Chapters 5 - 7)

Chapter 5, Users and Privileges describes the core concepts related to users for implementing security in Documentum. *Chapter 6, Groups and Roles* describes additional capabilities for facilitating security management for groups of users. *Chapter 7, Object Security* introduces permissions and ties them to users, groups, and privileges to realize the security model.

Part 3: **User Interface** (Chapters 8 - 9)

Chapter 8, Searching describes the features for finding relevant content stored in a repository. While other user interface aspects are covered throughout the book, searching is described separately because of its fundamental importance to content management. *Chapter 9, Webtop Presets* describes the new feature in version 6 for hiding screen options that are not relevant to user's tasks in particular situations.

Part 4: Application Development (Chapters 10 - 13)

Chapter 10, Documentum Projects describes how to package development artifacts for reuse and portability across repositories. *Chapter 11, Custom Types* describes how to create user-defined metadata structures for customization. *Chapter 12, Workflows* and *Chapter 13, Lifecycles* describe how to model and implement business processes in Documentum.

Part 5: Advanced Concepts (Chapters 14 - 15)

Chapter 14, *Aliases* describes a mechanism for dynamic assignment of ownership, locations, and permissions. Chapter 15, *Virtual Documents* describes how multiple documents can be managed as one larger document to facilitate collaboration.

The Appendices are available for free at http://www.packtpub.com/sites/default/files/0226EN_Appendices.zip.

The Practice Tests are available for free at http://www.packtpub.com/sites/default/files/0226EN_Practice tests.zip.

Appendices

Appendix A, *What's New in Documentum 6 and 6.5?* summarizes new features introduced in these versions, in the context of technical fundamentals. This information should be helpful for readers conversant with versions 5.x. Appendix B, *DocApps* describes the old way of packaging the development artifacts for reuse and portability across repositories. This material is included in the book primarily to meet the exam requirements.

Practice tests

There are three practice tests at the end covering all the topics in this book.

There is a set of questions for each chapter to test your understanding of the concepts discussed in the chapter. A good way to prioritize and focus your efforts is to use the questions to identify the areas where you score low and then work on those areas.

These questions, their answers, and the solutions to the practice tests have been provided at the end.

Example business scenario

A Documentum solution typically addresses one coherent set of needs, which often pertains to one business unit in an organization. This book uses one business scenario to illustrate content management concepts so that the examples relate to real-life and they belong to the same solution. For the sake of brevity and ease of understanding, the example scenario is a simplified version of the real-life process. As new concepts are introduced, the scenario will be expanded and refined to create specific examples where needed.

The scenario describes the primary operation of a lender that offers home loans. This scenario was selected because the loan approval process is highly document-centric and provides sufficient detail for illustrating the concepts. The process is illustrated in the next figure and is followed by its description:

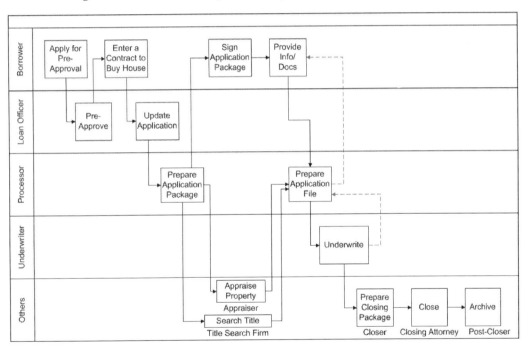

The preceding figure uses *bands* (aka *swim lanes*) where each band identifies a performer. The activities drawn in a band are performed by the performer associated with that band. The last band represents multiple performers where each performer owns a one-off activity. The process flow is explained below.

Doquent Mortgage provides home loans to *borrowers*. It engages home buyers early in the purchase process. A borrower can get a *pre-approval* to verify or prove the amount of loan he/she can get. The borrower fills out a *loan application* with personal information and provides it to a *loan officer*. At this stage the property information is not needed since the pre-approval simply states how much loan the borrower is likely to obtain.

The information in the application is used to issue a *Preliminary Underwriting Finding*. It indicates whether the borrower is eligible for the loan. If eligible, it also lists the documents needed to validate eligibility. If not eligible, the loan officer tries different parameters to identify if the borrower can be eligible at different terms, such as for a different amount of loan. If the loan officer succeeds, a *pre-approval letter* is issued under the new terms.

Once the borrower finds a house and signs a contract to purchase it, the property information is provided to the loan officer, who updates the loan application and hands it off to a *processor*.

The processor prepares an *application package* for the borrower to sign. The package includes various standard *forms* to be signed and specifies the list of required verification *documents*. The borrower signs the forms and returns the package along with the requested documents.

The processor orders an *appraisal* and a preliminary *title search*. The appraisal ensures that the property is valued sufficiently for the loan amount. The title search checks that the ownership of the property is not in question. Either of these checks can cause the application to be *denied*.

If no problems are encountered, the processor packages the forms and documents into an *application file*. The file includes a *cover summary sheet* and the forms and documents are stacked in a prescribed order. The processor also validates the file for completeness and accuracy. The processor takes about one week for these activities. The file is then handed off to an *underwriter* in the lending department.

The underwriter takes about four days to review the file. If the file violates guidelines or lacks any required information, the underwriter *suspends* the file and sends it back to the processor. The processor corrects the problems and sends the file back to the underwriter. Once everything is in order, the underwriter issues a *conditional approval* to the processor.

The conditional approval usually has *conditions*, which are requests for additional information or documents. The processor gathers the requested information/documentation and sends them to the underwriter.

The underwriter clears the conditions and issues a *commitment letter* to the processor. The file is forwarded to *closer* in the closing department.

The closer prepares the *closing package* and sends it to the *closing attorney*. The attorney performs the *closing* and the file is forwarded to *post-closer*.

The post-closer performs quality control and *archives* the file, which is kept for five years.

Learn more

The topics discussed in this chapter can be further explored using the following resources:

- A 15 Minute Guide to Enterprise Content Management—`http://www.aiim.org.uk/publications/ecm_at_work/pdfs/Ecm_15min_guide.pdf`
- Magic Quadrant for Enterprise Content Management (2009)—`http://www.gartner.com/technology/media-products/reprints/oracle/article101/article101.html`
- EMC Proven Professional Certifications for Content Management—`http://mylearn.emc.com/portals/home/ml.cfm?actionID=290`
- The Fundamentals Trap for Documentum Professionals—`http://doquent.wordpress.com/2008/08/01/fundamentals-trap-for-documentum-professionals/`
- Documentum/EMC Proven Professional Certification – Does It Matter?—`http://brilliantleap.com/blog/2009/03/documentum_emc_proven_professi.html`

Conventions

In this book, you will find a number of styles of text that distinguish between different kinds of information. Here are some examples of these styles, and an explanation of their meaning.

Code words in text are shown as follows: "Content Server uses `dmr_containment.order_no` (shown in the parent-child relationship figure earlier) to store a sequence number that orders the children of the virtual document."

A block of code is set as follows:

```
SELECT r_object_id, object_name
FROM dm_sysobject
IN DOCUMENT ID('090000108001193a')
WITH ANY r_version_label = 'CURRENT'
```

New terms and **important words** are shown in bold. Words that you see on the screen, in menus or dialog boxes for example, appear in the text like this: " Selecting a virtual document and using **Tools | Virtual Documents | Reorder Children** provides an interface to move components up or down in the order as shown here".

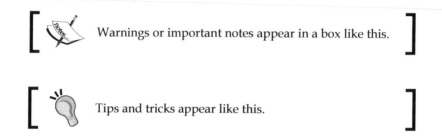

> Warnings or important notes appear in a box like this.

> Tips and tricks appear like this.

Reader feedback

Feedback from our readers is always welcome. Let us know what you think about this book—what you liked or may have disliked. Reader feedback is important for us to develop titles that you really get the most out of.

To send us general feedback, simply send an e-mail to feedback@packtpub.com, and mention the book title via the subject of your message.

If there is a book that you need and would like to see us publish, please send us a note in the **SUGGEST A TITLE** form on www.packtpub.com or e-mail to suggest@packtpub.com.

If there is a topic that you have expertise in and you are interested in either writing or contributing to a book on, see our author guide on www.packtpub.com/authors.

Errata

Although we have taken every care to ensure the accuracy of our content, mistakes do happen. If you find a mistake in one of our books—maybe a mistake in the text or the code—we would be grateful if you would report this to us. By doing so, you can save other readers from frustration and help us improve subsequent versions of this book. If you find any errata, please report them by visiting http://www.packtpub.com/support, selecting your book, clicking on the **let us know** link, and entering the details of your errata. Once your errata are verified, your submission will be accepted and the errata will be uploaded on our website, or added to any list of existing errata, under the Errata section of that title. Any existing errata can be viewed by selecting your title from http://www.packtpub.com/support.

Piracy

Piracy of copyright material on the Internet is an ongoing problem across all media. At Packt, we take the protection of our copyright and licenses very seriously. If you come across any illegal copies of our works, in any form, on the Internet, please provide us with the location address or website name immediately so that we can pursue a remedy.

Please contact us at copyright@packtpub.com with a link to the suspected pirated material.

We appreciate your help in protecting our authors, and our ability to bring you valuable content.

Questions

You can contact us at questions@packtpub.com if you are having a problem with any aspect of the book, and we will do our best to address it.

Good luck! Let's get started.

Part 1

Fundamentals

ECM Basics

Working with Content

Objects and Types

Architecture

1
ECM Basics

In this chapter, we will explore the following:

- Content and metadata
- Repository and Content Server
- Webtop Interface Concepts

This chapter introduces the fundamental concepts of the Documentum platform. The concepts are described at a high level to provide an overview of the breadth of the platform. These concepts are explored in detail in the rest of the book.

Webtop and **Documentum Administrator (DA)** are key applications for using and managing the Documentum platform. The examples and illustrations in this book utilize these two applications extensively. This chapter also introduces the user interface concepts related to these two applications.

 We will refer to EMC Documentum as Documentum for brevity. References to documentation will use the exact document titles.

Content and metadata

Databases are ubiquitous in modern technology solutions. This is a mature field and well-known best practices are routinely used for deploying databases. Databases provide standard means for accessing and manipulating structured data. **Structured** means that the data components (fields) are of specific type (integer, string, and so on) and this knowledge is helpful in querying and manipulating the data.

On the other hand, files stored on the file system are generally unstructured and can contain information in any form. Such files and the information they contain are collectively referred to as **content**. A check image, an email, a manual in PDF format, and a video clip are all examples of unstructured content. Some file formats, such as **comma-separated values (CSV)**, may contain data that may be considered as structured. However, every file can be considered content, irrespective of its format. While databases provide standard means of managing structured data, **content management systems (CMS)** are a relatively new technology. As the content itself is unstructured, it is not possible to read and understand the content without any prior knowledge of it. Therefore, each content item is associated with some structured data, which describes the content item. This data that provides information about the attached content item is called **metadata**. Metadata consists of a set of data items called **properties** or **attributes**.

Content management systems utilize metadata extensively to provide sophisticated functionality. For example, metadata is essential for making documents searchable in terms of their author, title, subject, or keywords. It is hard to imagine any functionality of Documentum that does not utilize metadata in one form or another. The following figure shows two content items and their associated metadata:

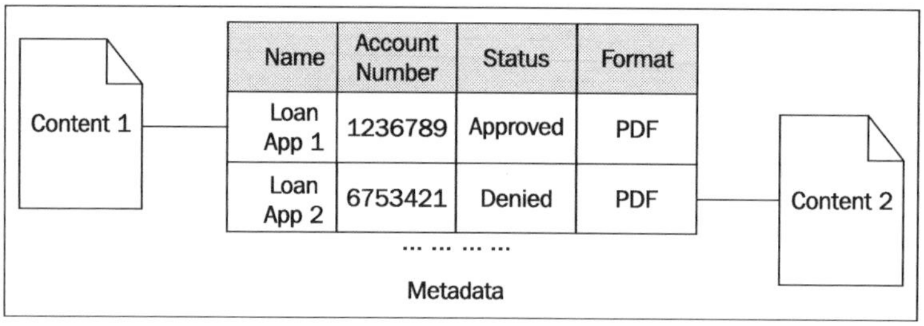

Name	Account Number	Status	Format
Loan App 1	1236789	Approved	PDF
Loan App 2	6753421	Denied	PDF
... ...			

Content 1

Content 2

Metadata

In the preceding figure, the content file Content 1 has the following details:

- Name: Loan App1
- Account Number: 1236789
- Status: Approved

The content file Content 2 has the following details:

- Name: Loan App2
- Account Number: 6753421
- Status: Denied

These content files represent two loan applications in PDF format.

Repository

Content management systems need to manage both content and metadata.
Documentum uses the host file system (by default) to store the content and a
Relational Database Management System (RDBMS) to manage metadata and its
association with the content items. Note that the content can also be stored in other
types of storage systems, including an RDBMS, a **content-addressed storage (CAS)**,
or external storage devices.

> EMC coined the term content-addressed storage (CAS) in 2002 when
> it released Centera. CAS provides a digital fingerprint for a stored
> content item. The fingerprint (also known as an ID or logical address)
> ensures that a retrieved item is exactly the same item that was saved.
> No duplicates are ever stored in CAS.

A **repository** is a managed unit of content and metadata storage and includes areas
on the file system and a database. The organizational details of files and metadata
in a repository are hidden from the users and applications that need to interact
with the repository. The repository is managed and made available to the users and
applications via standard interfaces by a **Content Server** process. The basic structure
of a repository is shown in the following figure:

The preceding figure shows the minimal structure of a repository. There are some
optional structural elements that can be added to the repository. It is possible for a
repository to use multiple content stores. This feature enables physical separation of
content storage based on various criteria. A repository can include **full-text indexes**
if an **Index Server** is a part of the installation. Full-text indexes enable rapid searching
within content files and metadata. A repository can also include an **XML store**
to provide native XML persistence and management capabilities. The repository
infrastructure can include **directory services** as an authentication mechanism.
However, we will represent the structure of a repository in the basic form used
previously, which remains valid and sufficient for the purposes of this book.

> The repository was officially referred to as **docbase** in pre-5.3 Documentum versions. The term docbase is still popular and is used interchangeably with repository.

Content Server

Content Server serves content to applications, which provide friendly interfaces to human users. Content Server brings the stored content and metadata to life and manages its lifecycle. It exposes a known interface for accessing content while hiding the details of how and where the files and metadata are stored.

> The term Content Server is used in two contexts — the **Content Server software** that is installed and resides on the file system and the **Content Server instance**, which is the running process that resides in memory and serves content at run time. However, there is little chance of confusion since the usage is often clear from the context and the term Content Server is typically used without additional qualification (software or process/instance).

A Content Server instance manages only one repository. However, multiple Content Server instances can be dedicated to the same repository. Multiple Content Server instances for one repository can provide the following benefits:

- Improved performance by dividing up the load for serving content among the instances
- Improved service for remote users via **Remote Content Server** instances
- Improved fault-tolerance by supporting **fail-over** and **disaster recovery**

The following figure shows two Content Servers serving one repository:

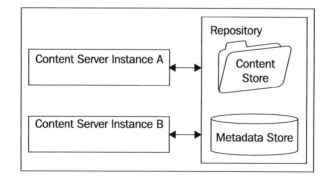

Content Server provides an **Application Programming Interface (API)** and therefore needs applications in front of it to expose a friendly interface to human users. Documentum provides desktop and web-based client applications and supports the creation of custom applications of either type. The following figure shows several client applications interacting with a Content Server instance:

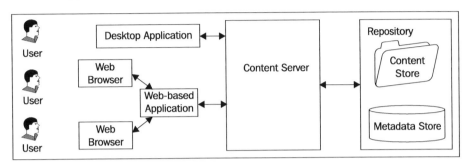

The full set of Content Server features is exposed via **Documentum Foundation Classes (DFC)**. DFC provides an API for interacting with the Content Server programmatically. Content Server functionality is also exposed through **Documentum Foundation Services (DFS)** in the form of **Web services**. It also provides a framework for developing custom Web services.

 Prior to version 6, **Documentum Client Library (DMCL)** provided another mechanism for interacting with Content Server. While DMCL is still available, the new features developed for DFC and DFS are not available through DMCL.

Documentum also provides a **Web Development Kit (WDK)** to facilitate development and customization of Web-based client applications.

Documentum provides two command-line utilities for interacting with the Content Server—**IDQL** and **IAPI**. IDQL supports query execution while IAPI supports direct invocation of the API functions.

 IAPI is available but deprecated as it works with DMCL. This means that it won't support new features and is expected to be discontinued in the future.

Content Server is the foundation of the Documentum platform and provides the following standard services:

- Content management services
- Process management services
- Security services
- Distributed services

These features are described here briefly and in more detail in later chapters.

Content management services

Content management services primarily deal with storage and retrieval, versioning, data dictionary, assembly and publishing, and search functionality.

Content Server uses an object-oriented model and stores everything as objects in the repository. It provides APIs for managing content and metadata together. Library services (checkin and checkout of objects stored in the repository) enable making changes to content in a safe manner. Content Server inherently provides versioning for objects. As users work with objects they can create new versions while keeping older versions intact.

Metadata can also be retrieved using **Document Query Language (DQL)**, which is a superset of Structured Query Language used with databases (ANSI SQL). DQL can query objects and their relationships, in addition to any database tables registered to be queried using DQL.

Data dictionary stores information about object types in the repository. The data dictionary can be altered by the addition of user-defined object types and properties.

Virtual documents link multiple component documents together into a larger document. An individual document can be part of multiple virtual documents. The assembly of virtual documents can also be controlled by business rules and data stored in the repository.

Content Server also provides indexing and search capabilities, which include the ability to search within content and to add third-party search providers to the installation.

Process management services

Process management features include workflows and lifecycles.

Workflows typically represent business processes and model event-oriented applications. Workflows can be defined for documents, folders (representing the contained documents), and virtual documents. A workflow definition acts like a template and multiple workflow instances can be created from one workflow definition.

Many documents created by an enterprise go through different stages during the lifetime of that document. For example, a document may be a draft when initially created, can be approved after successful review, and archived when no longer needed. **Lifecycles** define business rules that can be applied to different types of documents.

Security services

Security features include security for content and metadata and accountability for operations.

A repository uses **Access Control Lists (ACLs)**, also known as **permission sets**, as the security mechanism by default. The repository security can be turned off as well. When repository security is enabled, each object has an associated ACL. The ACL provides object-level permissions to users and groups. Using ACLs Content Server enforces seven levels of basic permissions and seven levels of extended permissions. There are additional user privileges and other security components, which are discussed in later chapters.

Content Server provides, a robust accountability capability via auditing, tracing, and electronic signatures. Accountability features help identify causes of specific system behavior. **Auditing** can track operations such as checkin or checkout that have been configured to be audited. **Tracing** can provide detailed run-time information useful for identifying causes of certain behavior and for troubleshooting issues. **Electronic signatures** can enforce sign-offs in business processes. A sign-off is analogous to a signature on paper and it is a way of authorizing or approving a decision electronically.

Distributed services

A Documentum installation can include multiple repositories and Content Server supports various distributed models, including single-repository and multi-repository models. In a single-repository distributed configuration, content is distributed across all sites configured to access the repository. In a multi-repository distributed configuration, content and metadata are distributed across all participating repositories.

Add-on services

In addition to the standard services described above, Content Server also offers the following optionally licensed functionality:

Trusted Content Services (TCS) provides additional security features such as digital shredding of content files, strong electronic signatures, content encryption, and enhanced ACLs.

Content Services for EMC Centera (CSEC) adds support for Centera storage for guaranteed retention and immutability. Centera storage is suitable for storing large amounts of infrequently changing data that needs to be retained for a specific period.

Content Storage Services (CSS) enables the use of content storage and migration policies, which automate the assignment of content to various storage areas. CSS can be used for optimizing the use of storage infrastructure in the enterprise. CSS also provides features for content compression and de-duplication.

Retention Policy Services (RPS) enables use of policies to manage the lifecycle of the objects stored in the repository. A retention policy defines the phases through which such an object passes and how it is finally disposed off or archived.

Collaborative Services can be deployed with an optional license to enable collaboration features in Webtop and, potentially, third-party and custom applications. Collaborative features include:

- **Room**: This is a secured area within a repository with defined membership and access restrictions.

- **Discussion**: This is a series of comments associated with an object.

- **Contextual folder/cabinet**: This is a folder with attached description and discussion.

- **Calendar**: This is a construct to enable organizing, scheduling, and tracking of events.

- **Data table**: This is a structured collection of similar data such as issues and tasks.

- **Note**: This is a simple document with built-in discussion and rich text content.

Internationalization

Internationalization (i18n) refers to the ability of Content Server to adapt to language and other regional differences. Content Server uses UTF-8 encoding of Unicode. The Unicode standard provides a unique number to represent every character in every language. UTF-8 is a way of representing these numbers in binary form. Unicode enables Content Server to store metadata using characters from different languages and to manage multilingual content.

Webtop user interface

Webtop is the primary web application for Documentum users. It is also the basis for several other Documentum web applications and custom applications developed to serve specific needs of organizations. Due to this shared basis, these applications share the same approach to the user interface. In this section, we look at the key elements of this user interface. The detailed functionality will be discussed via illustrated examples in the rest of the book.

Logging in

Webtop is accessed via a web browser using a URL of the form `http://host:port/webtop`. It presents the login page for authentication as shown in the following screenshot:

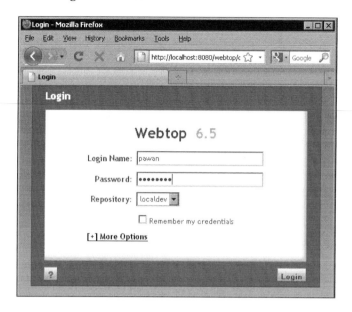

The user selects a repository to log into and provides the **Login Name** and **Password** for authentication. Clicking on **Login** authenticates the user and displays the main Webtop interface on successful authentication. If authentication fails, the login page is displayed again with an error message. Also note the **?** button, which is available on most screens to provide context-sensitive help.

A typical interaction using Webtop follows this sequence of steps:

1. Navigate to a location.
2. Select one or more items in the current location.
3. Perform an action on the selected items.

These interactions map nicely to the areas available on the Webtop **GUI (Graphical User Interface)**. Navigation can be performed using the **Browser Tree** on the left. Items can be selected in the **Work Area**. Actions can be performed using regular menus in the **Menu Bar** or the context menu. The main Webtop GUI is shown in the following screenshot:

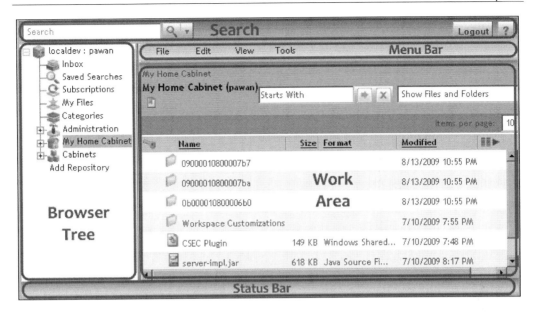

There are two other areas on the GUI— the **Status Bar** at the bottom for displaying messages, and a **Search** bar at the top which contains search controls, the **Logout** button, and the help (?) button.

These areas of the Webtop GUI are discussed next.

Browser tree

The browser tree is used for **navigation**—locating items within the repository. Structurally, it looks similar to the folder tree display within Windows Explorer:

The items displayed in the tree are called **nodes**:

- The root node (top node) represents the repository. It shows the name of the current repository and the name of the current user.

- **Inbox**: It is like the e-mail inbox, which displays notifications and tasks for the current user.

- **Saved Searches**: This node displays saved searches accessible to the current user.

- **Subscriptions**: This node displays the items that the user has subscribed to. This is a means of accessing an item directly, rather than navigating to it in the usual manner. Other means of directly accessing documents are discussed in *Chapter 8, Searching*.

- **My Files**: This node shows the items recently used by the user. Specifically, these are the items currently checked out or recently checked in by the user. These operations are discussed in detail in *Chapter 2, Working with Content*.

- **Categories**: This node can be used to navigate categories which provide an alternative to organizing documents by cabinets and folders. **Content Intelligence Services (CIS)** can be used to automatically assign categories to documents.

- **Administration**: This node provides access to limited administration functionality, depending on the user's privileges.

- **My Home Cabinet**: This node shows the contents of the user's default folder.

- **Cabinets**: This node provides access to the folder structure containing documents and other objects.

- **Add Repository**: This link can be used to log into another repository.

Clicking on a node in the browser tree usually updates the work area.

Work area

The work area displays a list of items with one item per row. Usually, they are items linked to a folder such as documents and subfolders. When a search is performed the items displayed in this area are search results. In general, the items shown in this area depend on the node selected in the browser tree or the result of some action.

The top left area indicates what is being shown in the work area. The controls at the top provide a means of filtering what is shown in the list. For example, the **Starts With** control lets the user shortlist items by their names. The **Show Files and Folders** control restricts the kinds of items being displayed. The options in this control may change depending on what is being shown in the list. The **Items per page** control allows the user to select the number of items to show on one page. When the list has items spread over more than one page, a pagination control appears, as shown below. This control allows the user to jump to the first page or the last page, to scroll back and forth one page at a time, or to jump to a particular page number by typing it in the text field.

The column headers identify what is displayed in each column. The first column header on the left indicates a key and it identifies whether an item is checked out. Checking out and checking in are discussed in detail in *Chapter 2, Working with Content*. If a column header is clickable, the list can be sorted by that column. The column selection icon in the header in the rightmost column allows the user to select the columns to be displayed. Column widths can be adjusted by dragging the vertical separators in the header row.

The user can operate on one or more items in the list by selecting those items. An item can be selected by clicking on its row, which becomes highlighted as shown in the following screesnshot:

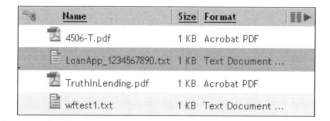

A set of contiguous items can be selected by selecting the first item and then selecting the last item with *Shift*+click. A set of non-contiguous items can be selected by selecting each item using *Ctrl*+click. The selected items can be operated upon using menus.

Menus

There are two kinds of menus available to users for performing actions—menus in the menu bar above the work area and the **context menu** displayed by right-clicking on a selection of items.

Menus in the menu bar contain actions that the user can perform. Some actions can only be performed on selected items and become unavailable (grayed out and not clickable) when no items have been selected. Other actions do not act on selections and are available even when no items have been selected. Actions can also become unavailable when the user is not allowed to perform those actions due to security or other configuration settings.

Note that some actions have a corresponding key combination shown in the menu. This is called a hot key or keyboard shortcut. An action can also be invoked by pressing the hot key combination rather than clicking on the menu and action. For example, pressing *Shift+I* will invoke the import action.

Available actions on selections can be quickly accessed via a streamlined context menu by right-clicking on the selection. The same actions are also accessible via the menus in the menu bar; however, they are conveniently listed in one place in the context menu while the disabled actions are hidden. A context menu is shown in the following screenshot:

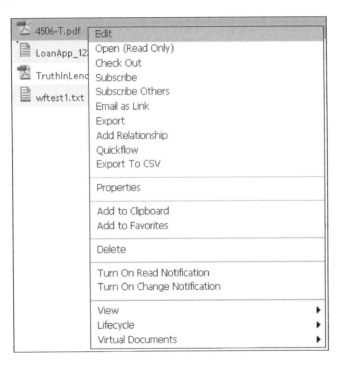

Double-clicking a row invokes the default action for an item. For example, a document is opened for viewing while a folder is "opened" to display its contents, by default.

Search

The browser tree enables the user to locate items by navigating through folders or looking under specific nodes in the tree. On the other hand, searching enables the user to find items based on their properties or contents. The items could be present anywhere in the repository and even outside the repository, depending on the installation configuration and search parameters. *Chapter 8* is dedicated to the discussion of search functionality.

Search functionality can be accessed via the bar at the top, which also contains the **Logout** and help (**?**) buttons.

Status bar

The Status Bar at the bottom of the GUI is used to display messages, usually when an action has been performed. It displays both informational and error messages.

Logging out

A user needs to log in if the user does not have an active session in Webtop. An active session can expire if the user doesn't interact with Webtop for an extended period of time. The session is terminated if the browser window interacting with Webtop is closed. The user may also terminate the session by explicitly logging out by clicking on the **Logout** button showed earlier.

Documentum Administrator (DA)

DA is a WDK application and has a very similar user interface to Webtop, as shown in the following screenshot. The key difference between the two is that DA offers extensive functionality under the **Administration** node. The relevant DA functionality will be illustrated with examples and concepts throughout the book.

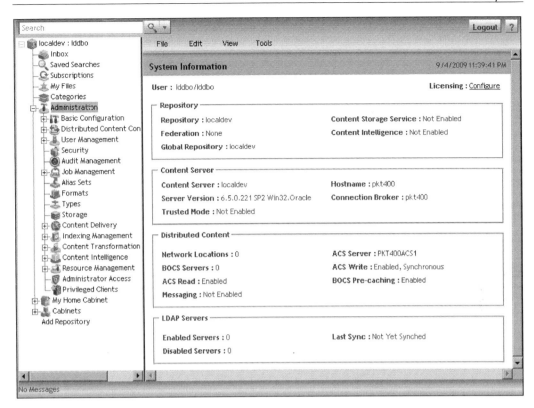

Checkpoint

At this point you should be able to answer the following key questions:

- What is content and what is metadata?

- What is a repository and what is Content Server? What is the relationship between the two?

- What services are provided by Content Server? What features are enabled by these services?

- What are the key features of the Webtop user interface? What is the key difference between the DA and Webtop user interfaces?

Learn more

The topics discussed in this chapter can be further explored using the following resources:

- EMC Documentum Content Server 6.5 Fundamentals
- EMC Documentum Content Server 6.5 SP2 Release Notes
- EMC Documentum Content Server 6.5 Distributed Configuration Guide
- EMC Documentum Process Builder 6.5 SP2 Release Notes
- EMC Documentum Foundation Classes 6.5 SP2 Release Notes
- EMC Documentum Webtop 6.5 SP2 User Guide
- EMC Documentum System 6.5 Object Reference Manual
- White Paper – Building on the EMC Documentum Platform: The Cost-Effective Strategy for Developing Content-Related Solutions

2
Working with Content

In this chapter, we will explore the following concepts:

- Importing and exporting content
- Linking to folders
- Checking out and checking in
- Versioning
- Formats and renditions
- Deleting versions

We have placed this chapter before *Chapter 3, Objects and Types* because it is more intuitive to think about working with files than with the metadata associated with them. It is also easier to illustrate and grasp the concepts in the context of working with files. However, objects and content are closely coupled in a Documentum repository. Objects can exist without content but content cannot exist without the associated objects in the repository. Therefore, it may be beneficial to revisit this chapter after going through Chapter 3.

 Content import and export, formats, and renditions are concepts specific to content. The other concepts discussed in this chapter apply to objects in general, irrespective of whether they have associated content or not. Object and content relationship will be explored in detail in Chapter 3. This chapter will use the term *document* to represent the combination of object and content in the repository, to avoid any confusion.

Although all Content Server operations are governed by the Documentum security model, this chapter leaves security out of discussion for the sake of simplicity. The discussion on security is deferred until Chapter 5, *Users and Privileges*, Chapter 6, *Groups and Roles*, and Chapter7, *Object Security*, which all describe the security model comprehensively.

Interacting with content

Content and metadata stored in the repository are managed and served by the Content Server. However, human users interact with Content Server through several types of applications. Depending upon their job roles, the users may use one of the following means to interact with the Content Server:

- A web application such as Webtop or Documentum Administrator. This is the most common means of interacting with the Content Server.

- A desktop application such as Documentum Composer. This is also quite common, as it is the primary development tool for Documentum.

- A query tool such as IDQL or IAPI. These tools are often used by administrators or developers for precise and low-level interaction with the Content Server.

- A custom application, which uses DFC, DFS, or integration technologies such as **Documentum Process Integrator** to interact with Content Server. Such an application may provide higher-level operations, which bundle multiple low-level operations in some sequence.

Irrespective of the interface used by the end users, Content Server offers the same core capabilities to all entities directly interacting with it, as shown in the following figure:

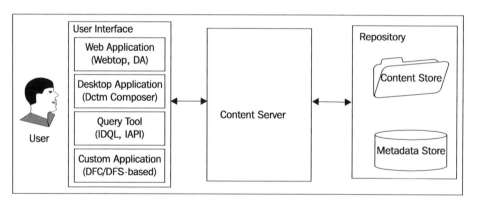

The Content Server capabilities for working with content are the subject of this chapter and Webtop features exposing these capabilities are used for illustration.

Importing content

Content is usually created using desktop tools such as Microsoft Office. It could also take the form of reports created by enterprise applications. There is no limit to the possible sources and kinds of content. Typically, content must be brought into a repository in order to be managed by Documentum. Content is brought into a repository by **importing** it. Once a content item has been imported into the repository, it is potentially available to all repository users.

Objects in a repository are organized in a folder structure similar to the hierarchical structure evident in most operating systems. This hierarchical structure is also referred to as a **folder tree**. Before importing a file using Webtop, the user should navigate to the destination folder in the repository. The import action is initiated by using the **File | Import** menu item or the *Shift+I* shortcut. The **File Selection** screen allows selection of one or more files and folders to be imported, as shown in the following screenshot. The user can select files and folders from multiple locations using **Add Files** and **Add Folders** buttons repeatedly. Selecting a folder copies the complete folder tree into the repository, including the selected folder. The text in the heading—**1234567890**, indicates the name of the destination folder in the repository where the files are being imported.

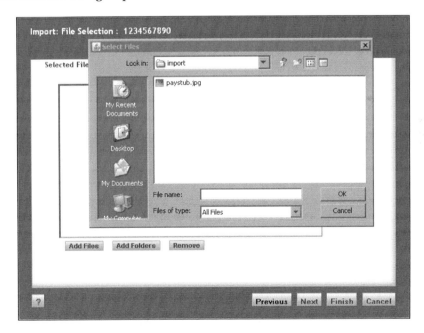

Clicking on **Next** displays the **Object Definition** screen, as shown in the following screenshot. Here properties can be specified for the file being imported. This screen provides convenient defaults, which are sufficient for our current purpose. The properties shown on this screen are a subset of the available ones. Available properties can be modified after importing the file. If multiple files were selected for import this screen would iterate through them, gathering metadata for all of them. There is also an option to apply common metadata, such as object type, to all the selected files without iterating through them one at a time.

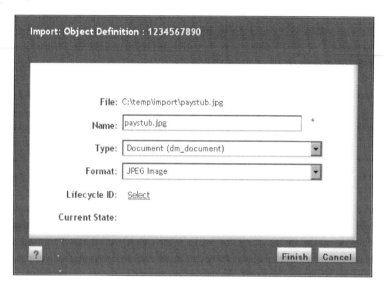

Clicking **Finish** completes the import action and the imported document shows up in the destination folder, as shown in the following screenshot. Note that a newly imported document gets version labels 1.0 and CURRENT. Versions are discussed later in this chapter.

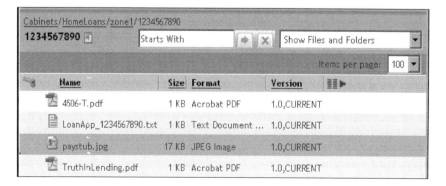

Linking to folders

Recall that before importing a file with Webtop, the user navigates to the destination folder within the repository. In addition to creating a document in the repository, the import operation also **links** the document to the selected folder. In simple terms, the document is imported into the folder. When a document is linked to a folder, it can be listed in that folder's contents.

Similarly, folders can be created within (and linked to) another folder using the **File | New | Folder** menu item. Nested folders lead to a hierarchical folder structure (**folder tree**) similar to the structure found in operating systems such as Microsoft Windows or UNIX. Indeed, there is a concept of **folder path** within the repository and it is used to browse or navigate around the repository.

In our example scenario, suppose that the mortgage business is organized by geographic zones. The folder structure for a particular home loan application is /HomeLoans/<zone>/<loanaccount>. For example, the last figure indicates that **paystub.jpg** has been imported in the path **/HomeLoans/zone1/1234567890**, where zone is **zone1** and the loan account is **1234567890**.

Sometimes we need to access a document from two or more paths. For example, suppose that the approved loan applications for zone1 also need to be listed in the path /HomeLoans/zone1/Approved. Documentum allows a document to be linked to multiple folders. In this case, when the application has been approved, LoanApp_1234567890.txt can be linked to the folder /HomeLoans/zone1/Approved.

Using Webtop, linking an existing document to a folder is a two-step process. First, the document is added to **clipboard** using the **Edit | Add to Clipboard** menu item or the shortcut *Shift+C*. Then the user navigates to the target folder (where the document needs to be linked) and uses the **Edit | Link Here** menu item or the shortcut *Shift+L* to establish the link. The right-click context menu can also be used in each step. The **Edit** menu also has options for moving or copying the document to the target folder.

The first folder that a document is linked to is called the **primary folder** of the document. After the document has been linked to a second folder it is visible in both locations and there is no visual indication of whether a folder is the document's primary folder or not.

 When drag-and-drop is enabled in Webtop, Internet Explorer can be used to link an object to a new folder by dragging it with the *right-click*. In this case, the user also has the options to **move** or **copy** the object. Using drag-and-drop with *left-click* moves the object to the new folder.

Folder links of a document can be removed as well. **Unlinking** a document from a folder removes it from that folder path. When an object is linked to multiple folder paths, it can be unlinked from any of those paths. In Webtop, this is achieved by attempting to delete the object and then selecting **Just the link** option. Object deletion is discussed later in this chapter. If the document is unlinked from its primary folder the second folder link becomes the primary folder. Documents and folders cannot be unlinked if they have only one link. Programmatically, the last link can be removed as long as another link is created before saving the changes.

Exporting content

In real-life, we often need to make a copy of a document to take with us or to give to someone else. It is particularly useful when the person needing the copy does not have routine access to the original. Similarly, a document ("original") in a repository can be **exported** to create a copy outside the repository, typically on a file system. The document inside the repository is not modified by exporting it and the external copy is no longer associated with the document inside the repository. Furthermore, users other than the one who imported a document can export it.

Suppose that the loan officer needs a copy of the paystub image that was imported earlier. She navigates to the document and selects it by clicking on its row. The export action can be initiated by using the **File | Export** menu item, the shortcut *Shift+E*, or by using the right-click context menu.

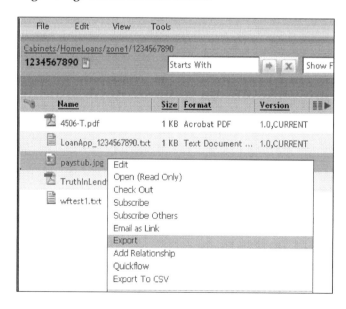

Webtop prompts the user to select the destination folder for the exported document using a folder selector dialog. Once the destination folder has been specified, the selected document is exported to that folder. Note that it is possible to select multiple documents before initiating export. In this case, all the selected documents are exported to the specified destination folder. If a folder is included in the selection, that folder and the documents linked to that folder are exported.

By default, exporting a folder only exports the folder and the documents directly linked to it. It does not export any subfolders within the selected folder. However, **deep export** functionality can be enabled via the custom app.xml file in Webtop installation. Once deep export has been enabled, exporting a folder exports the subfolders within it recursively. Deep export enables the creation of a local copy of the repository folder structure. A sample execution of deep export is shown in the following image:

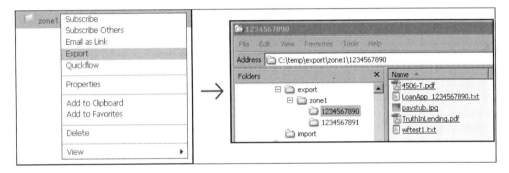

Checking out

A repository has multiple users and it is possible that two users may try to access the same document at one time. It is not a problem if they are just trying to view the document or to export a copy of the document. However, it becomes a problem if they both try to edit the document. Who gets to edit the document? Whose changes will supersede if they are both allowed to edit the document? Fortunately, this problem is not unique to Documentum, or even to the content management discipline. In its general form, this concern is known as **concurrency control**. Documentum uses a simple approach to resolve this problem—exclusive access for modification.

A user must **check out** a document from the repository before he/she can make changes to it. This operation **locks** the document in the repository, preventing other users from checking it out and modifying it. The user checking out the document is known as the **lock owner** for that document. Other users can still access the locked document or any of its existing versions for viewing or exporting. Versions are discussed later in this chapter.

This book uses the terms *check out* or *check in* as verbs and *checkout* and *checkin* as the corresponding nouns.

Using Webtop, checkout is performed just like export. The menu item is **File | Check Out** with the shortcut **O**. The right-click context menu can also be used as usual.

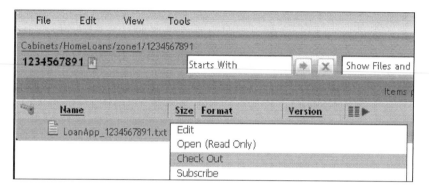

On checkout, Webtop performs an additional step and creates a copy of the content on the user's desktop, where the user can work on this file. Unlike export, the destination folder is predetermined via checkout preferences, as shown in the following screenshot. Preferences can be accessed using the **Tools | Preferences** menu item.

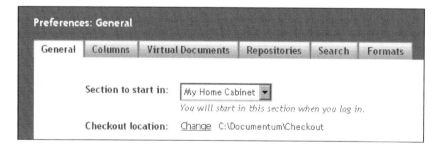

On successful completion of checkout, Webtop returns to the list view and shows a success message in the status bar, as shown in the following screenshot:

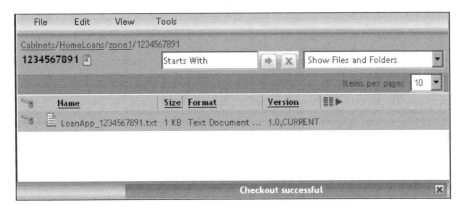

Webtop makes a visual distinction for a checked out document depending on whether the user is the lock owner for that document or not. It uses the column with a key icon in the header to indicate whether a document is currently checked out. A checked-out document is displayed with a *key* for its lock owner, as shown in the previous screenshot. For other users, a *lock* is displayed for the document, as shown in the following screenshot. Users seeing a lock on a document cannot check it out.

Webtop also provides a convenient **edit** action, which checks out the document and launches an application for editing it, based on the format of the document. If the document is already checked out, edit is only available to the lock owner and it launches the application to open the local copy for editing. In this process, Content Server is only involved in the checkout step. Edit can be invoked via the **File | Edit** menu item, the shortcut **E**, or the right-click context menu.

In some cases, the user may decide against modifying the checked out document. A checkout can be canceled using the **cancel checkout** action, which releases the lock on the document. No changes are made to the document in the repository and the local changes, if any, are discarded. The cancel checkout action is available to the **lock owner** or a **superuser**. We will learn about superusers in the chapters dealing with security. In Webtop, checkout can be canceled using the **File | Cancel Checkout** menu item or via the right-click context menu.

Checking in

The primary purpose of checking out a document is to modify its content and then **check in** the modified content. The user modifying the content can take a long time before it is ready to be checked back into the repository. When Webtop makes a local copy of the content on checkout, it remembers the association of the external copy with the document in the repository that was checked out. Webtop utilizes this *memory* at the time of checking in to locate the modified file.

What happens to the existing content for a document when the modified content is checked in? Is it overwritten? Is a new copy of the document created? The answer could be either, depending on the options specified by the user.

In Webtop, checkin can be initiated by the **File | Check In** menu item, shortcut **I**, or the right-click context menu.

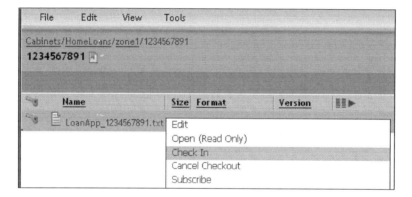

Content Server maintains a history of the changes applied to documents using **versions**. It creates a new version when the checkin operation is invoked. Each version is a separate document (content and metadata) but is aware of the document from which it was created. Versioning is described in detail in the next section.

When a checked out document is checked back in using Webtop, the user gets several options to influence the behavior of checkin, particularly with regard to versioning as shown in the following screenshot:

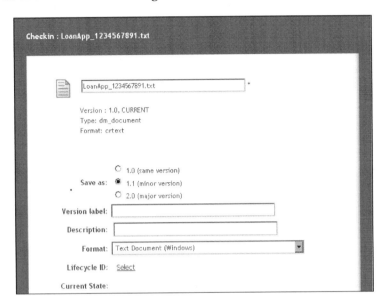

The user can decide what to do about versioning:

- Choose not to create a new version and replace the existing content with the content being checked in. Note that this is a convenience option and Webtop will perform a **save** operation rather than a checkin operation in this case.

- Choose to increment the major version or the minor version. See the next section for information about major and minor versions.

- Add a version label.

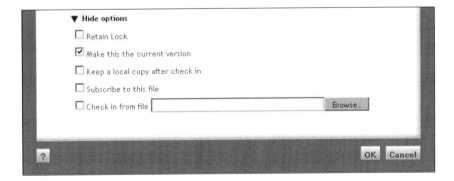

As shown in the preceding figure, the following additional options are available for checkin:

- Choose to keep the document checked out for more changes (also known as *retain lock* as opposed to *release lock*).

- Make the version current. If the version is checked in as a non-current version, a version label must be provided. After checkin, Webtop doesn't display the new version since it is not the current version.

- Keep a local copy of the document even after checkin. If this option is not selected the local copy of the file is deleted.

- Subscribe to the document. **Subscriptions** provide bookmark-like functionality and are discussed in Chapter 8, *Searching*.

- Manually select another local file to use as the new content. This option is useful if a new content file needs to be used or if Webtop is expecting the updated file to be in a path different from the actual location of the file.

The range of checkin options described above give the user significant control over the behavior of the checkin operation. However, the default options (as shown in the previous screenshots) lead to the following behavior:

- A new minor version is created and made the current version.

- Most of the properties on the new version are copied from the version checked out.

- The local file created by checkout becomes the content for the new version. Typically, this file is modified by the user before checkin.

- The document is unlocked and the local file is removed.

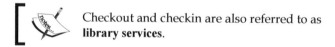

[Checkout and checkin are also referred to as **library services**.]

It is evident by now that versioning is closely tied to the checkin process. Even as multiple versions are created for a document, they retain information that identifies them as versions of the same document. This relationship leads to a **version tree** for the document. Let's look at some general tree concepts before we dive into details of version trees.

Talking about trees

Let's digress briefly to talk about **trees** in computer science. In this book, we will discuss at least three kinds of trees—folder trees, version trees, and virtual document trees. It is important to be unambiguous, succinct, and consistent about tree terminology to avoid confusion.

The tree structure borrows its name from the trees in nature due to its analogous features. It can have a root, a trunk, branches, and leaves like the natural trees. It also defines nodes and edges or links as additional concepts. The concepts of a trunk and branches are typically useful when talking about version trees. These two concepts may already be familiar to you if you have used a **revision control system** (also known as **source control**, **version control**, or **source code management**) for software development such as Subversion, CVS, or Microsoft Visual SourceSafe.

A tree is a hierarchical structure consisting of **nodes** connected by **links** or **edges** that follow some simple rules. All the nodes in a tree are **connected**; that is, we can go from any node in a tree to any other node in the tree by traversing the links. Each link is referred to as a parent-child relationship; that is, when two nodes are connected through a link in a tree, one of them is a **parent** and the other one is a **child**. Each node can have 0 or more children nodes. One node in a tree has 0 parent nodes while each of the other nodes has 1 parent node. The figure below illustrates these concepts with an example, where the numbers on the nodes are just labels and have no special meaning:

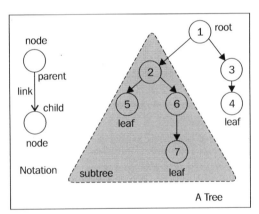

In this figure, an arrowhead is drawn on each link to identify the child node (and implicitly the parent node). However, the arrowhead is not needed and it could even be drawn on the parent side. In any case, the convention should be consistent on all the links within a tree.

The tree here has been drawn from top to bottom with the root node at the top. It is also a common practice to draw it from left to right. Also, it is a common practice to refer to a parent node as parent, a child node as child, and so on.

There are some other terms that are commonly used with trees. The node with no parent is called **root**. The nodes with no children are called **leaf** nodes. For a given node, its parent's parent is called an **ancestor** and an ancestor's parent is also called an ancestor. In general, a parent is also considered an ancestor. A node is a **descendant** of its ancestors. A node and all its descendants along with their associated links constitute a **subtree** rooted at that node. For example, the subtree rooted at node 2 is highlighted in the previous figure.

We can always traverse from one node to another in a tree using successive links without repeating a link in this traversal. Such a sequence of links is called a **path**. Equivalently, the path consists of a sequence of nodes on these links and that is how it is usually expressed, as it is a common practice to only label (name) the nodes. For example, in the preceding figure a path from node 2 to node 4 is (2,1,3,4).

In certain contexts, paths originating from the root have special significance and among them one path is more significant than the others. This most significant path from the root is called the **trunk**. A **branch** forms when a path breaks away from the trunk. A branch can also form by a path breaking away from another branch. The following figure illustrates this view of a tree. The numbers on nodes are just labels and don't have any special meaning.

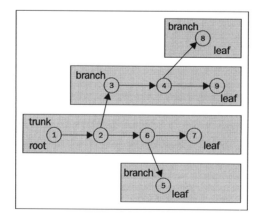

Equipped with this terminology regarding trees, we are ready to explore versioning in Documentum. Folder trees were introduced earlier in this chapter and they are discussed in multiple places, including Chapter 7, *Object Security*. Virtual document trees are discussed in Chapter 15, *Virtual Documents*.

Versioning

Recall that importing or creating a new document assigns version 1.0 to it, by default. Checking out and checking in this document creates a new version of the document, which is a separate document with its own content and metadata. Repeating this process, several versions can be derived from one original document.

A **version tree** is a visualization of multiple versions derived directly or indirectly from the same **root** document. A version tree is typically drawn from top to bottom or from left to right, with the root version drawn first. The figure below shows a simple version tree, which only has a trunk:

Content Server applies an **implicit version label** to each document and the label is of the form *major.minor*, where major is an integer greater than 0 (1, 2, 3, and so on) and minor is a non-negative integer (0, 1, 2, and so on). For example, 2.3 is an implicit version label. The implicit version label is also called a **numeric version label** due to the use of numbers. Additional **symbolic version labels** can be added to an object's metadata, which are descriptive and more appropriate for the end user. For example, Approved is a symbolic version label.

Numeric version labels are *not* decimal numbers. The decimal numbers 1.1, 1.10, and 1.100 are identical but the version labels 1.1, 1.10, and 1.100 are three distinct version labels.

If the checkin operation increments the *minor* version, the *major* portion is left unchanged. For example, the version label changes from 2.3 to 2.4 when the object is checked in as minor version. If the checkin operation increments the major version, the minor portion is reset to 0. For example, the version label changes from 2.3 to 3.0. In general, the implicit version labels of the form x.0 are referred to as **major versions** and the others are referred to as **minor versions**.

It is not necessary to create a new version to make changes to an object. The **save** operation can be used for updating an object without creating a new version. If the object has been checked out, saving it updates the version that was checked out and then unlocks it. In Webtop, this option is labeled as **Save as same version** on the checkin screen.

Duplicate versions are not allowed in a version tree as the purpose of the version tree is to enable distinction among versions of a document. The implicit version labels are generated by the Content Server and its numbering mechanism ensures uniqueness within the version tree. When a symbolic version label is assigned to a version, Content Server removes any existing label in the version tree that matches the new label. Note that this matching is case-sensitive; so, approved and Approved are treated as two different labels.

Normally checkin sets the new version as the **current version**, which means that the label CURRENT is assigned to it. However, an older version can be left as current instead. There is only one current version in a version tree though any of the versions can be the current one. Typically, applications and DFC queries use the current version as the default where multiple versions could be considered. Applications require explicit actions for accessing non-current versions.

A document always has a version and a version tree, even if it consists of just one version. All operations on existing documents operate on one or more versions of documents. Thus "document" is often an abbreviation for "current version of document" or "a version of document".

Webtop displays and exports only the current version, by default. In the normal list view all versions can be displayed using the filter **Show All Objects and Versions**. The user can list all versions of a particular document for performing various actions upon non-current versions. The **View | Versions** menu item or the right-click context menu can be used to view versions of a document, as shown in the following screenshot:

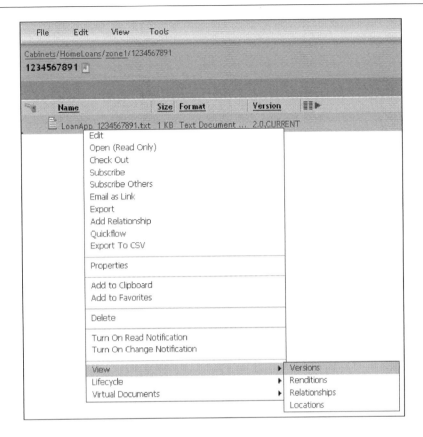

Webtop shows the version list for the document, as shown in the following screenshot. From this screen, the user can act upon the non-current versions as well. The non-leaf versions don't allow editing of properties other than certain system properties such as owner name and lifecycle ID. Most other operations are also available for non-leaf versions.

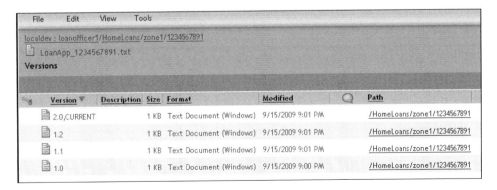

A folder object inside the repository cannot be versioned. However, applications can allow users to *check out a folder* with the semantics that the documents linked to that folder need to be checked out. This is just a usability enhancement for the user interface.

Branching

In our example scenario, suppose that a loan officer is preparing a loan application for a borrower. As she updates it she saves the following versions of the document—1.0, 1.1, 1.2, and 2.0 (CURRENT). At this point, she has some doubts about the likelihood of the terms in version 2.0 to be approved. She also realizes that the version 1.1 is close to what she can offer with a better likelihood of the loan getting approved. She wants to take version 1.1 and make small changes to it to create an alternative application, without discarding the version 2.0. What should she do?

Content Server allows checkout of a non-leaf version in the version tree. When this document is checked in, two options are available as usual, check in as major version or as a minor version. If major version is chosen, the next higher (higher than the highest major version present in the version tree) major version is used. If minor version is chosen, a **branch** is created in the version tree. The sequence of versions *splits off* as a new branch at this point. The version for the checked in document at the point of branch origin is obtained by appending .1.0 to the implicit version of the document that was checked out (parent version). Thus, branching enables users to work from an older version while still retaining the latest changes.

 If a second branch is created by checking out the same parent version as for the first one, the new version will be created by appending .2.0, and so on.

Let's return to our example to see how this works. The loan officer needs to work with version 1.1 and make some changes to it. She checks out version 1.1 and then checks it back in as a minor version. A branch is created with version 1.1.1.0. Note that even though this label ends in .0 it is a minor version since major versions always have the form x.0.

Branch version labels provide another reminder that implicit version labels are not decimal numbers. Decimal numbers cannot have more than one decimal point while branch version labels have multiple dots.

Once there are branches in the version tree, checking in along the branches becomes more interesting. Incrementing minor version works in the same way for a new child version of a leaf version, with the rightmost number getting incremented. However, incrementing the major version results in the next higher major version after the highest major version in the complete tree. So `2.3.1.6` can lead to `5.0` if `3.0` and `4.0` are already present in the version tree. This is obvious once we remember that duplicate version labels are not allowed in a version tree.

Let's explore this behavior by continuing with our example. After creating `1.1.1.0`, she realizes that she needs to make some more changes. So she checks out `1.1.1.0`, makes the changes, and checks it back in as a minor version resulting in the creation of version `1.1.1.1`. The resulting version tree is shown in the following figure:

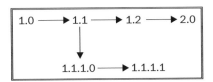

As new versions are created, various versions may become current in a version tree one after another. However, there is exactly one current version in each version tree at any time.

As a variation of this scenario, suppose that she chose to use major version on the last checkin. The new version would be `3.0` and the version tree would look like the following:

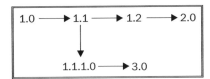

Let's look at one last variation on this example. Suppose that after checking out version 1.1 she chose to check it back in as a major version. In this scenario the new version would be 3.0. It is not called a branch even though it was created from an old version. The version tree would look like the following. The dotted line indicates the parent version of the major version; *it is not considered a branch.*

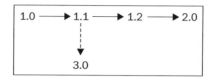

 When a branch is being created, it is not possible to save the document as the same version.

How does Content Server remember which documents are part of the same version tree? The name of a document is not required to be unique so that is not a guaranteed way to keep track of such information. Further, something more is needed to track the structure of each version tree. Content Server assigns a unique (within the repository) identifier called **object ID** to each document. The object ID is stored in a property (metadata element) called r_object_id. Object ID is discussed in detail in Chapter 3, *Objects and Types*.

Each document also has a property called i_chronicle_id. All the documents in a version tree have the same value for this property and it is the value of the r_object_id property of the root version in the version tree. The following figure illustrates the use of these properties to relate the documents in a version tree:

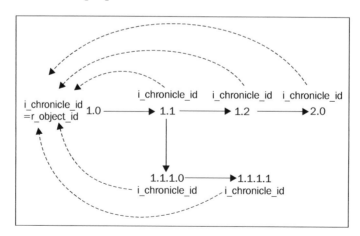

Another key property related to versioning is `i_antecedent_id`, which relates a version to its parent version, known as **antecedent** in Documentum terminology. The following figure illustrates how `i_antecedent_id` is used in a version tree. We will learn more about objects, properties, and object relationships in later chapters.

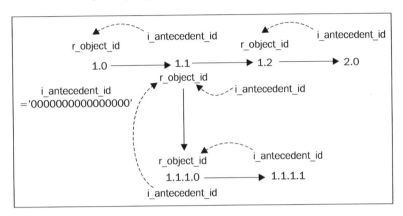

Deleting versions

Recall that every document is a version in a version tree. So deleting a document is synonymous to deleting a version. Let's look at how to delete a document using Webtop and the impact of deleting a version on its version tree.

One or more documents can be deleted by selecting them and then using the **File** > **Delete** menu item, the shortcut *Delete*, or the right-click context menu. Webtop iterates through the selected documents and asks whether the selected version or all versions need to be deleted.

Deleting a folder offers the following options, as shown in the next screenshot:

- An empty folder can be deleted
- Current versions of all documents in the folder and its subfolders can be deleted recursively
- All versions of all documents in the folder and its subfolders can be deleted recursively

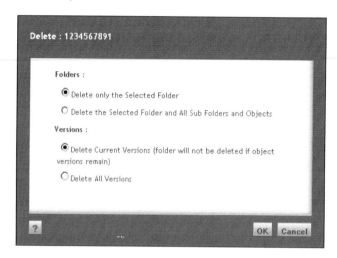

When a document version is deleted, Content Server preserves the integrity of its version tree. The remaining versions in the version tree are not renumbered but a version that loses its antecedent gets a new antecedent, which is the antecedent of the version deleted. In the following figure, version 1.1 is deleted and versions 1.2 and 1.1.1.0 get new antecedents as a result:

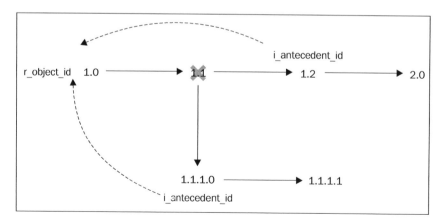

This behavior leads to an interesting scenario—what happens if the root version of a version tree is deleted? The child versions of the root now have no version to make an antecedent. Removing the root version will also make the chronicle ID of the whole version tree invalid. Content Server handles deletion of a root version in a special manner. Instead of deleting the root version, it lets it stay but marks it as deleted using the property `i_is_deleted`. Thus the integrity of the version tree is maintained and the deleted version is excluded from all normal operations.

Formats

Documents can be created from various sources, including desktop and enterprise applications. These sources use varying approaches for organizing the content within the document and use different file name extensions. A Documentum repository can store any kind of document but it associates a **format** with each document. The format is typically used to identify the application that can understand the contents of the document.

Within Documentum, a format captures information such as file name extensions related to the format. For example, `pdf` and `doc` are document formats which are associated with *Adobe Acrobat* and *Microsoft Word* applications, respectively. Formats play a key role in terms of document renditions, as will be discussed next.

Format preferences

Webtop behavior related to formats can be modified via **format preferences**. Format preferences associate a format for editing (primary format) and a format for viewing with an object type. Every document in the repository is associated with an object type. Object types are discussed in detail in Chapter 3, *Objects and Types*. The preferred viewing and editing applications can also be specified in format preferences. Format preferences are available on the **Formats** tab on the preferences screen, as shown below. Preferences can be accessed via the **Tools | Preferences** menu item.

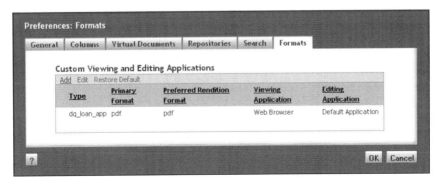

Renditions

Suppose that the loan officer in our example is gathering supporting documentation for the loan application. She imported a scanned image of a pay stub in JPEG format. However, she is required to use a PDF format for it if she needs to email it. Should she replace the original image with a PDF document containing the image? Should she keep the PDF and JPEG formats as two separate documents and then relate them by name or some other mechanism? Fortunately, Documentum supports storage of multiple formats for one document via renditions.

Each document has a **primary format**, which we usually refer to as the format of the document. However, it is possible to represent the same document in other formats and attach them to the same document. These non-primary formats are called **renditions** of the document. For example, it is possible to have text and PDF renditions of a document whose primary format is DOC.

 Differences among renditions are not limited to format, though it is probably the most common criterion; other criteria can be resolution (for images) and language (for translations).

Renditions can neither be *edited* nor *versioned*. A rendition is not stored as a separate document within the repository. Each rendition is attached to an existing document. In fact, the only properties tied to a rendition are the object ID of the primary format document and the format of the rendition itself.

When a document is versioned using checkin, the rendition of the previous version is not copied to the new version. Each version needs to get its own renditions, if any. This is shown in the following figure:

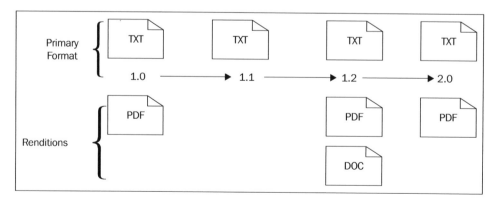

Using Webtop, renditions can be added to or removed from a document. Adding a rendition manually requires that the rendition be generated and be available for import. The user selects a document and uses the **File | Import Rendition** menu item for adding a rendition to the document.

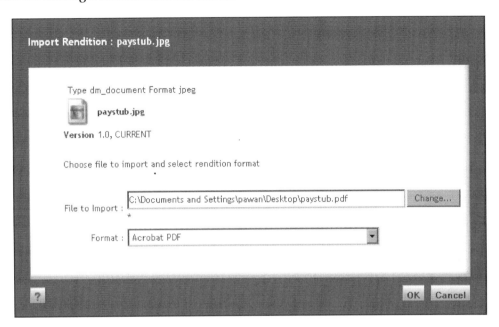

Existing renditions of a document can be viewed by selecting the document and using the **View | Renditions** menu item or the right-click context menu. The list of renditions appears as in the following figure. Renditions can be opened for viewing, exported, or deleted from this screen:

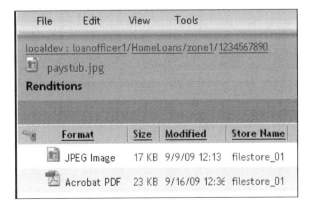

Manual management of renditions is suitable if the renditions are rarely needed and a mechanism for generating renditions is readily available to the users. Documentum also provides the **Content Transformation Services (CTS)** suite for automating the generation and management of renditions. This approach is particularly useful when a large number of renditions need to be generated, the formats make it difficult to generate renditions manually, or a uniform policy needs to be implemented for generating renditions. The format transformation features of the products in the CTS suite are listed below:

- **DTS**: **Document Transformation Services** can create PDF and HTML renditions.

- **ADTS**: **Advanced DTS** adds more formats to the list supported by DTS. It also provides capabilities for extracting metadata and for retaining bookmarks and hyperlinks in PDF renditions.

- **MTS**: **Media Transformation Services** can create various media formats, such as a TIFF file from a Photoshop file.

- **AVTS**: **Audio Video Transformation Services** address the specific needs of audio and video formats, such as frame rate, bit rate, resolution, and encoding.

- **MITS**: **Medical Imaging Transformation Services** add support for **Digital Imaging and Communications in Medicine (DICOM)** medical image format.

- **XTS**: **XML Transformation Services** can transform and render XML documents into a variety of formats.

- **Custom converters**: Custom converters can also be plugged in to support formats not covered by the above services or to use alternative means of creating these renditions.

Documentum product notes

It is important to distinguish the behavior of Content Server from that of Webtop or other applications that users directly interact with. Content Server offers content-related operations at a fine granularity. Applications, such as Webtop, present these operations in a form suitable for the usage patterns of human users. For example, the "same version" option during Webtop checkin doesn't even invoke checkin on Content Server. It performs a save but the inclusion of this option is both intuitive and convenient for human users. Similarly, the interaction taking place on the user's desktop may not include Content Server. For example, launching an application to view or edit a document is a capability of the client application and not of the Content Server.

Learning more

The topics discussed in this chapter can be further explored using the following resources:

- EMC Documentum Content Server 6.5 Fundamentals
- EMC Content Management and Archiving Product Summary Guide
- White Paper – EMC Documentum Content Transformation Services: Putting Your Information to Work
- EMC Documentum Webtop 6.5 SP2 User Guide
- EMC Documentum System 6.5 Object Reference Manual

Checkpoint

At this point you should be able to answer the following key questions:

1. What are the core Content Server features for working with content?
2. What is the difference between import and checkin? What is the difference between export and checkout?
3. How can a document be linked to or unlinked from folders?
4. What are versions? What is a version tree? What are branches?
5. What is the impact of deleting versions on a version tree?
6. What are formats? What are renditions?
7. How is Webtop used for working with content?
8. Which Documentum products provide features for format conversion?

3

Objects and Types

In this chapter, we will explore the following concepts:

- Objects and types
- Type hierarchies and type categories
- Object and content persistence
- Lightweight and shareable object types
- Aspects
- Querying objects

Objects

Documentum uses an object-oriented model to store information within the repository. Everything stored in the repository participates in this object model in some way. For example, a user, a document, and a folder are all represented as objects. An **object** stores data in its **properties** (also known as **attributes**) and has **methods** that can be used to interact with the object.

Properties

A content item stored in the repository has an associated object to store its metadata. Since metadata is stored in object properties, the terms *metadata* and *properties* are used interchangeably. For example, a document stored in the repository may have its title, subject, and keywords stored in the associated object. However, note that objects can exist in the repository without an associated content item. Such objects are sometimes referred to as **contentless objects**. For example, user objects and permission set objects do not have any associated content. Users and permission sets are discussed in chapters related to security.

Each object property has a data type, which can be one of `boolean`, `integer`, `string`, `double`, `time`, or `ID`. A `boolean` value is `true` or `false`. A `string` value consists of text. A `double` value is a floating point number. A `time` value represents a timestamp, including dates. An `ID` value represents an object ID that uniquely identifies an object in the repository. Object IDs are discussed in detail later in this chapter.

A property can be **single-valued** or **repeating**. Each single-valued property holds one value. For example, the `object_name` property of a document contains one value and it is of type `string`. This means that the document can only have one name. On the other hand, `keywords` is a repeating property and can have multiple `string` values. For example, a document may have `object_name='LoanApp_1234567891.txt'` and `keywords='John Doe','application','1234567891'`.

The following figure shows a visual representation of this object. Typically, only properties are shown on the object while methods are shown when needed. Furthermore, only the properties relevant to the discussion are shown. Objects will be illustrated in this manner throughout the book:

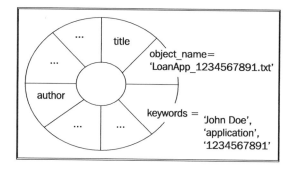

Methods

Methods are operations that can be performed on an object. An operation often alters some properties of the object. For example, the `checkout` method can be used to check out an object. Checking out an object sets the `r_lock_owner` property with the name of the user performing the checkout. Methods are usually invoked using Documentum Foundation Classes (DFCs) programmatically, though they can be indirectly invoked using API. In general, Documentum Query Language (DQL) cannot be used to invoke arbitrary methods on objects. DQL is discussed later in this chapter. DFC is discussed in *Chapter 4, Architecture* but DFC programming is beyond the scope of this book.

Note that the term *method* may be used in two different contexts within Documentum. A method as a defined operation on an object type is usually invoked programmatically through DFC. There is also the concept of a method representing code that can be invoked via a job, workflow activity, or a lifecycle operation. This qualification will be made explicit when the context is not clear.

Working with objects

In *Chapter 2, Working with Content* we used Webtop for performing various operations on documents, where the term document referred to an object with content. Some of these operations are not specific to content and apply to objects in general. For example, checkout and checkin can be performed on contentless objects as well. On the other hand, import, export, and renditions deal specifically with content. Talking specifically about operations on metadata, we can view, modify, and export object properties using Webtop.

Viewing and editing properties

Using Webtop, object properties can be viewed using the **View | Properties** menu item, shortcut **P**, or the right-click context menu. The following screenshot shows the properties of the example object discussed earlier. Note that the same screen can be used to modify and save the properties as well.

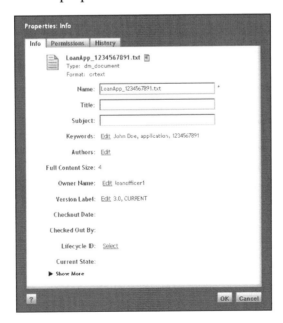

Multiple objects can be selected before viewing properties. In this case, a special dialog shows the common properties for the selected objects, as shown in the following figure. Any changes made on this dialog are applied to all the selected objects.

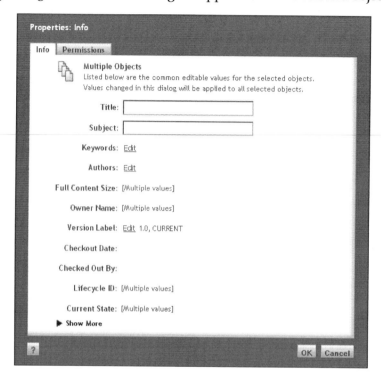

On the properties screen, single-valued properties can be edited directly while repeating properties provide a separate screen for editing through **Edit** links. Some properties cannot be modified by users at any time. Other properties may not be editable because object security prevents it or if the object is immutable. Security is discussed in other chapters while object immutability is discussed next.

Object immutability

Certain operations on an object mark it as **immutable**, which means that object properties cannot be changed. An object is marked immutable by setting `r_immutable_flag` to `true`. Content Server prevents changes to the content and metadata of an immutable object with the exception of a few special attributes that relate to the operations that are still allowed on immutable objects. For example, users can set a version label on the object, link the object to a folder, unlink it from a folder, delete it, change its lifecycle, and perform one of the lifecycle operations such as promote/demote/suspend/resume. The attributes affected by the allowed operations are allowed to be updated.

An object is marked immutable in the following situations:

- When an object is versioned or branched, it becomes an old version and is marked immutable.
- An object can be frozen which makes it immutable and imposes some other restrictions. Some virtual document operations can freeze the involved objects as discussed in *Chapter 15, Virtual Documents.*
- A **retention policy** can make the documents under its control immutable.

Certain operations such as unfreezing a document can reset the immutability flag making the object changeable again.

Exporting properties

Metadata can be exported from repository lists, such as folder contents and search results. Property values of the objects are exported and saved as a .csv (**comma-separated values**) file, which can be opened in Microsoft Excel or in a text editor. Metadata export can be performed using **Tools | Export to CSV** menu item or the right-click context menu. Before exporting the properties, the user is able to choose the properties to export from the available ones.

Object types

Objects in a repository may represent different kinds of entities – one object may represent a workflow while another object may represent a document, for example. As a result, these objects may have different properties and methods. Every time Content Server creates an object, it needs to determine the properties and methods that the object is going to possess. This information comes from an **object type** (also referred to as **type**).

The term **attribute** is synonymous with *property* and the two are used interchangeably. It is common to use the term attribute when talking about a property *name* and to use property when referring to its *value*.

We will use a *dot notation* to indicate that an attribute belongs to an object or a type. For example, objectA.title or dm_sysobject. object_name. This notation is succinct and unambiguous and is consistent with many programming languages.

An object type is a template for creating objects. In other words, an object is an *instance* of its type. A Documentum repository contains many predefined types and allows addition of new user-defined types (also known as **custom types**). User-defined types offer important capabilities and are described in detail in *Chapter 11, Custom Types.*

The most commonly used predefined object type for storing documents in the repository is dm_document. We have already seen how folders are used to organize documents. **Folders** are stored as objects of type dm_folder. A **cabinet** is a special kind of folder that does not have a parent folder and is stored as an object of type dm_cabinet. Users are represented as objects of type dm_user and a group of users is represented as an object of dm_group. Workflows use a process definition object of type dm_process, while the definition of a lifecycle is stored in an object of type dm_policy. These object types are described in more detail in later chapters. The following figure shows some of these types:

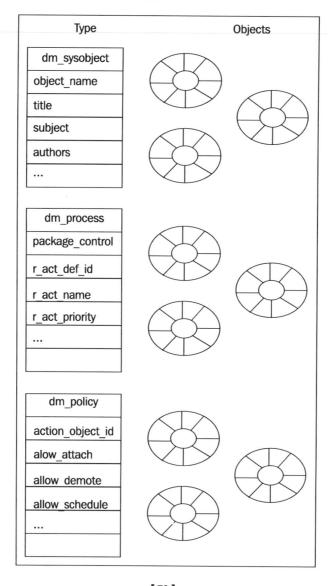

Just like everything else in the repository, a type is also represented as an object, which holds structural information about the type. This object is of type dm_type and stores information such as the name of the type, name of its supertype, and details about the attributes in the type. The following figure shows an object of type dm_document and an object of type dm_type representing dm_document. It also indicates how the type hierarchy information is stored in the object of type dm_type.

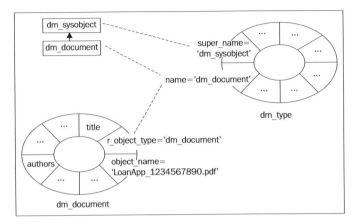

The types present in the repository can be viewed using Documentum Administrator (DA). The following screenshot shows some attributes for the type dm_sysobject. This screen provides controls to scroll through the attributes when there are a large number of attributes present. The **Info** tab provides information about the type other than the attributes.

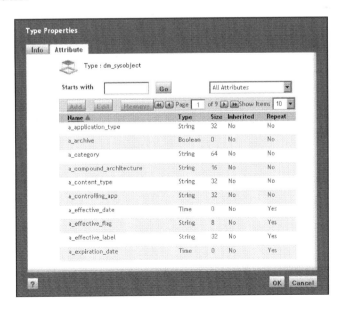

While the obvious use of a type is to define the structure and behavior of one kind of object, there is another very important utility of types. A type can be used to refer to all the objects of that type as a *set*. For example, queries restrict their scope by specifying a type where only the objects of that type are considered for matches. In our example scenario, the loan officer may want to search for all loan applications assigned to her. This query will be straightforward if there is an object type for loan applications. Queries are introduced later in this chapter.

As another example, audit events can be restricted to a particular object type resulting in only the objects of this type being audited. Auditing is described in more detail in the *Chapter 5, User and Privileges*.

Type names and property names

Each object type uses an *internal type name*, such as dm_document, which is used for uniquely identifying the type within queries and application code. Each type also has a *label*, which is a user-friendly name often used by applications for displaying information to the end users. For example, the type dm_document has the label Document.

Conventionally, internal names of predefined (defined by Documentum for Content Server or other client products) types start with dm, as described here:

- dm_: (general) represents commonly used object types such as dm_document, which is generally used for storing documents.
- dmr_: (read only) represents read-only object types such as dmr_content, which stores information about a content file.
- dmi_: (internal) represents internal object types such as dmi_workitem, which stores information about a task.
- dmc_: (client) represents object types supporting Documentum client applications. For example, dmc_calendar objects are used by **Collaboration Services** for holding calendar events.

Just like an object type each property also has an internal name and a label. For example, the label for property object_name is Name. There are some additional conventions for internal names for properties. These names may begin with the following prefixes:

- r_: (read only) normally indicates that the property is controlled by the Content Server and cannot be modified by users or applications. For example, r_object_id represents the unique ID for the object. On the other hand, r_version_label is an interesting property. It is a repeating property and has at least one value supplied by the Content Server while others may be supplied by users or applications.

- `i_`: (internal) is similar to `r_` except that this property is used internally by the Content Server and normally not seen by users and applications. As discussed in the previous chapter, `i_chronicle_id` binds all the versions together in to a version tree and is managed by the Content Server.

- `a_`: (application) indicates that this property is intended to be used by applications and can be modified by applications and users. For example, the format of a document is stored in `a_content_type`. This property helps Webtop launch an appropriate desktop application to open a document. The other three prefixes can also be considered to imply *system* or non-application attributes, in general.

- `_`: (computed) indicates that this property is not stored in the repository and is computed by Content Server as needed. These properties are also normally read-only for applications. For example, each object has a property called `_changed`, which indicates whether it has been changed since it was last saved. Many of the computed properties are related to security and most are used for caching information in user sessions.

Type hierarchy

It is common for different types to be related in some way and to share attributes and methods. In true object-oriented style, Documentum allows persistent types to be organized in an **inheritance**-based **type hierarchy**. A type can have none or one **supertype** and it inherits all the supertype attributes as its own. The complete set of attributes belonging to a type is the union of the inherited attributes and attributes explicitly defined for that type. In this relationship, the new type is called a **subtype**.

> A type with no supertype is called a **null type**. Null types are discussed in *Chapter 11, Custom Types*.

The *super* and *sub* prefixes are based on the visual representation of this relationship where the supertype is positioned logically higher than the subtype, as shown in the following figure:

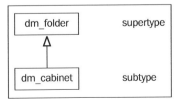

Note that supertype and subtype are *relative* terms. This means that when using either of these terms we refer to two types. A type can be a *subtype* for one type and *supertype* for another type at the same time. When many such relationships are visually represented together, they create a tree structure known as a **type hierarchy**. Readers familiar with object-oriented modeling will recognize this type hierarchy as a *class-inheritance hierarchy*. The following figure shows a portion of the type hierarchy for the predefined Documentum types:

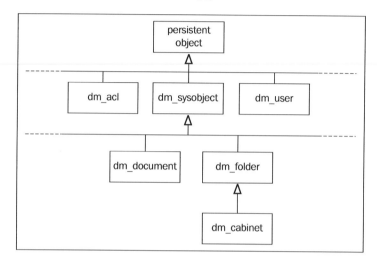

dm_document is an important type since it represents a document and is one of the most commonly used types. It is an interesting type because it has no properties of its own and it inherits all its properties from dm_sysobject.

One may question the point of having a separate type without any properties of its own. Recall the comment about using a type for treating the objects of that type as a set. dm_document as a separate type enables us to refer to all the objects of this type and subtypes as a set. It can also be used for the complementary set, for example, identifying all the objects of type dm_sysobject and its subtypes which are not of the type dm_document.

Object ID

r_object_id is a special property of every persistent object. It is used to uniquely identify the object and encodes some information within the property itself. It is a 16-character string value where each character is a hex (hexadecimal) digit.

The first two digits constitute a **type tag** representing the type of the object. For example, 09 means that the object has a type that is dm_document or its subtype – the object represents a document rather than a user, group, or something else. The next six digits represent the **repository ID** – a numeric identifier assigned to the repository. The last eight digits represent a *unique ID within the repository* and this ID is generated by the Content Server. The following figure illustrates the structure of the object ID and also shows the decimal values corresponding to the hex values.

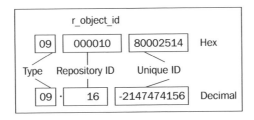

 Note that EMC assigns a unique range of repository IDs to each of its customers for the various repositories served by their Content Server installations. As long as these assigned repository IDs are used uniquely, r_object_id will uniquely identify an object across all repositories.

Type categories

Object types are categorized into **standard** and special categories for internal management by Content Server. A type is a standard type if it is not in one of the special categories. Most of the commonly used types are standard types.

The special object type categories are:

- **Shareable**: Shareable object types work in conjunction with lightweight object types. A single instance of a shareable type can be shared among many lightweight objects.

- **Lightweight**: Lightweight object types are used to minimize storage for multiple objects that share common system information. The shared properties reside in an instance of a shareable type and the rest of the properties reside in the lightweight objects. A lightweight type is a subtype of a shareable type.

- **Aspect property**: **Aspects** enable addition of properties to any object regardless of its type. Aspect property object types are used internally for managing properties associated with aspects. Users and client applications are not aware of these types.

- **Data table**: Data table is a collaboration feature that enables users to manage structured collection of information.

Since shareable and lightweight object types are used together they are discussed together later in this chapter. Aspect property types are internal types not visible to the users so they are not discussed further. However, the corresponding feature for users – aspects, is discussed later in this chapter. Data table object types are used by the optional Collaboration Services and are not discussed further.

Content Server explicitly identifies the category of an object type using the dm_type. type_category attribute, which can have the following values:

Value	Description
0	Standard object type
1	Aspect property object type
2	Shareable object type
4	Lightweight object type
8	Data table type

Object persistence

Objects stored in the repository are called **persistent** objects and their types are referred to as **persistent types**. All persistent types are part of a type hierarchy rooted in the internal type **persistent object**, which has the following attributes:

- r_object_id: This is used for uniquely identifying the object and is assigned by Content Server. This property has been described earlier in this chapter.

- i_vstamp: This is used internally for managing object updates and holds the number of committed transactions that have altered this object.

- i_is_replica: This is used in replication and determines whether an object is a **replica** of another in a different repository. Object **replication** replicates (copies) objects, both content and metadata, from a source repository to a target repository. The object copies in the target repository are known as replica objects.

Objects are stored in the repository using **object-relational technology** where properties are stored in (relational) database tables. Each persistent type is represented by two tables in the repository database – one for storing the single-valued properties and the other for storing the repeating properties. Single-valued properties for a type are stored in a table named *type_name*_s, while repeating properties are stored in a table named *type_name*_r.

For both single-valued and repeating properties, the property names map to the column names in the tables. Further, all of the _s and _r tables also have a column named r_object_id. The r_object_id column is used to join the single-valued and repeating properties along with the inherited properties to bring all the properties of an object together.

The structure of the _r tables is worth paying extra attention to. Each object can have multiple rows in the _r table where each column represents one repeating property. There is also an internal attribute named i_position, which defines the order of the values. Usually, two repeating properties of an object are not related to each other. For example, authors and i_folder_id are two repeating properties of dm_sysobject and there is no relation between an author and the ID of a folder that the object is linked to. Yet, these two values may be present in the same record in the table dm_sysobject_r.

> While there is no requirement for two repeating attributes to be related there is no prohibition either. Indeed, various types have two or more repeating attributes that are related and correspond to one another by index position. For example, dm_policy represents a lifecycle and has several repeating attributes which correspond to each other by index position where each index represents one state. Among these attributes, state_description[3] will hold the description for the state named in state_name[3], whose internal state number is stored in i_state_no[3]. Lifecycles are the subject of *Chapter 13*.

This storage scheme lets us determine the number of records for an object in its _r table. It is equal to the maximum number of values in any of the repeating properties that is not an inherited property for the object's type.

Consider an example where a custom type `dq_document` has `dm_document` as its supertype, as shown in the following figure:

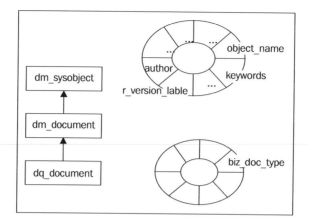

The following figure illustrates persistence for an object of `dq_document`. This figure only shows a small number of attributes for brevity. Note that the tables used for persisting objects of a particular type only store the properties explicitly defined for that type. Inherited properties are stored in the tables for the supertypes where they belong. However, all such persistence tables have the `r_object_id` column, which is used for joining information from other tables. Also note that `dm_document` does not add any properties of its own and `dq_document` does not add any repeating properties so the corresponding tables are absent from this figure. Another example of a type that doesn't use one of the tables is `dm_folder`, which has two repeating properties but no single-valued properties of its own.

dm_sysobject_s

object_name	r_object_id
LoanApp_1234567890.pdf	0900001080002514

dm_sysobject_r

r_object_id	keywords	authors	r_version_label
0900001080002514	John Doe		1.1
0900001080002514	application		CURRENT
0900001080002514	1234567890		

dq_document_s

biz_doc_type	r_object_id
Loan Application	0900001080002514

Looking at the figure above, you may be wondering how we would know that this is an object of `dq_document` since the table name doesn't indicate that. In fact, these tables hold information for objects of all subtypes of `dm_sysobject` as well. The exact object type of an object is identified by the `dm_sysobject_s.r_object_type` column (not shown in the figure above).

It is useful to know how properties are stored in database tables though all the properties of an object can be queried together using DQL without any reference to these tables. Internally, Content Server uses database views that join appropriate tables to retrieve all the needed properties of the type together. Further, when multiple types are used in one DQL query the DQL parser applies appropriate table joins to achieve the intended effect.

While most of the types represent persistent objects, there are some types whose objects are used for temporarily storing information in memory. These objects are not stored in the repository and are called **non-persistent** objects. For example, a *client config* object holds the configuration parameters for sessions when a client attempts to connect to the Content Server.

Content persistence

We have seen so far how metadata is persisted but it is not obvious how content is persisted and associated with its metadata. All **sysobjects** (objects of type `dm_sysobject` and its subtypes) other than folders (objects of type `dm_folder` and its subtypes) can have associated content. In *Chapter 2, Working with Content* we saw that a document can have content in the form of renditions as well as in primary format. How are these content files associated with a sysobject? In other words, how does Content Server know what metadata is associated with a content file? How does it know that one content file is a rendition of another one? Content Server manages content files using **content objects**, which (indirectly) point to the physical locations of content files and associate them with sysobjects.

Locating content files

Recall that Documentum repositories can store content in various types of storage systems including a file system, a Relational Database Management System (RDBMS), a content-addressed storage (CAS), or external storage devices. Content Server decides to store each file in a location based on the configuration and the presence of products like **Content Storage Services**. In general, users are not concerned about where the file is stored since Content Server is able to retrieve the file from the location where it was stored. We will discuss the physical location of a content file without worrying about why Content Server chose to use that location.

Content object

Every content file in the repository has an associated **content object**, which stores information about the location of the file and identifies the sysobjects associated with it. These sysobjects are referred to as the **parent objects** of the content object.

A content object is an object of type `dmr_content`, whose key attributes are listed as follows:

Attribute	Description
parent_count	Number of parent objects.
parent_id	List of object IDs of the parent objects.
storage_id	Object ID of the store object representing the storage area holding the content.
data_ticket	A value used internally to retrieve the content. The value and its usage depend upon the type of storage used.
i_contents	When the content is stored in turbo storage, this property contains the actual content. If the content is larger than the size of this property (2000 characters for databases other than Sybase, 255 for Sybase), the content is stored in a `dmi_subcontent` object and this property is unused.
	If the content is stored in content-addressed storage, it contains the content address.
	If the content is stored in external storage, it contains the token used to retrieve the content.
rendition	Identifies if it's a rendition and its related behavior.
	0 means original content.
	1 means rendition generated by server.
	2 means rendition generated by client.
	3 means rendition not to be removed when its primary content is updated or removed.
format	Object ID of the format object representing the format of the content.
full_content_size	Content file size in bytes, except when the content is stored in external storage.

Object-content relationship

Content Server manages content objects while performing content-related operations. Content associated with a sysobject is categorized as **primary content** or a **rendition**. We have already learned about renditions in *Chapter 2, Working with Content*. A rendition is a content file associated with a sysobject that is not its primary content.

Content in the first content file added to a sysobject is called its primary content and its format is referred to as the **primary format** for the parent object. Any other content added to the parent object in the same format is also called primary content, though it is rarely done by users manually. This ability to add multiple primary content files is typically utilized programmatically by applications for their internal use.

While a sysobject can have multiple primary content files it is also possible for one content object to have multiple parent objects. This just means that a content file can be shared by multiple objects.

Putting it together

The details about content persistence can become confusing due to the number of objects involved and the relationships among various attributes. It becomes even more complicated when the full Content Server capabilities (such as multiple content files for one sysobject) are manifested. We will look at a simple scenario to visually grasp how content persistence works in common situations.

> Documentum provides multiple options for locating the content file. DFC provides the getPath() method and DQL provides get_file_ url administration method for this purpose. This section has been included to satisfy the reader's curiosity about content persistence and works through the information manually. This discussion can be treated as supplementary to technical fundamentals.

Let's revisit the renditions we saw in *Chapter 2, Working with Content*. The sysobject is named paystub.jpg. The primary content file is in jpg format and the rendition is in pdf format, as shown in the following figure:

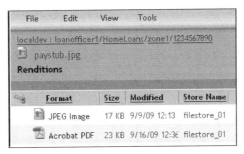

The following figure shows the objects involved in the content persistence for this document. The central object is of type `dm_document`. The figure also includes two content objects and one format object. Let's try to understand the relationships by asking specific questions.

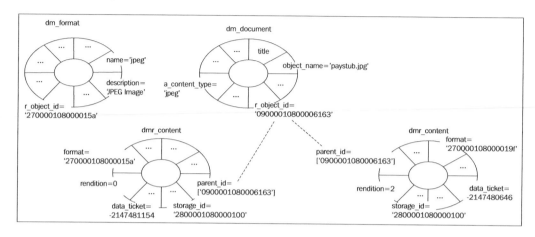

How many content files, primary or renditions, are there for the document `paystub. jpg`? This question can be answered by looking for the corresponding content objects. We look for `dmr_content` objects that have the document's object ID in one of their `parent_id` values. This figure shows that there are two such content objects.

Which of these content objects represents the primary content and which one is a rendition? This can be determined by looking at the rendition attribute. The content object on the left shows `rendition=0`, which indicates primary content. The content object on the right shows `rendition=2`, which indicates rendition generated by client (recall that we manually imported this rendition).

What is the primary format for this document? This is easy to answer by looking at the `a_content_type` attribute on the document itself. If we need to know the format for a content object we can look for the `dm_format` object which has the same object ID as the value present in the `format` property of the content object. In the figure above, the format object for the primary content object is shown which represents a JPEG image. Thus, the format determined for the primary content of the object is expected to match the value of `a_content_type` property of the object. The format object for the rendition is not shown but it would be PDF.

What is the exact physical location of the primary content file? As mentioned in the beginning of this section, there are DFC and DQL methods which can provide this information. For understanding content persistence, we will deduce this manually for a file store, which represents storage on a file system. For other types of storage, an exact location might not be evident since we need to rely on the storage interface to access the content file. Deducing the exact file path requires the ability to convert a decimal number to a hexadecimal (hex) number; this can be done with pen and paper or using one of the free tools available on the Web. Also remember that negative numbers are represented with what is known as a **2's-complement** notation and many of these tools either don't handle 2's complement or don't support enough digits for our purposes.

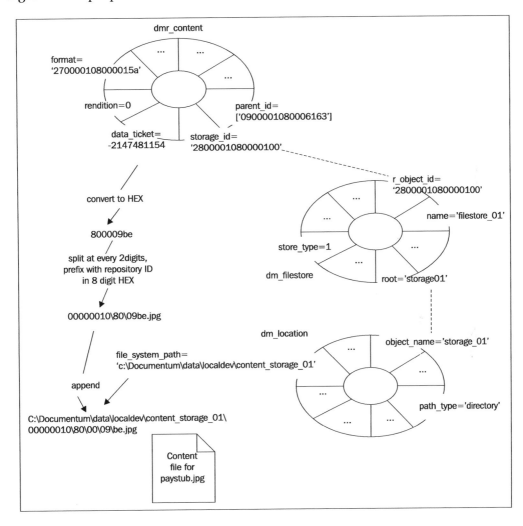

There are two parts of the file path—the *root path* for the file store and the path of the file *relative* to this root path. In order to figure out the root path, we identify the file store first. Find the `dm_filestore` object whose object ID is the same as the value in `storage_id` property of the content object. Then find the `dm_location` object whose object name is the same as the `root` property on the file store object. The `file_system_path` property on this location object has the root path for the file store, which is `C:\Documentum\data\localdev\content_storage_01` in the figure above.

In order to find the relative path of the content file, we look at `data_ticket` (data type integer) on the content object. Find the 8-digit hex representation for this number. Treat the hex number as a string and split the string with path separators (slashes, / or \ depending on the operating system) after every two characters. Suffix the right-most two characters with the file extension (`.jpg`), which can be inferred from the format associated with the content object. Prefix the path with an 8-digit hex representation of the repository ID. This gives us the relative path of the content file, which is `00000010\80\00\09\be.jpg` in the figure above. Prefix this path with the file store root path identified earlier to get the full path of the content file.

Content persistence in Documentum appears to be complicated at first sight. There are a number of separate objects involved here and that is somewhat similar to having several tables in a relational database when we normalize the schema. At a high level, this complexity in the content persistence model serves to provide scalability, flexibility by supporting multiple kinds of content stores, and ease of managing changes in such an environment.

Lightweight and shareable object types

So far we have primarily dealt with standard types. Lightweight and shareable object types work together to provide performance improvements, which are significant when a large number of lightweight objects share information. The key performance benefits are in terms of savings in storage and in the time it takes to import a large number of documents that share metadata. These types are suitable for use in transactional and archival applications but are not recommended for traditional content management.

The term **transactional content** (as in *business* transactions) was coined by Forrester Research to describe content typically originating from external parties, such as customers and partners, and driving transactional back-office business processes. **Transactional Content Management (TCM)** unifies process, content, and compliance to support solutions involving transactional content. Our example scenario of mortgage loan approval process management is a perfect example of TCM. It involves numerous types of documents, several external parties, and sub-processes implementing parts of the overall process. Lightweight and shareable types play a central role in the **High Volume Server**, which enhances the performance of Content Server for TCM.

A **lightweight object type** (also known as **LwSO** for **Lightweight SysObject**) is a subtype of a **shareable type**. When a lightweight object is created, it references an object of its shareable supertype called the **parent object** of the lightweight object. Conversely, the lightweight object is called the **child object** of the shareable object. Additional lightweight objects of the same type can share the same parent object. These lightweight objects share the information present in the common parent object rather than each carrying a copy of that information.

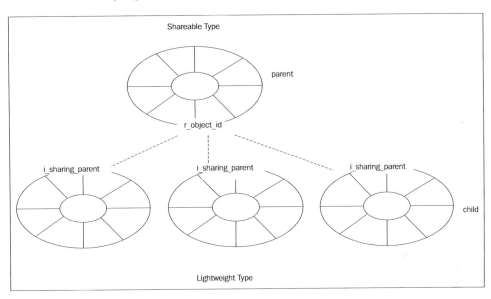

In order to make the best use of lightweight objects we need to address a couple of questions. When should we use lightweight objects? Lightweight objects are useful when there are a large number of attribute values that are identical for a group of objects. This redundant information can be pushed into one parent object and shared by the lightweight objects.

What kind of information is suitable for sharing in the parent object? System-managed metadata, such as policies for security, retention, storage, and so on, are usually applied to a group of objects based on certain criteria. For example, all the documents in one loan application packet could use a single ACL and retention information, which could be placed into the shareable parent object. The specific information about each document would reside in a separate lightweight object. ACLs define permissions on objects and are discussed in *Chapter 7, Object Security*.

Lightweight object persistence

Persistence for lightweight objects works much the same way it works for objects of standard types, with one exception. A lightweight object is a subtype of a shareable type and these types have their separate tables as usual. For a standard type, each object has separate records in all of these tables, with each record identified by the object ID of the object. However, when multiple lightweight objects share one parent object there is only one object ID (of the parent object) in the tables of the shareable type. The lightweight objects need to refer to the object ID of the parent object, which is different from the object ID of any of the lightweight objects, in order to access the shared properties. This reference is made via an attribute named `i_sharing_parent`, as shown in the last figure.

Materialization of lightweight objects

A group of lightweight objects sharing a parent object can be considered to be tethered to the parent object. They are forced to share the parent object's properties with the other lightweight objects and are said to be **unmaterialized** in this state. Suppose that one (or several) of the lightweight objects needs to change some of the shared properties while others need to retain the existing values. In this scenario, it is not possible to just change the property on the parent object. The lightweight object needs to break away from the rest and also needs to take a private copy of the properties of the parent object so that it can have different values for these properties.

When a lightweight object gets its own private copy of the parent object, it is said to be **materialized**. This terminology is similar to that used by RDBMS systems where materialized views may result in copies of previously shared column values. The private copy of the parent object uses the object ID of the materialized lightweight object. This state is similar to the standard type persistence, except that the join continues to use `i_sharing_parent` on the lightweight object table.

Materialization also results in a behavior change related to deletion. Deleting an unmaterialized lightweight object leaves the parent object alone, even if it was the last lightweight object pointing to the parent object. Deleting a materialized lightweight object always deletes its private copy of the parent object.

A lightweight object type definition includes specification of the materialization behavior, with the following options:

- Auto materialization—materialize automatically when certain operations occur

- Materialization on request—only materialize when explicitly requested

- Disallow materialization—do not materialize

Aspects

Aspects extend behavior and attributes for objects. An object type defines the properties and behavior of all objects of that type (and of its subtypes, via inheritance). In contrast, aspects enable us to attach additional behavior and attributes to an object, *regardless of its type*. Using aspects can speed up development and improve code reuse because they offer the possibility of extending attributes and behavior without altering the underlying type definitions.

In our example scenario, suppose that the mortgage lending company has a training program and they want to enhance it by providing examples of real-life situations and how their organization handles them. For this purpose, they want to tag documents that serve as good examples for handling specific scenarios. Irrespective of the type of document, they want to be able to add the following attributes to an example document:

Attribute	Description
example_title	A single-valued string describing the example in a few words.
example_detail	A repeating string where each value describes a reason why this is an example.

In this scenario, we could create an aspect named `Exemplary` with these two attributes. We don't need to modify any of the existing types nor do we have to create any new standard types. These attributes can be attached to any document and only to the documents that need it.

Restrictions

Even though aspects can be attached regardless of the type of object, aspects *cannot* be attached to arbitrary types of objects. Aspects can be attached under the following restrictions on types:

- An aspect can be attached to any sysobject
- An aspect can be attached to any object of null type (type with no supertype), once the type has been altered to allow aspects

It is also possible to attach multiple aspects to one object but one aspect cannot be attached multiple times to the same object.

If an aspect's name contains a dot, such as `jumbo.loan`, it cannot have any properties. Why would we want an aspect without any properties? An aspect without any properties can serve as a flag where the presence of this flag can be checked on objects.

Default aspects

Even though aspects are not automatically tied to object types sometimes we may have a need to do just that (often for convenience). For example, we may have an existing type called dq_loan_doc and we may want all of its objects (and of its subtypes) to have an aspect dq_web_viewable attached. If an aspect is associated with an object type, the aspect is automatically attached to each new object of the specified object type. Such an aspect is called a **default aspect** for the specified type. Of course, this aspect can still be attached to objects of other types (subject to the restrictions mentioned earlier). Default aspects for an object type are recorded in dmi_type_info.default_aspects for the type.

What is the benefit of having a default aspect? If we need an aspect on every object of a type then making it a default aspect saves the effort of manually or programmatically attaching the aspect to each object. Why wouldn't we just alter the type to add those attributes to the type definition? Maybe the type is not allowed to be altered. Maybe it really needs to be an aspect and it is applicable to objects of other types as well.

Multiple default aspects can be associated with one object type. An object type inherits all the default aspects defined for its supertypes. When we add a default aspect to a type, the newly added aspect is only associated with new instances created after the addition of the default aspect. Existing instances of the type or its subtypes are not affected. Similarly, removal of a default aspect does not affect the existing instances of the type.

Content Server creates and manages an internal object type for each aspect. The names and definitions of aspect properties are stored in this internal type. The internal type is named dmi_*type_id*, where *type_id* is the object ID of the internal type.

Aspects provide an alternative to placing attributes on a standard object type. However, this option should be exercised carefully as a large number of aspects or ill-designed aspects can make usage and maintenance difficult. Remember that aspects are most useful when they are not needed on all the objects of a type but may be needed on objects of types that are unrelated via an inheritance hierarchy.

Querying objects

Document Query Language (DQL) is a query language for Documentum just as **Structured Query Language (SQL)** is a query language for databases. In fact, DQL is a superset of ANSI SQL, which means that a well-formed query in ANSI SQL is also a well-formed DQL query. However, successful execution of a well-formed query depends on various factors such as existence of tables and availability of functions used in the query. DQL queries can be executed using **IDQL** (Interactive DQL shell), Documentum Administrator, Webtop, or programmatically through DFC applications. The results returned by a query are collectively referred to as a **result set**. When executing a query programmatically, the result set is represented by a **collection** object, which is a non-persistent object.

DFC provides a rich set of functionality for interacting with objects, including creating, querying, and modifying objects. DFC is a programmatic means of interacting with objects and is used in applications. DQL is used both for scripting and with DFC in applications.

In this section, we will examine the SELECT, UPDATE, and DELETE DQL queries used for manipulating objects. However, this is just a small overview of DQL capabilities and the *DQL Reference Documentation* should be used to explore the full set of DQL capabilities.

SELECT query

A DQL query can be used to inspect or affect one or more objects in a repository. The most common type of DQL query is the SELECT query, which retrieves the properties of one or more objects. For example, consider the following query:

```
SELECT r_object_id, r_creation_date
FROM dm_document
WHERE object_name = 'LoanApp_1234567890.txt'
```

This query shows three keywords—SELECT, FROM, and WHERE. These keywords divide up the query into three parts:

- *SELECT clause (selected values list)*: The selected values list specifies the properties to be retrieved.
- *FROM clause*: The FROM clause specifies the object types to be queried.
- *WHERE clause*: The WHERE clause is optional and specifies the conditions for matching the objects whose properties will be returned by the query. When the WHERE clause is present, the query is also called a *conditional* query.

A DQL query can also directly query database tables, though the tables need to be registered first. A **registered table** is a table from the underlying database that has been registered with the repository. This registration allows the table to be specified in a DQL query, either by itself or in conjunction with a type. A registered table can be used in place of an object type in most DQL queries and its columns can be used as properties in a DQL query.

Now, let's try to understand the semantics of this query. The FROM clause specifies that we want to consider objects of type dm_document. All the subtypes of dm_document are also included in the scope of this query. Among these objects, we only want to look at *current versions* of objects that have 'LoanApp_1234567890.txt' in their object_name property. The query will return the object ID (r_object_id property) and creation date (r_creation_date property) for all the resulting objects. Selection of non-current versions is discussed later.

No matter how (DFC or DQL) objects are queried, Content Server always enforces the configured security. Content Server will not return all documents just because a query requests all documents. It will only return the documents that the currently authenticated user is allowed to retrieve. Of course, the results can be further narrowed by conditions and arguments that are part of the query.

The same rules apply to the operations other than querying. Repository security is discussed in more detail in later chapters.

Basics

The comma-separated list after SELECT identifies the values to be returned. These values typically come from object properties, though they may include constants and calculations on properties as well. The allowed properties depend on the types specified in the FROM clause. For example:

```
SELECT object_name, title
FROM dm_document
```

Here the selected values are the properties object_name and title for the type dm_document. It is possible to rename the values being returned using the following syntax:

```
SELECT object_name AS Name, title AS Title
FROM dm_document
```

This capability is more useful and desirable when multiple types are present in the FROM clause:

```
SELECT d.r_object_id AS ObjectId, f.r_object_id AS FolderId
FROM dm_document d, dm_folder f
WHERE ...
```

Note that the selected attributes are both `r_object_id`, so renaming enables us to distinguish between them. Also note that we need to associate the property name with the type name in this case and it is done by using the prefixes `d.` and `f.`, where `d` and `f` are *aliases* (unrelated to the aliases in alias sets to be discussed in later chapters) for the types in the FROM clause. It is a good practice to use aliases for types and prefix them to property names when multiple types are present in the FROM clause.

When one or more repeating attributes are included in the selected attributes, the results may be returned in two ways. If `r_object_id` is included in the selected attributes, the values of each repeating attribute are returned as one string containing comma-separated values. In this case, one row is returned per matching object. The following query and its result illustrate this behavior. There are two values in `r_version_label` and three in `keywords` but they are all returned in one row per object:

```
SELECT r_object_id, object_name, r_version_label, keywords
FROM dm_document
WHERE object_name = 'LoanApp_1234567891.txt
```

r_object_id	object_name	r_version_ label	keywords
0900001080007932	LoanApp_1234567891.txt	3.0,CURRENT	Application, 1234567891,Loan

If `r_object_id` is not present in the selected attributes, only one value per row is returned even for repeating attributes. This means that multiple rows may be returned for one object. The following query and its result illustrate this behavior. There are two values in `r_version_label` and three in `keywords`. As a result, only one value per row but multiple rows per object are returned:

```
SELECT object_name, i_position, r_version_label, keywords
FROM dm_document
WHERE object_name = 'LoanApp_1234567891.txt'
ORDER BY i_position DESC
```

object_name	i_position	r_version_label	keywords
LoanApp_1234567891.txt	-1	3.0	Loan
LoanApp_1234567891.txt	-2	CURRENT	Application
LoanApp_1234567891.txt	-3		1234567891

Note the use of ORDER BY clause and `i_position` attribute for sorting the results. DESC indicates descending order. Multiple comma-separated attributes can be specified in the ORDER BY clause for sorting.

It is possible to use an asterisk (*) instead of a list of attribute names to be returned. In general, the * returns a set of predefined attributes but the exact behavior depends on the queried types and the presence of certain hints in the query. For full details about the behavior of *, see the *DQL Reference Manual*.

A DQL query only works on the current versions of objects unless (ALL) is used after the type name. For example, the following query retrieves name and title for all versions:

```
SELECT object_name, title
FROM dm_document (ALL)
```

It is rare to run a select query without a WHERE clause because it doesn't filter objects of the specified type(s). A query without a WHERE clause may take an inordinately long time to return the results. The WHERE clause provides conditions or search criteria for narrowing down the search scope to find relevant objects.

WHERE clause

The WHERE clause specifies a condition, which may consist of multiple conditions that an object must satisfy to be a part of the result set. An object participates in the conditions via its properties. Functions, expressions, logical operations, and literals are used along with the properties to define the condition. The following examples illustrate the usage of the WHERE clause.

The following example shows the use of a string literal in the WHERE clause. Note that a string literal is placed within single quotes:

```
SELECT r_object_id, title, subject
FROM dm_document
WHERE object_name = 'LoanApp_1234567890.txt'
```

The following example shows that a numeric value does not use quotes. This query retrieves objects that have been updated at least once:

```
SELECT object_name
FROM dm_document
WHERE i_vstamp > 0
```

An object ID literal is placed within single-quotes. The following query retrieves one specific object from the repository using its object ID:

```
SELECT object_name
FROM dm_document
WHERE r_object_id = '0900001080002514'
```

A repeating property in a WHERE clause is used with the keyword ANY, as shown in the next example. This query retrieves all current documents that have any of the keywords set to application:

```
SELECT object_name
FROM dm_document
WHERE ANY keywords = 'application'
```

Another commonly used condition relates to dates and the DATE function is useful for such situations. The following query retrieves objects that have not been modified since 09/09/2009:

```
SELECT object_name
FROM dm_document
WHERE r_modify_date < DATE('09/09/2009')
```

In addition to a comparison with exact values, pattern matching can be performed against string attributes. The character % represents zero or more characters while _ represents exactly one character. Pattern matching is performed using LIKE and NOT LIKE predicates as shown in the following example.

```
SELECT r_object_id, title, subject
FROM dm_document
WHERE object_name LIKE 'LoanApp%'
```

This query matches all current documents whose names start with LoanApp. The use of NOT LIKE would match all current objects that LIKE would not have matched.

Pattern matching is great but how would we find names containing %rate, for example? Since % has a special meaning for the LIKE predicate, it needs to be escaped. Essentially, we need to distinguish the literal % from the pattern matching %. The following query illustrates how to escape a pattern-matching character.

```
SELECT r_object_id, title, subject
FROM dm_document
WHERE object_name LIKE '%\%rate%' ESCAPE '\'
```

Next we look at UPDATE queries, which are used for modifying objects.

UPDATE query

An UPDATE query updates one or more objects and has the following syntax:

```
UPDATE <type_name> OBJECT
<property_updates>
WHERE <condition>
```

The WHERE clause works just as in the SELECT query. As before, the WHERE clause is optional but it is highly recommended that the WHERE clause not be omitted as far as possible because omitting it would lead to all objects of the type being updated (that are not otherwise restricted because of lack of permissions, immutability, or being checked out by another user).

<type_name> is the type or an *ancestor type* of the object(s) to be updated. Recall from the tree terminology discussed in *Chapter 2, Working with Content* that an ancestor can be the parent or an ancestor's parent in a tree. Therefore, an ancestor type could be the supertype, supertype's supertype, and so on. Sometimes, the ancestor type is loosely referred to as supertype to include all these possibilities.

<property_updates> specify the property names and the corresponding values to be set.

The following example illustrates these concepts:

```
UPDATE dm_document OBJECT
SET title = 'John''s Loan Application',
SET subject = '1234567890'
WHERE r_object_id = '0900001080002514'
```

This query shows several new features. Note that the keyword OBJECT (OBJECTS is also acceptable) is required, since we are trying to update the objects. If OBJECT is omitted, the query will attempt to modify a registered table. <property_updates> usually takes the form SET <property_name> = <value>. If multiple properties are being updated, each SET clause is separated using a comma.

Also note that for title we used two apostrophes where we needed one in the value. It is true for all DQL queries that an apostrophe inside a string literal should be replaced with two to escape the special meaning of the apostrophe.

In addition to setting literal (constant) values, it is possible to copy a value from one attribute to another, as shown here. This query copies the value of object_name into title:

```
UPDATE dm_document OBJECT
SET subject = object_name
WHERE r_object_id = '0900001080002514'
```

The following query updates or sets repeating attributes:

```
UPDATE dm_document OBJECT
SET authors[0] = 'John',
SET authors[1] = 'Jane'
WHERE r_object_id = '0900001080002514'
```

Note that if a repeating property, like `authors` in this example, needs to be updated, an individual value needs to be set using this format – SET <property_name>[<index>] = <value>. <index> specifies the position in the list of repeating values for the property and the positions start with 0. However, if we just need to append values at the end of the list we can use this format – APPEND <property_name> = <value>. Multiple values can be appended by using multiple APPENDs within the same update query.

Repeating values can be removed using TRUNCATE, as shown in the following example:

```
UPDATE dm_document OBJECT
TRUNCATE authors
WHERE r_object_id = '0900001080002514'
```

This query removes all values for `authors`. In another variation, TRUNCATE authors [2] will remove all values at index 2 and higher.

DELETE query

A DELETE query has a similar structure to an UPDATE query except that there are no properties to be set. A DELETE query has the following format:

```
DELETE <type_name> OBJECT
WHERE <condition>
```

This query does not have many new features. In fact it is probably one of the simplest DQL queries. Again, the WHERE clause is optional but omitting it will result in all objects of the specified type and its subtypes being deleted.

> We need to be very careful when using DELETE queries because there is no easy way to undo such a deletion, which destroys the objects in the database.

Let's look at an example of the DELETE query:

```
DELETE dm_document OBJECT
WHERE owner_name = USER
AND FOLDER('/Temp')
```

This query deletes all current objects of type `dm_document` or any of its subtypes that are owned by the currently authenticated user and linked to the folder path /Temp. Note the keyword USER – it gets dynamically replaced with the currently authenticated user when the query is executed. Similarly, TODAY is a keyword that gets replaced with the date on which the query is executed. Some other useful keywords are YESTERDAY, TOMORROW, and NOW. These keywords are used in queries that utilize date or time values.

Further, note the use of the keyword AND—it enables conjunction of two conditions in the WHERE clause. OR and NOT can also be used in a similar manner.

The query also illustrates how to search certain folders for objects. The folder predicate can specify one or more folder paths and whether the subfolders of those folders should be included in the search recursively. Consider the modified version of this query:

```
DELETE dm_document OBJECT
WHERE owner_name = USER
AND FOLDER('/Temp/a','/Temp/b',DESCEND)
```

This query deletes all current objects of type dm_document or any of its subtypes that are owned by the currently authenticated user and linked to the folder path /Temp/a, /Temp/b or any subfolders of these paths. Note that multiple folders can be specified in the folder predicate and, optionally, DESCEND specifies that the subfolders should be included for all folder paths listed.

API

API methods can be issued via IAPI or Documentum Administrator in addition to programmatic access through DFC. IAPI can send individual method calls to the server. The API can be used to create scripts for administrative or development purposes. One of the most common uses of the API is to dump an object to view all of its properties. For example, the following API command prints the names and values for all the properties of the object identified by the given object ID:

```
dump,c,'0900006480001126'
```

 The API will not be discussed in detail in this book. API is no longer officially supported since most API methods have been mapped to DFC methods.

Documentum product notes

Normally, there is one content object per content file in the repository. However, if **Content Storage Services** are deployed and content duplication checking and prevention is enabled, multiple content objects may become associated with one content file. This happens when identical copies of a content file are found and removed.

Since objects, content objects, and content files can have many-to-many relationships; Content Server uses certain attributes on content objects to track these relationships. In order to uniquely identify these relationships, each content file is assigned a **page number** per parent object and the page number identifies this content file uniquely among the content files associated with that sysobject. Page numbers are useful for identifying the primary content that is the source of a rendition.

Typically, a rendition is associated with a parent object via a content object. However, renditions created by the media server can be alternatively connected to their source via a relation object.

High Volume Server provides transactional capabilities (as in business transactions) and features for rapid ingestion, efficient database storage, and reliable access to content. It can be used as a standalone repository for store-and-retrieval applications or as a transaction processing accelerator when coupled with a Documentum Content Server.

Each repository has some cabinets created for use by Documentum software. These cabinets are called *system* cabinets. `Temp` is a system cabinet which is frequently used for holding temporary objects. Aspects are a relatively new feature and its support in the product suite is still maturing.

Learn more

The topics discussed in this chapter can be further explored using the following resources:

- EMC Documentum Content Server 6.5 Fundamentals
- EMC Documentum Webtop 6.5 SP2 User Guide
- EMC Documentum System 6.5 Object Reference Manual
- EMC Documentum System 6.5 SP2 DQL Reference Manual
- EMC Documentum Retention Policy Services Administrator 6.5 SP1 User Guide
- EMC Documentum Transactional Content Management—A Detailed Review
- DFC Javadocs
- Two's complement—`http://en.wikipedia.org/wiki/Two%27s_complement`
- New in D6 Platform: Aspects—`http://doquent.wordpress.com/2007/09/26/new-in-d6-platform-aspects/`

Checkpoint

At this point you should be able to answer the following key questions:

1. What is the difference between objects and types? How are objects related to types?

2. What information is encoded in the `r_object_id` attribute?

3. What are the object type categories?

4. What is a type hierarchy? How are objects of standard types persisted in the repository database?

5. What are lightweight and shareable types? How are objects of these types persisted?

6. What are aspects? When should they be used?

7. What are the various ways of querying objects in a repository? What are some common DQL queries?

4
Architecture

In this chapter, we will explore the following concepts:

- Documentum architecture layers
- Platform component groups and components
- Patterns of communication with Content Server

Documentum platform

The term *Documentum* means different things to different people. Some people think of the repository, some think of Webtop, and others think of a custom content application developed for their business.

In order to grasp the full capabilities and organization of the Documentum platform, it may be best to think of it as a set of *core product components*, an additional set of *optional product components* (some of which are used frequently), and an unbounded set of *custom applications*.

The Documentum platform includes a large number of product components. A large number of interacting components bring complexity to the platform but this complexity is made manageable by organizing the platform as a framework. The framework provides guidelines, standards, and tools for using and extending the platform.

The Documentum platform is organized in layers, just like the well-known *n-tier* architecture for enterprise applications. However, the similarity is in terms of the benefits of using layers rather than a one-to-one correspondence with the traditional tiers. Instead of mapping on to the traditional application tiers, Documentum layers typically cross multiple traditional application tiers, as will be discussed in the next section.

Layered architecture

Layered architectures are a norm in enterprise applications today. Layers can separate components by various criteria such as purpose or role, technology, and dependence on other components. There are various benefits of layered architectures, including the following:

- Complexity becomes manageable from multiple perspectives — comprehension, design, implementation, testing, and deployment

- Encapsulated implementation of a layer makes it possible to replace the layer with another implementation

- Multiple higher-level layers can utilize the functionality of the lower-level layers, thus promoting reuse

In this discussion, we will use the term *tiers* in the popular sense — *presentation (view)*, *logic*, and *persistence (data/content storage)*. We will describe the Documentum platform architecture in terms of layers.

The following figure shows a very high-level organization of the architecture, with the top layer being closest to users and the bottom layer being closest to the system. In general, each layer utilizes the layer directly below it but the tools layer can interact with all the other layers.

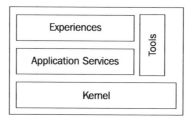

The Documentum platform is organized in four layers — **Kernel Layer, Application Services Layer, Experiences Layer**, and **Tools Layer**. Each layer serves a specific purpose and consists of product components that contribute towards that purpose. Thus, each layer can also be thought of as a conceptual group of components. Let's look at the purpose of each layer:

- Kernel provides the core content management capability for storing, accessing, and securing content.

- Application services provide capability for organizing, controlling, sequencing, and delivering content to and from the repository.

- Tools enable development and deployment of enterprise content applications. A **content application** implements a business process that relies on content. Tools also include web services to enable content-based integration with other applications.

- Experiences provide the framework and interfaces for presenting content management capabilities in desktop or web-based applications.

The following figure maps Documentum architecture layers to traditional architecture tiers. Note how most layers span multiple tiers.

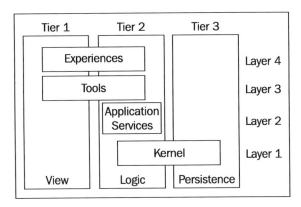

Next, we explore the capabilities encapsulated in each layer and the key product components that provide those capabilities. Note that many products have components that span multiple layers. In such cases, a product will most likely be discussed in the layer that contains its core capability.

Product names in this chapter have been abbreviated to avoid repetition of EMC Documentum prefix on each occurrence. Products listed here are EMC Documentum products unless they are qualified by another prefix such as Microsoft or Adobe.

Kernel

The **Kernel Layer** components can be categorized into **Repository Infrastructure**, **Repository Services**, and **Security Services**, which together provide storage, access, and security for the repository. The following figure outlines these categories and the associated products:

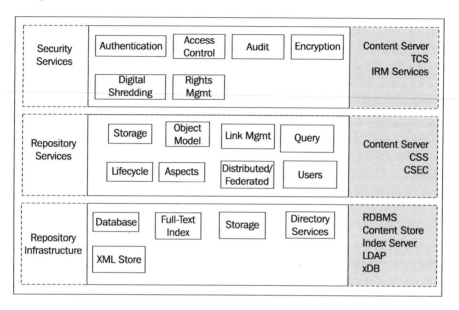

Repository infrastructure

Repository infrastructure establishes a repository physically using **database, full-text indexes, content storage**, and **directory services** capabilities. It can also include native **XML storage** separately from database and content storage.

A database is used for storing metadata and this capability is often provided by one of the well-known RDBMS products such as **Oracle** or **Microsoft SQL Server**.

Content storage is usually provided by the file system of the host operating system (OS) or a **Content-Addressed Storage (CAS)**, such as **EMC Centera**. CAS uniquely identifies a content item using a digital fingerprint (also known as ID or logical address) of the content item rather than a file system path of the content item. Other alternatives such as **Network Attached Storage (NAS)**, **Storage Area Networks (SAN)**, streaming servers, and even relational databases can be used for content storage.

Optionally, the repository can also maintain a **full-text index** of all text-based content assets stored within the repository. For example, such content may include documents, text files, HTML files, XML content, and close-captioned video content. The full-text index includes all words from the content and the metadata identified for full-text indexing. The full-text index supports words in multiple languages and more than 70 languages are supported. Full-text indexes are created by **FAST Index Server**, however alternative engines could be used for indexing. **Documentum OEM Edition** is designed to be embedded in content-rich applications and uses **Apache Lucene** for indexing, which is an open source alternative to FAST. A new product—**Enterprise Search Server (ESS)**, is in the works and it will provide another alternative to FAST full-text indexing. It will leverage the new XML capabilities along with the existing open search architecture to provide better scalability, performance, and support for distributed configurations, among other goals.

Directory services provide user directories as common infrastructure for implementing security and a Documentum repository can utilize such directories as sources of user information. Directory Services are often provided by LDAP server products such as **Microsoft Active Directory**, **Sun ONE Directory Server**, **Oracle Internet Directory**, **IBM Tivoli Directory Server**, and **Novell eDirectory**.

XML Store brings XML-enabled ECM and ECM-enabled XML capabilities to a repository. XML can add structure and intelligence to content and ECM can provide management and governance for XML. XML Store is provided by the native XML database **xDB**, which is fully optimized for managing large volumes of XML content.

Repository services

Repository services make the repository available via a unified view by hiding the disparate components of the repository infrastructure. These capabilities are primarily provided by Content Server; additional relevant products are mentioned here as applicable.

The **storage management** capability makes the specifics of the storage infrastructure transparent to the rest of the platform. If EMC Centera is used in the repository infrastructure, **Content Services for EMC Centera (CSEC)** is needed to enable its functionality. EMC Centera is optimized to store content, such as archived content, for long periods.

It is possible to add an optional storage policy engine via **Content Storage Services (CSS)** to automate storage allocation and migration based on policies. For example, frequently accessed content can be stored in a high-performance storage environment while rarely accessed content can be migrated to a more economical storage environment based on configured policies.

The **object model** represents everything in the repository as objects. We have already seen how objects, types, and content are represented and managed in a repository. Essentially, an object can have metadata, content, and operations that can be performed on the object.

Objects can be associated with other objects. A particularly important association is provided by the links between objects and folders. The **link management** capability manages these links.

The **query** capability supports execution of queries against the repository. This capability helps find objects based on specified conditions and uses full-text index when available. Query results are filtered by object security applicable for the user executing the query.

Objects in a repository can be associated with a **lifecycle**, which defines a sequence of states the object goes through. This capability provides checks and automation as objects move through their lifecycles.

We have already seen that **aspects** enable the addition of attributes and operations directly to objects, independently of the types of the objects.

Content Server understands and can participate in **distributed** or **federated** architectures. In a distributed architecture, a repository has parts of the infrastructure spread over multiple Content Server installations. These separate installations work together to provide a unified view of the repository at each installation. In a federated architecture, multiple repositories cooperate to share users, groups, and security.

The capability of representing and managing **users** is the foundation on which security services rely.

Security services

Security services secure the functionality provided by the repository services. The key security capabilities include identifying the user, allowing only the permitted activities for the user, and keeping track of activities being performed on the repository. Once again, the key capabilities are provided by Content Server and additional relevant products are mentioned as applicable.

Authentication identifies the user through a configured mechanism in the repository. It is possible to use the Operating System security or the system database for this purpose. The repository can also utilize existing directories which may be part of the repository infrastructure. **RSA Access Manager** is supported for single sign-on. It is also possible to extend the authentication mechanism to use **Kerberos** or **CA Netegrity** when these products are part of the existing security infrastructure.

Access control or **authorization** restricts access to repository contents and functionality based on configured access rules. Controls may be applied to users such as restricting a user from creating groups. Fine-grained controls can be applied to objects in terms of permissions via access control lists.

Auditing provides the capability for tracking operations being performed on the repository. It can track the old and new values on modified objects and the user who performed the change. Auditing comes in handy when there is a security breach – it can help figure out the cause of the breach, so that the security configuration can be corrected. Similarly, it can help identify causes of performance issues and guide system optimization.

Content Server can **encrypt** all communication with its clients and other infrastructure components using SSL encryption to protect the information being exchanged with it on the network.

Trusted Content Services (TCS) enhances the security capabilities of the platform for application-specific security needs in the following ways:

- Enables encryption of file stores to protect content from being accessed directly, bypassing the Content Server.

- Enables **digital shredding** of deleted content so that it cannot be recovered at the Operating System level.

- Supports verifiable electronic signatures.

- Enhances authorization via **Mandatory Access Control (MAC)**, which works on top of the core security model and can provide overriding capabilities. It can require membership in an externally defined group, restrict user access globally, and allow application-specific security settings on ACLs.

Information Rights Management (IRM) Services extends the security and access control beyond the limits of the repository. Normally, once content leaves the repository users are free to do with it what they wish as long as it is permitted by the document format. IRM Services add an **IRM Policy Server** which can host policies defining whether documents can be opened, displayed, printed, or further distributed once they leave the repository. Out of the box, it supports Microsoft Office, Adobe PostScript, HTML, RIM BlackBerry, and Lotus Notes formats for IRM control. When the content leaves the repository it is in encrypted form and it is decrypted only after the policy server has verified that the requested operation is allowed on the content according to configured policies.

Application services

The **Application Services Layer** components can be categorized into **Compliance Services**, **Content Services**, and **Process Services**, which together provide content management capabilities. The following figure outlines these categories and the associated products:

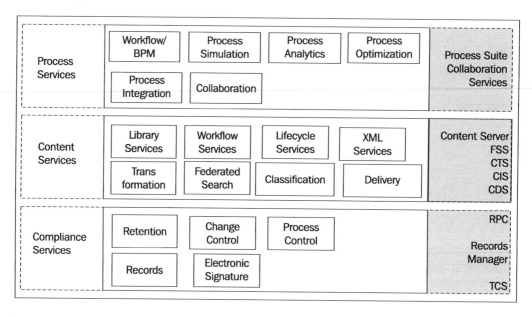

Compliance services

Compliance is the process of following guidelines and rules, typically established by external bodies such as government agencies. Almost all regulations require **retention** in some form, which means that assets such as documents must be preserved in unaltered form for a predetermined period of time. For example, US employers are required to retain employee I-9 forms according to Immigration and Nationality Act and HR stipulations.

Compliance services enable the platform to enforce retention policies and to manage content as records. These capabilities are provided by **Retention Policy Services (RPS)**, **Records Manager (RM)**, and TCS.

RPS adds a retention engine to the platform providing the capability to fulfill legal requirements and to comply with regulations. It enables definition of **retention policies** and their application to objects, folders, workflows, and lifecycles. A retention policy specifies how long an object needs to be kept in the repository. Such retained objects become immutable for the duration of the policy. Policies can also specify rules for content disposal, including the options of permanent archival and destruction of content at appropriate time. Further, objects can be put *on hold temporarily* in response to unplanned events such as an external audit, which may not be covered by a policy. Such on-hold objects cannot be disposed of even if the applied retention policy allows it.

RPS also enhances the platform capabilities by adding notification related to progress through retention phases, auditing for retention-related events, and reporting related to record-keeping activities.

RM builds upon the platform capabilities and RPS features to provide record-keeping capabilities to users. Its architecture makes its capabilities available to external systems for easy integration using web services.

RM provides the following features:

- **Retention Policy Management**: Using RPS as the underlying engine, RM enables users to create, manage, and use retention policies.

- **Security and Access Control**: Enhances the security model by providing non-cumulative permissions and the ability to associate permissions with object types. Enhances access control by requiring membership of one or all of a set of designated groups.

- **File Plans**: A file plan provides an automated control mechanism for permanent system-wide record classification. It specifies how to name, classify, organize, and retain/dispose records.

- **Containment Policies**: Specify rules for using a folder hierarchy or a file plan in terms of how it can grow and what actions are permitted within portions of the hierarchy.

- **Naming Policies**: Configure naming conventions and enforce them through validation and dynamic name generation.

We have already seen that TCS provides **electronic signature** capability for signing a document electronically and for verifying the integrity of the signed document.

Content services

Content services provide the core set of capabilities for working with objects and content.

Library services provide the fundamental capabilities of checking in, checking out, versioning, and managing renditions. We have already seen these features in *Chapter 2, Working with Content.*

Workflows in Documentum automate business processes. Just like everything else in the repository, process definitions and workflow instances are stored in the repository as objects. This enables the platform to support a large number of concurrent workflow instances since the state of each instance can be persisted. Workflow capabilities of the platform are discussed in *Chapter 12, Workflows*. Process Services build on top of the core workflow features provided by Content Services and are discussed later in the chapter.

Lifecycles enable enforcement of policies around content. A lifecycle defines a sequence of states that an object goes through over time. The lifecycle state changes for a document can check conditions and trigger actions that can enforce desired policies. Lifecycle capabilities are discussed in detail in *Chapter 13, Lifecycles*.

XML services provide essential features for managing XML content items in their native format and include **XML content validation** and **XML chunking**. XML validation ensures that XML elements are well-formed and conform to the associated definition (that is, **DTD** or **schema**). The process of chunking segments XML documents into their elements, which are then managed as discrete content objects available for reuse in multiple contexts. **XML Store** offers a high-performance and scalable architecture for full-featured management of XML documents.

Federated Search Services (FSS), formerly named **Enterprise Content Integration Services** (ECIS), enable the platform to provide **federated search** capabilities, which can go outside Documentum repositories to integrate, query, and access content. A large number of content sources are supported for this integration, including **FileNet**, **OpenText**, **Microsoft SharePoint**, **IBM Lotus Notes**, **SAP**, **Oracle**, **Lexis/ Nexis**, **Factiva Infobases**, **Autonomy** search engine, **Google Enterprise Search Appliance**, **Google Desktop**, and online search engines such as **Google** and **Yahoo**.

Content Transformation Services (CTS) convert various kinds of content from one format and resolution to others. For example, these content types may include documents, images, and videos. In *Chapter 2, Working with Content* , we saw that CTS consists of Document Transformation Services (DTS), Advanced DTS (ADTS), Media Transformation Services (MTS), Audio Video Transformation Services (AVTS), Medical Imaging Transformation Services (MITS), and XML Transformation Services (XTS). CTS also allows custom converters to support formats not covered by the previous services or to use alternative means of creating these renditions.

Content Intelligence Services (CIS) analyze the text within content objects and automatically set their metadata. They can also classify these objects into categories according to predefined rules.

Content Delivery Services (CDS) deliver and deploy content to web servers, portals, and application servers using configurable rules. CDS can also deliver metadata along with the content. These services include **Interactive Delivery Services (IDS)**, which were formerly **Site Caching Services (SCS)** and **Interactive Delivery Services Accelerated (IDSx)**, which were formerly **Site Deployment Services (SDS)**. SCS enables delivering content to disparate target environments. SDS complements SCS by automating content delivery to multiple external web servers or web server farms.

Process services

Process Services enable collaboration and business process management on the platform.

Collaborative Services enable users to collaborate on common documents in the repository. In *Chapter 1, ECM Basics*, we saw that collaboration features include rooms, discussions, contextual folders, calendars, data tables, and notes, which are stored and managed as regular objects. These services also expose service-oriented interfaces facilitating integration with other services.

The **Process Suite** provides capabilities to define, execute, and manage automated business processes that can go beyond the Documentum platform when needed. A **Process Engine** and a **Business Activity Monitor (BAM)** engine extend the workflow capabilities of the Content Server. Processes running in this environment can act on any content object in the repository. **Process Builder** and **Forms Builder** are used to visually design and define processes that can be packaged in Documentum projects to be deployed to repositories. BAM provides analytical reporting for monitoring the state of the processes in execution. **Process Analyzer** provides modeling, simulation, and analysis capabilities. **Process Integrator** enables integration with the rest of the enterprise infrastructure and systems outside the enterprise using a service-oriented architecture, which may utilize standards such as SMTP, HTTP, and web services. The Process Suite can also incorporate external tools such as **ILOG Rules Engine**, **Cognos Analytics Engine**, and the **IDS Scheer Optimizer/Simulator**.

Experiences

The **Experiences Layer** components consist of **Client Infrastructure** and **Applications**, which together make the functionality of the platform usable for the end user. Client infrastructure provides shared components which provide application-independent capabilities that are needed by the clients of the platform. Applications present the platform to end users for a targeted use. The following figure outlines these categories:

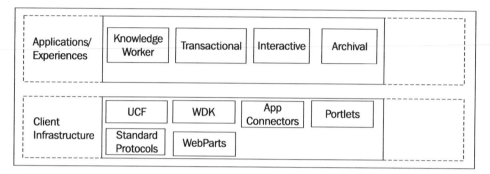

Client infrastructure

In general, a client is any entity that interacts with the platform. Client infrastructure provides shared components which provide application-independent capabilities needed by clients. For example, a client needs to be able to exchange content with the platform irrespective of the context of this transfer.

Unified Client Facilities (UCF) is a lightweight client-based service for content transfer between the client, application server, and Content Server. The UCF APIs provide a presence on the client for accessing the client file system, registry, and network resources. On the application server, a UCF server component provides access to library services.

Web Development Kit (WDK) is a library of components as well as a framework for developing web applications on the Documentum platform. The WDK framework uses a form-control-event approach which is consistent with **.NET WebForms** and the **Java Server Faces** standard (**JSF** or **JSR-127**).

The WDK components provide basic web application functionality for interacting with content and allow custom applications to be built on top of them. The custom applications are able to add to and alter the behavior provided by WDK. Documentum web application products such as **Webtop**, **Documentum Administrator (DA)**, **Web Publisher (WP)**, **Digital Asset Manager (DAM)**, **Records Manager (RM)**, **Documentum Compliance Manager (DCM)**, and so on are also built on the WDK framework.

Application Connectors make the repository accessible within desktop applications such as **Microsoft Office**. They are WDK components that utilize an open plug-in framework. In Microsoft Word, Excel, and PowerPoint, the connectors appear as menu items and directly interact with the server-side components. For example, a user could open a repository document directly from Microsoft Word using the connector. An Application Connector **Software Development Kit (SDK)** is available for development of additional application connectors.

Portlets are pluggable user interface components that are managed and displayed in a web portal. WDK supports portlet development using the **JSR-168** standard to provide native access to Documentum from a portal environment. While developers can build custom standards-compliant portlets using WDK, a set of pre-packaged WDK-based portlets with functionality such as *Inbox* and *Search* are available from EMC. Some portals, such as the **SAP Portal**, are not JSR-168 compliant. In such cases, the portlets are built using the native technology of the portal.

Documentum also provides client-infrastructure for the Microsoft platform via **WebParts**, which correspond to portlets. For example, **Documentum Content Services for Sharepoint** are implemented as a group of WebParts.

The Documentum repository is also accessible via standard protocols, which include the following:

- **Java Database Connectivity (JDBC)**, **Open Database Connectivity (ODBC)**, and **ActiveX Data Objects (ADO.NET)**: These APIs make a repository appear as a database and make it accessible in the form of a relational database.

- **Web-based Distributed Authoring and Versioning (WebDAV)**: WebDAV is an extension of the HTTP protocol that enables web-based distributed access to content. The Documentum platform includes a WebDAV server, which provides access to a repository via the WebDAV protocol.

- **File Transfer Protocol (FTP)**: Documentum includes an FTP server that enables content exchange with the repository using the FTP protocol.

- **File Share Services**: These services make a Documentum repository look like a network drive, enabling simpler access to the repository via desktop applications.

- **Documentum Foundation Services (DFS)**: These services make the repository accessible via web services. Interaction with Content Server using DFS is discussed later in the chapter.

Content Management Interoperability Services (CMIS) is a standard proposal defining a common interface for content repositories provided by different vendors. EMC is one of the proponents of the standard and Documentum currently offers an early-access CMIS implementation.

Applications/Experiences

EMC categorizes Documentum products for end-users in the following categories – **Knowledge Worker Applications**, **Transactional Content Management**, **Interactive Content Management**, and **Archiving**.

We have looked at several products while discussing the other architecture layers. This section may mention them again to indicate the experience that they align with, even if they don't have a user interface.

Knowledge Worker Applications

Knowledge Worker Applications deal with document management, classification, search, and collaboration around content. In simple terms these applications help users manage, find, and share content as a part of their work processes. These products are discussed as follows.

Document management

The products that enable document management are listed as follows:

- **Webtop** is the primary web interface for working with a Documentum repository.

- **Content Management Portlets** provide customizable out-of-the-box portlets— *Cabinets, Recent Files, Home Cabinet, Inbox, Subscriptions, Workflow View, Browse by Category, Search* and *Advanced Search*. These are familiar features from Webtop that have been made available for portal environments.

- **Content Services for Sharepoint** is a set of **ASP.NET WebParts** (controls) that expose Documentum Content Server access from SharePoint pages.

- **Documentum Client for Outlook (DCO)** provides easier navigation and management for email and documents through Microsoft Outlook. When using DCO, repository contents appear in folder views within Outlook. It enables automatic metadata capture from emails and also supports locking down emails stored in the repository for compliance purposes.

- **PDF Annotation Services** brings the review and commenting capabilities of Adobe Acrobat and PDF format to the Documentum platform.

- **CTS** provides content transformation and analysis capabilities.

Search and classification

The products that support search and classification are listed as follows:

- **FSS** extends the search capabilities of the platform beyond Documentum repositories.

- **FSS Adapters** bring various sources of information under the umbrella of FSS so that they can participate in federated searches. Federated searches scan multiple sources of information to gather results in one place.

- **Discovery Manager** allows users to search the desktop, web, and the enterprise with a single query as it makes the FSS capabilities available to end users.

- **FSS Portlet** makes the federated search capabilities available in a portal environment.

- **FSS Multilingual Services** allow users to perform searches in their preferred languages and to perform on-the-fly translations. Support for English, French, German, Italian, and Spanish is built-in.

- **CIS** automates classification of documents by automatically extracting information from documents and populating their metadata.

Content collaboration

The products that support content collaboration are listed as follows:

- **Collaboration Services** provide a client-extension to extend a WDK-based application (including Webtop, Web publisher, DAM, and DCO) with a collaborative environment.

- **CenterStage** provides a rich interface to the repository and includes numerous collaboration features. The **Essentials** version provides the shared team workspaces along with the core document management features. The **Pro** version adds Web 2.0 features such as wikis and blogs.

- **Documentum eRoom** provides a web-based collaborative workspace for distributed teams. eRoom can work independently of a Documentum repository but the enterprise edition provides native integration with Documentum repositories.

Transactional Content Management

Transactional Content Management (TCM) addresses the needs of content-rich (business) transactional processes by providing support for electronic capturing of documents and business process management.

Capture

The capture capabilities include electronic capturing and management of this input process from the perspective of the repository. These capabilities are provided by the Captiva suite of products.

- **Captiva InputAccel** can capture information from paper and electronic sources, transform it into usable content, and deliver it to a variety of backend systems, including Documentum repositories.
- **Captiva Dispatcher** provides intelligent recognition and classification capabilities to streamline handling of vast amounts of incoming data.
- **Captiva Input Management Console** provides browser-based analysis, reporting, and trend results of capture products (primarily Captiva-based).
- **Captiva eInput** is a front-end for a distributed capture system where images can be captured at remote locations and submitted to a content management solution. It is a web-based system that obviates the need for desktop scanning software at each remote location.

The suite also includes various products for specific applications, such as claims processing, invoice processing, and healthcare industry needs.

Business process management

Process Suite provides capabilities for orchestrating, analyzing, and optimizing content-oriented business processes. It includes **Process Builder**, which enables implementation of process models and their deployment for execution in the Process Engine. **Forms Builder** can be used with Process Builder to create user interfaces for workflow activities. **Process Connectors** enable application integration for tools such as rules engines, simulation environments, analysis and reporting tools with the products in the Process Suite.

Process Engine adds the capabilities to execute, orchestrate, and manage business processes. **Process Integrator** enables integration of Documentum process, content, and repository services with external systems and processes.

The Process Suite also includes a set of products for monitoring and analysis of executing processes. **Business Activity Monitor** provides reports, alerts, and dashboards for monitoring business processes. **Process Navigator** provides a browser-based interface for viewing and analyzing process models. **Process Analyzer** enables users to define business processes and to associate metadata for activities within a process. **Process Simulator** provides performance simulation for processes and a testing environment.

TaskSpace provides a highly configurable interface for users to quickly access high-volume transactional workflows with a focus on job functions or tasks. Typical transactional business processes include loan-origination processing, accounts payable management, case management, and claims processing.

Documentum Process Services for SAP enables integration of SAP content and transactional content management applications with the Process Suite. It makes SAP-related activity templates available for Documentum processes.

Interactive Content Management

Interactive Content Management solutions require the ability to create, manage, and deliver web-based and digital assets. The Document platform provides **Web Content Management (WCM)**, **Digital Asset Management (DAM)**, and **Editorial Publishing** products for this purpose.

Web Content Management

- **Web Publisher** enables creation and management of content for web sites and portals. It provides authoring tools as well as workflows for creation, approval, and management of the content.

- **Web Publisher Page Builder** provides a WYSIWIG (what-you-see-is-what-you-get) editor with page creation, layout, and display capabilities for business users. It also provides a site-creation wizard as a well as a framework for building sites using Web Publisher.

- **Web Publisher Portlet Builder** enables non-technical users to create, administer, and deploy portlets.

- **Content Delivery Services** includes **IDS** and **IDSx**, as discussed earlier, for distribution of accurate and reliable content from a Document repository to web servers and web farms.

Digital asset management

Digital assets include rich media as well as traditional documents. Documentum digital asset management products enable management of digital assets through a unified interface and provide extended capabilities that address special needs for rich media.

Digital Asset Manager (DAM) provides transformations and content preview capabilities such as thumbnails and PowerPoint previews to manage digital assets through this WDK application.

Authoring Integration Services (AIS) provide standards-based integration between authoring tools and Documentum repositories. AIS consists of File Share Services, WebDAV Services, and FTP Services, which have been described earlier.

CTS can also transform content for multi-purpose use and multi-channel publishing. **Media Transformation Services**, **Audio Video Transformation Services**, and **Medical Imaging Transformation Services** cater to these needs.

Learning Services facilitate the creation, management, and reuse of learning materials. It also provides interoperability with other **Learning Management Systems (LMS)** by using standards such as **Package Exchange Notification Services (PENS)** and **Shareable Content Object Reference Model (SCORM)**.

Editorial publishing

Content Services for WoodWing integrates Documentum with authoring tools for book and magazine publications. This enables automation of publishing workflows, and publication of the same content for multiple channels.

Archiving

Archiving products support preserving content for the long term and for archival.

Email archiving

SourceOne Email Management (formerly **Email Xtender)** products provide capabilities for archiving emails from Lotus Notes and Microsoft Exchange.

 The **SourceOne** suite of products focuses on **discovery**, which involves finding, safely holding, efficiently culling, and defensibly producing responsive content. Email management is only one aspect of discovery.

SAP archiving

EMC offers a suite of SAP integration products for archiving and content management.

Content Services for SAP enables management of documents and content within the context of SAP applications. **Content Services for SAP Portal** enables access to content in Documentum repositories from SAP Portal.

Archive Services for SAP enables archiving of SAP content into Documentum repositories. **ViewPoint for SAP** enables viewing of archived SAP content from SAP. **External Viewing Services for SAP** allows SAP and non-SAP users to view archived SAP content.

Integrated archiving

Integrated archiving products provide a unified software platform and consistent policies for storage management for various types of information such as reports, images, and content from SharePoint and SAP.

Archive Services for Reports enable archiving for reports and application output, format transformation to PDF, and automatic classification. It can also retain documents as parts of an individual print stream to maximize storage efficiency.

Archive Services for Imaging offers scalable archiving of paper-based information in electronic form.

Archive Services for SharePoint provides centralized control, retention, and reuse of SharePoint content in Documentum repositories.

Tools

The Tools Layer is made up of a consistent set of APIs, a unified object and programming model, and some readymade components. This layer enables development of clients and server-side components that work with the content repository.

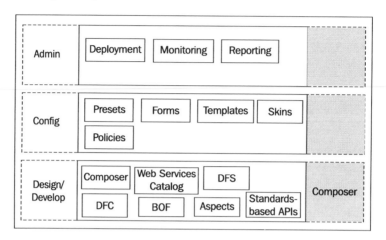

Design/Development

Among Design/Development components, Composer is the development tool while others are features used for development.

Documentum Composer, an Eclipse-based integrated development environment (IDE), is the primary tool for developing, deploying, and configuring applications running on the Documentum platform. Composer is discussed in detail in *Chapter 10, Documentum Projects.*

Documentum Foundation Services (DFS) provides a **Service Oriented Architecture (SOA)** development framework and API, which includes a set of out-of-the-box business objects and services. DFS also provides a Java SDK for developing custom services and Service-based Business Objects (SBO). SBOs are discussed later in this section.

DFS also includes a set of web services—**Enterprise Content Services (ECS)**, which expose the Documentum platform via web services. The core services in ECS are **Object, Version Control, Access Control, Lifecycle, Schema, Query, Query Store, Virtual Document**, and **Repository Inquiry** services.

ECS includes additional services related to BPM, Collaboration, Content Intelligence, Search, CTS, Enterprise Integration, Compliance Management, and Interactive Delivery.

Documentum Foundation Classes (DFC) expose the Documentum object model as an object-oriented library for applications to use in the form of Java and Component Object Model (COM) libraries. DFC provides high-level capabilities such as *virtual document management*, *XML content-management*, and *business objects*. Virtual documents combine component documents into a larger document. Virtual document management is described in *Chapter 15, Virtual Documents*.

Business Object Framework (BOF) is a structured environment for developing content applications. BOF enables developers to create reusable components that can be shared by multiple applications. There are two types of business objects:

- **Type-based Business Object (TBO)**: TBOs are the most common types of business objects. They are tightly linked to an existing or custom object type. New methods (custom business logic) can be added to such a type via a TBO. For example, a business object representing a loan is suitable to be implemented as a TBO.

- **Service-based Business Object (SBO)**: An SBO implements logic of procedures that are not specific to an object type. In fact, an SBO typically interacts with objects of multiple types in order to accomplish its function. Another way to think about SBOs is that they provide global or common services to multiple object types in a repository. For example, the Documentum Inbox service is an SBO and is not tied to a particular type of object.

Aspects provide a framework for extending object behavior and attributes. Aspects are a type of BOF entity that can be dynamically attached to object instances to provide fields and methods beyond the standard ones for the object type. Aspects were discussed in *Chapter 3, Objects and Types*.

 DFS, BOF, and DFC offer a range of choices for developing customizations for the Documentum platform. DFS can be used to manage content via web services from disparate environments. BOF can be used to develop server-side application capabilities that remain available to all clients. DFC can be used to develop clients or logic where the previous two concerns are not critical. Note that both DFS and BOF are built on top of DFC.

The standards-based APIs—JDBC, WebDAV, FTP, and File Share Services enable interaction with a repository using well-known standard protocols. These APIs have been discussed under client infrastructure.

Configuration

The configuration group includes features that support configuration in various products:

- **Webtop Presets** define actions or selections available in various situations, such as when a user from a particular group is trying to perform actions or the action is going to be performed in a particular folder location. Presets are discussed in *Chapter 9, Webtop Presets*.

- **Forms** can be used to create custom interfaces in workflows.

- **Templates** provide initial content for creating new documents.

- **Skins** offer an alternative look and feel for applications without altering the logic or functionality.

- **Policies** can be used to control behavior. For example, a retention policy can dictate where the content is stored based on the state of the content and the criteria specified in the policy.

Administration

Just like the configuration features, administration features are spread throughout various products. These features relate to deployment, monitoring, and reporting. For example, Process Suite provides a rich set of features related to monitoring and reporting. Composer can deploy the artifacts developed or modeled with it.

Communication patterns

Operation of the Documentum platform involves basic communication patterns, which are repeated during interaction with Content Server. In order to understand these patterns, it is important to first identify the components that participate in such communication.

Key components

The following figure shows the key components involved in communication with Content Server:

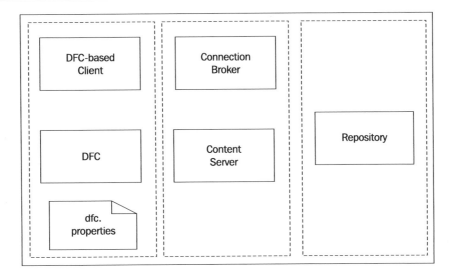

We are already familiar with Content Server—it manages the repository. Any content management communication ultimately needs to reach it.

DFC is implemented in Java and it also provides a *Java-COM Bridge* for access from Visual Basic or Visual C++. It also provides a **Primary Interop Assembly (PIA)** that supports access from the .NET platform. A DFC-based client uses an instance of DFC running locally within a Java Virtual Machine (JVM). DFS-based communication is discussed later.

A DFC-based client is any application or component that connects to the Content Server using DFC. In the rest of this section *client* would mean *DFC-based client* unless mentioned otherwise.

A **Connection Broker** (also known as **DocBroker**) is Documentum's *name server* or *registry* and it provides status and other information about Content Servers in response to request for such information. Each Content Server instance reports its status to one or more connection broker instances via a process known as projection, which is discussed in the next section.

Each DFC instance is configured via a file named `dfc.properties`. Among other configuration details, this file contains the name and port of a connection broker. Optionally, it can contain information about additional (also known as *secondary*) connection brokers.

Projection

A client is usually concerned about accessing a repository to perform content management operations on objects in that repository. However, repositories are accessed via Content Server instances and multiple Content Server instances may serve one repository. Therefore, there is a need to translate the request for a repository into a connection with a Content Server instance serving that repository. A connection broker provides a mapping of available Content Server instances serving a repository. The connection broker builds this map based on information provided by various Content Server instances.

Content Server instances regularly broadcast, or **project**, information to at least one connection broker to be considered active. Each Content Server broadcast to a connection broker is called a **checkpoint** and the connection broker receiving the checkpoint is called the **projection target**. A checkpoint contains connection and availability information for the Content Server instance sending the checkpoint. The interval between successive checkpoints from a Content Server instance is called its **checkpoint interval**. Each checkpoint also specifies the duration for which the checkpoint information is valid and this duration is called **keep entry interval**.

How does a Content Server instance know which connection brokers are its projection targets? Each Content Server instance has a file named `server.ini` which it reads on start-up. Each Content Server instance also has a server configuration object (of type `dm_server_config`). Projection targets can be specified in the `server.ini` file and the server configuration object.

The following figure illustrates three Content Server instances projecting to three connection brokers. The Content Server instance A (CS-A) for `repo1` only projects to connection broker A (CB-A) while the Content Server instances (CS-B and CS-C) for `repo2` project to the connection brokers B (CB-B) and C (CB-C). This means that CB-B and CB-C are not aware of the existence of `repo1` and CB-A is not aware of `repo2`.

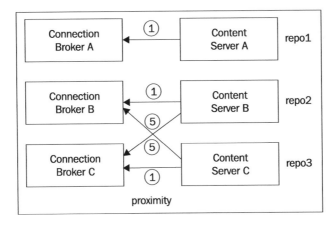

If a client wishes to connect to `repo2` via CB-B, which Content Server instance will be used, assuming both are available? Each checkpoint also includes a **proximity** value, which generally represents an ordering with lower values being preferred. This value is quite useful when various Content Server instances are located in distinct geographical locations. For example, we would prefer to use a local Content Server over a remote Content Server for connecting to the same repository. Based on the proximity values shown in the figure, the mentioned client will be connected to CS-B.

Fundamental communication pattern

The fundamental communication pattern with a Content Server is discussed in this section using the key components described earlier. The figures use arrows to indicate the initiation of action (component at the tail reaching out to the component at arrowhead).

Note that the discussion that follows uses a minimal configuration of one connection broker and one Content Server instance. If there are multiple connection brokers present, DFC will work with the first one aware of the desired repository. If there are multiple Content Server instances serving the desired repository, the pattern will apply after one instance has been selected for connection.

The fundamental communication pattern consists of these stages:

1. A session (connection) is established with a Content Server instance.

2. Requests are issued using this session and the Content Server instance processes these requests.

3. The session is released.

Establishing a session

The following figure illustrates the process of establishing a session with a Content Server instance:

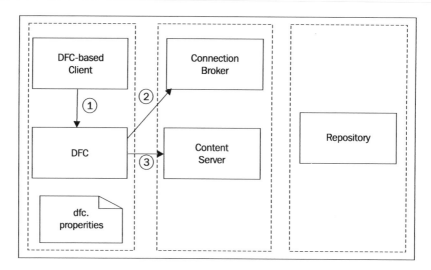

DFC is initialized before it can be utilized for performing any operations. During initialization, DFC reads `dfc.properties`, which provides connectivity information for connection brokers among other configuration parameters. The initialization step is not shown in the previous figure for simplicity.

Using an initialized DFC instance, a session is established as follows:

1. A client issues a connection request to DFC with the repository name and user credentials.

2. DFC requests the connection broker to provide information about the Content Server instances serving the specified repository. The connection broker provides this information.

3. DFC performs network communication using the remote-procedure call (RPC) capability and establishes a session with a Content Server instance. This session is provided to the client for performing operations.

Processing a request

The following figure illustrates the processing of a request by a Content Server instance:

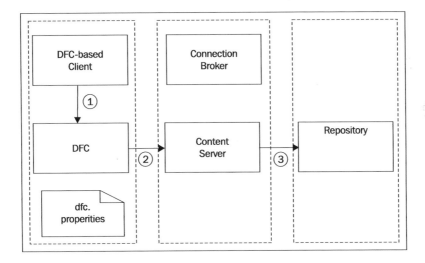

Client requests are processed by the Content Server instance as follows:

1. The client issues a request to the DFC instance along with the session.
2. Using the session, the DFC passes the request to the Content Server instance.
3. The Content Server instance processes the request and interacts with the repository. This processing may involve interaction with the database and the file stores that constitute the repository. Once the processing is complete the results are passed back on the reverse path back to the client.

Any number of requests can be processed in this manner using an existing session.

Releasing the session

Once the session is no longer needed it can be released. After this point, any additional requests will require establishing a new session.

DFS communication pattern

DFS provides a framework and web services for using the capabilities of the Documentum platform. When DFS is used for interacting with a repository, the application or the client interacts directly with the web service using standards and protocols related to web services. However, the web service itself becomes a DFC-based client described in the fundamental pattern earlier.

While the communication pattern between the web service and the Content Server instance is the same as that described for a DFC-based client, the pattern between a web service client and the web service is different. Usually, a DFS client sends a request to the DFS web service and that leads to an interaction with the Content Server instance. The interaction between a DFS web service and its client follows web service standards and a typical usage of these protocols is shown in the following diagram:

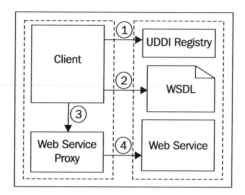

In general, web services refer to a category of technologies but, in practice, they are also used to refer to a set of standard protocols and technologies. The interaction illustrated in the figure is described as follows:

1. A **discovery protocol** is used for discovering available web services. **UDDI (Universal Description Discovery and Integration)** is a common protocol used for this purpose. A **UDDI registry** stores information about the location of web services and their descriptions. A client uses a UDDI registry to discover the location of a web service description file for the web service it needs.

2. A **description protocol** describes the public interface for a web service. **WSDL (Web Service Description Language)** is used for this purpose. Using the information from the UDDI registry, the client fetches the **WSDL document** for the web service.

3. A **web service proxy** provides code for communicating with the web service using the standard protocols and facilitates the creation of web service clients. Web service development tools can usually generate a proxy for the web service. Using information from the WSDL document, the client initiates a request for the web service and passes it to the proxy.

4. The proxy passes the request on to the web service using a standard **messaging protocol**, such as **SOAP (Simple Object Access Protocol)**, **XML-RPC**, and **REST**. The messaging protocol defines an **encoding** for messages in a common format. These messages are sent over the network using a **transport protocol** such as **HTTP (HyperText Transfer Protocol)**, **FTP (File Transfer Protocol)**, and **SMTP (Simple Message Transfer Protocol)**. The web service then interacts with Content Server using the fundamental pattern described earlier and passes the results back through the proxy to the client.

It is also possible to *chain* web services—a web service client could itself be a web service and have other clients interacting with it.

WDK application communication pattern

WDK is a library and framework for developing web applications for Documentum. A WDK application runs in a J2EE-compliant application server (more specifically, a *servlet engine*). A WDK application is organized into components where each component consists of the following:

- Component XML configuration
- Pages that are part of the component presentation
- Java classes encoding the behavior of the component
- Resource bundles for localization

A WDK application is also organized in layers and each layer has a directory (folder) of its own on the file system. The foundation layers of WDK applications are wdk and webcomponent on top of that. Applications add more layers above these foundation layers. For example, the layers in Webtop are shown in the following screenshot:

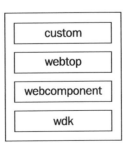

The role of each Webtop layer is described as follows:

- wdk: The wdk layer provides the base WDK framework layer.
- webcomponent: The webcomponent layer provides components for the core web interface.
- webtop: The webtop layer provides interface and behavior specific to the Webtop application.
- custom: The WDK framework is designed to be extended and customized and the custom layer is provided specifically for this purpose. A separate layer for customization prevents upgrades from overwriting the custom code. It also keeps most of the customization code together under one folder. The customization model supports small and selective customization, as well as large scale behavior and user interface changes.

A user usually interacts with a WDK application through a browser. In this case, the browser is not a client of the Content Server, since it is communicating with the application server. It is the WDK components on the application server that are the clients for the Content Server. The communication between the WDK components and the Content Server follows the same fundamental pattern where the WDK components become DFC-based clients. The dfc.properties used by Webtop can be found within the application folder on the application server.

In summary, the browser client may interact with the WDK application in any pattern but the WDK components interact with the Content Server in the same fundamental pattern as described earlier.

Documentum product notes

Each Documentum installation designates a repository as the **global registry**. The global registry is the repository used for storing installation-wide elements such as SBOs. All repositories in an installation connect to the global registry for accessing the installation-wide elements.

In a Documentum deployment, the Content Server, the file store, and the database can all be hosted on separate physical machines. All normal access to the repository should occur through the Content Server. In order to avoid accidental or malicious direct access, the content storage on the file system is secured by permissions to the **installation owner** only. The installation owner is the OS user account used for installing Content Server.

The interaction of Content Server with a repository deserves some attention. One Content Server serves one repository but multiple Content Server instances can also serve the same repository. This is usually done for performance reasons (**load balancing**), where the expected number of concurrent requests to one instance may cause it to become overloaded.

Multiple Content Server instances may also be used for **high availability (fail-over)** where failure of one Content Server instance doesn't make the repository unavailable since the other instance(s) can serve the repository.

The Content Server is supported by **Method Servers**, which can execute **methods**. In this context, a method is a piece of code that can be scheduled to run as a job or can be invoked from a workflow activity or a lifecycle action. There are two kinds of Method Servers:

- **Dmbasic Method Server**: This executes methods written in **Docbasic**. Docbasic is a programming language, somewhat similar to Visual Basic, and supported by Documentum. A Docbasic program can access the Content Server functionality via API calls.

- **Java Method Server**: This executes methods written in Java. However, these methods are not literally the methods on a Java class. A Documentum Java Method is a class that implements a specific interface in order to be accepted as a Documentum Java Method. The Java Method Server is just a J2EE application server (currently JBoss, by default) that hosts the web application responsible for executing Documentum Java methods.

In Documentum versions prior to 6.0, **Documentum Client Library (DMCL)** was a low-level API exposing full Content Server functionality. DFC used to wrap around DMCL exposing a higher-level API for the clients to use. Since version 6.0, DMCL is still available to use but does not incorporate any new features.

Prior to version 6.0 the WDK application were installed using installers. Since Documentum version 6.0, WDK applications are available to deploy in the JEE standard WAR format.

Learn more

The topics discussed in this chapter can be further explored using the following resources:

- EMC Documentum Content Server 6.5 Fundamentals
- EMC Documentum System 6.5 Object Reference Manual
- EMC Content Management and Archiving Product Summary Guide
- EMC Documentum Webtop 6.5 SP2 User Guide
- EMC Documentum Web Development Kit 6.5 Development Guide
- EMC Documentum Documentum Foundation Services 6.5 Development Guide
- (White Paper) EMC Documentum Architecture: Delivering the Foundations and Services for Managing Content Across the Enterprise, A Detailed Review
- (White Paper) Leveraging Web Services to Integrate with EMC Documentum in an SOA, Applied Technology
- (White Paper) SOA Meets Compliance: Compliance Oriented Architecture—A conceptual framework for considering Documentum Retention Policy Services
- (White Paper) Federated Search Services: Reaching Out to Information Beyond EMC Documentum—A Detailed Review
- (White Paper) Managing the XML Revolution: Organizing and Delivering Content Components for Engaging Applications—Best Practices Planning
- JSR-168 Portlet Specification—`http://jcp.org/aboutJava/communityprocess/review/jsr168/`
- Technology Reports: Content Management Interoperability Services (CMIS)—`http://xml.coverpages.org/cmis.html`
- EMC World 2009: Enterprise Search Server (ESS)—`http://www.alexandra.st/?p=466`

Checkpoint

At this point you should be able to answer the following key questions:

1. What are the layers of Documentum architecture? What are their roles? What are the key component groups of each layer?

2. What is the fundamental communication pattern for interacting with the Content Server? How is it different from interaction with a DFS web service or a WDK application?

Part 2

Security

Users and Privileges

Groups and Roles

Object Security

5
Users and Privileges

In this chapter, we will explore the following concepts:

- Documentum security at a high level
- Users and authentication
- User authorization including privileges and client capabilities
- User management with DA

Documentum security

At a high level, the security model in Documentum is similar to that used in contemporary enterprise applications. There are *resources* (information, objects) that need to be secured, there are *operations* that can be performed on the resources, and there are *users* who wish to perform these operations. The *security configuration* defines what is allowed for various combinations of users, operations, and resources. At run time, a user attempts to perform an operation and the components of the Documentum architecture resolve rules for the specific user, operation, and resource combination to allow or disallow the attempted operation. In our example scenario, there can be a requirement that a loan application for a loan that has been approved may only be edited by a manager. In this example, the resource is an approved loan application and the restricted operation is editing.

At a detailed level, security implementation is specific to the Documentum architecture. This is the first chapter on Documentum security and introduces the concept of users and security aspects that are tied to users.

In general, the term security is used with the semantics of controlling access, which involves two parts—**authentication** and **authorization**. While authorization deals with what a user is allowed to do, the first step is to identify the user reliably. Therefore, first the user *identity* is authenticated and then each attempted operation by this user is checked against the authorization rules configured for this user.

Information security deals with *confidentiality, integrity,* and *availability* of information. Controlling access contributes towards the confidentiality and integrity goals. Encryption of information also serves these two goals. Availability is often addressed via architectural means. For example, multiple Content Server instances can serve one repository and keep it available if one of the instances fails.

Just like everything else, security configuration is also stored in the repository as objects and properties on objects. Various components of the Documentum architecture enforce the configured security rules. In some cases, it may be possible to use external (non-Documentum) components to assist with security enforcement. For example, an LDAP server or a product such as Netegrity SiteMinder can participate in the user authentication process. This is an important feature since Documentum is just one component of enterprise infrastructure and its ability to integrate with other components facilitates the overall management and deployment of infrastructure.

The following figure illustrates the security features specific to users. We will see later that **permissions** are tied to objects and provide the foundation for **object security**. Permissions indicate what can be done to an object by different users. On the other hand, restrictions can be placed on users, irrespective of the specific objects that they may want to interact with. **Privileges** are tied to users and are enforced by the Content Server. **Client capabilities** are also tied to users but they are *optionally* enforced by Documentum client applications. Both privileges and client capabilities are attached to the user representation and stored within the repository, as shown in the following screenshot. The representation of a user in the repository is discussed in detail later in this chapter.

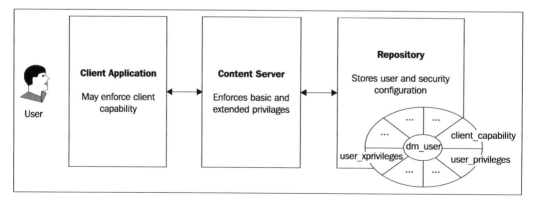

There are two important objects in a Documentum repository that store configuration information influencing the operation of the Documentum platform:

- **Repository configuration** (type dm_docbase_config): A repository configuration object contains configuration information about a repository. Each repository has a single repository configuration object whose object name matches the name of the repository. It provides configuration information related to security and other repository-specific properties. This object is created as a part of the repository creation process.

- **Content Server configuration** (type dm_server_config): A server configuration object contains information that a Content Server uses to define its operation and operating environment, such as the number of allowed concurrent sessions, maximum cache sizes, the storage area locations, and the locations of executables that the server calls. There is one server configuration object per instance of Content Server serving a repository. One of these objects is created as a part of the repository creation process. Other instances may be created via administrative actions.

Since they affect the whole range of platform behavior, these objects and their relevant properties will be discussed at the relevant points in the rest of the book.

Users

The term **user** is typically used in one of two ways—a *human* interacting with a system or the *representation of identity* within the system. The representation of identity within the system may or may not correspond to a real human user. Identities not representing human users are typically referred to as *generic, system,* or *application* users or accounts. A user is represented as an object of type dm_user within the repository.

Authentication

Typically, a user logs into an application to authenticate the claimed identity. For example, WDK applications such as Webtop and Web Publisher challenge a user with a login screen for authentication. The user selects the repository to be accessed and presents an identity as a login/password combination. The information identifying a user for the purpose of authentication is called **credentials**. The following screenshot shows the Webtop login screen:

Once the credentials are submitted, Content Server verifies these credentials using one or more of the following ways:

- OS (Operating System) account: This is the default authentication mechanism. Content Server uses an internal program to match the credentials against OS accounts. It is also possible to use a custom program to perform authentication against the OS. In this mechanism, the password is not stored in the repository. On UNIX systems, Content Server uses the `dm_check_password` program for OS authentication. EMC also provides the source code for this program, which can be customized to meet any specific authentication requirements.

- **LDAP (Lightweight Directory Access Protocol)** server entry: Content Server contacts an LDAP server to authenticate the credentials against an entry present in the LDAP server. LDAP is a technology used for security implementations such as central authentication and authorization.

- **Inline password**: Content Server matches the provided password against a password stored in the repository. The `dm_user.user_password` property stores inline passwords. The appropriate `dm_user` object is identified by the login (and potentially domain) and the password is compared against the `user_password` property of that object.

- **Authentication plug-in**: An authentication plug-in may be used, which takes over the responsibility of authentication. This mechanism provides freedom to use external authentication sources such as Netegrity SiteMinder and RSA Access Manager. Documentum provides two plug-ins—**RSA** and **Netegrity SiteMinder**.

The following figure illustrates these various sources against which Content Server may authenticate a user:

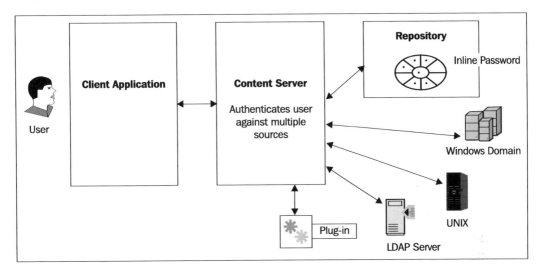

By default, Content Server runs in **no-domain-required** mode, which is indicated by a blank in `dm_docbase_config.auth_protocol`. In this case, users don't need to specify a domain and user names must be unique in the repository.

On the other hand, if Content Server is running in **domain-required** mode, the `auth_protocol` property is set to `'domain-required'`. In this case, multiple users can have the same name as long as they have different domains. Further, users are required to specify a domain name for authentication.

Content Server determines the method of authentication for each user based on the `dm_user.user_source` property. The values of this property and their semantics are as follows:

User source	Implication
LDAP	Authentication through an LDAP server. This requires at least one LDAP config (`dm_ldap_config`) object to be present in the repository. Documentum supports several LDAP sources as discussed in *Chapter 4, Architecture*.
unix only	Authentication using UNIX, domain is not used.
domain only	Authentication against Windows domain.
unix first	Authentication against UNIX first; if that fails, authentication against Windows domain.
domain first	Authentication against Windows domain first; if that fails, authentication against UNIX.
inline password	Authentication against the password stored in `dm_user.user_password` object.
plug-in identifier	Authentication with the plug-in identified by the identifier (such as `dm_netegrity`, which represents Netegrity SiteMinder authentication plug-in).

An **LDAP configuration object** (type `dm_ldap_config`) stores configuration for Content Server to use for interacting with an LDAP server. For example, it contains the host name and port number of the LDAP server, information about the structure of the directory tree, and credentials for connecting to the LDAP server.

There can be multiple LDAP configuration objects in a repository but one Content Server uses only one LDAP configuration object at any given time (identified by `dm_server_config.ldap_config_id`).

An LDAP configuration object can be created through Documentum Administrator or through DQL. Creation and modification of an LDAP configuration object requires Superuser privileges. Privileges are discussed later in this chapter.

Special users

There are two special users in a repository. They are as follows:

- **Installation owner**: Installation owner is the OS account used for installing the Content Server. A corresponding user is automatically created in the repository.

- **Repository owner**: The repository owner is the *database owner* (DBO) of the underlying database for the repository. The repository owner can be referred to as `'dm_dbo'` in some DQL queries. Note that the repository owner does not need to have an OS account.

Both of these users automatically get Superuser privilege in the repository. Privileges are discussed later in this chapter.

Authorization

Recall that authorization pertains to controlling access to functionality. User-specific authorization can be enforced by the client applications as well as the Content Server. Client applications utilize a user's **client capability** to enforce access control for functionality within the client application. They can also utilize **roles** to manage access to functionality within the applications. Roles are discussed in *Chapter 6, Groups and Roles*.

On the other hand, Content Server utilizes basic and extended **privileges** to enforce access control. As we will see in later chapters, Content Server also enforces object security in addition to these privileges.

Client capability

The `dm_user.client_capability` attribute stores the **client capability** level for users. This information is available for all users, but it is up to the client applications to utilize this information for enforcing additional access control.

Documentum's client applications such as Webtop assign specific meanings to these capabilities. These capabilities are hierarchical in the sense that one level can also imply another level. There are four levels of client capability:

- **Consumer**: Consumers can search, view, and copy documents and forward tasks in workflows. This is the default capability.

- **Contributor**: The contributor capability includes consumer capability. In addition, a contributor can create documents and folders, modify regular documents and virtual documents (including checkin and checkout), delete documents, initiate workflows, and perform workflow tasks.

- **Coordinator**: The coordinator capability includes contributor capability. In addition, a coordinator can create cabinets and virtual documents and can view hidden objects.

- **System Administrator**: The system administrator capability includes the coordinator capability. In addition, a system administrator can manage Content Server, repository, and users and groups.

> Note that client capabilities only allow what a user can *attempt* to do within a client application. These attempts are further subject to the Content Server scrutiny using privileges and object permissions. For example, suppose that a user has coordinator client capability but no privilege for creating a cabinet. In this case, the user will not be able to create a cabinet.

Basic privileges

While client capabilities may be enforced by a client application, privileges are enforced by the Content Server. A user's **basic privileges** are set in the `dm_user.user_privileges` property as described in the following table:

Privilege	Value	Description
None	0	None of the basic privileges. This is the default value.
Create Type	1	Can create custom object type.
Create Cabinet	2	Can create, modify, and delete cabinets.
Create Group	4	Can create, modify, and delete groups.
Sysadmin	8	Can perform basic administration tasks.
Superuser	16	Can perform all administration tasks.

Unlike client capability, privileges are not hierarchical and each privilege needs to be specified explicitly. Multiple basic privilege values can be combined by adding the corresponding integer values. Thus, if we want to grant Create Type and Create Cabinet privileges to a user, the `user_privileges` property needs to be set to 3 (=1+2).

While the first four privilege values are straightforward, Sysadmin and Superuser privileges need some elaboration. A user with Sysadmin privilege has following abilities:

- It has lower privileges as well (Create Type, Create Cabinet, Create Group)
- It can activate/deactivate a user
- It can manipulate users and groups
- It can grant and revoke the lower privileges to other users
- It can create or modify system-level permission sets
- It can administer full-text indexing and repository
- It can manage lifecycles
- It can manipulate workflows

On the other hand, a user with Superuser privilege has the following features:

- It has Sysadmin privileges as well
- It can grant and revoke Sysadmin and Superuser privileges and extended privileges
- It can delete system-level permission sets
- It can become owner of all objects in the repository
- It can unlock checked out objects
- It can manipulate others' custom types
- It can create null types (types with no supertypes)
- It can manipulate others' permission sets
- It can query any underlying RDBMS tables, even if they are not registered
- It can view all audit trail entries even if it doesn't have explicit View Audit extended privilege
- It can register and unregister others' tables

Extended privileges

Each user also gets extended privileges, which pertain to **audit trails**. Auditing is a very important feature of the Documentum platform since it enables tracking of different types of events, which can be used later for diagnostic or research purposes. Each occurrence of an audited event is recorded as an object of the type `dm_audittrail`.

 Note that only the events configured to be audited generate audit trail entries. By default Content Server audits dm_audit, dm_unaudit, dm_signoff, dm_adddigsignature, dm_addesignature, dm_addesignature_failed, dm_purgeaudit, dm_logon_failure, and the set of events represented by dm_default_set. Among these events, auditing can be turned off for dm_logon_failure and dm_default_set only.

A user normally does not get any privileges related to audit trails. The extended privileges are set in the `dm_user.user_xprivileges` property and can be a combination of one or more of the following:

Ext privilege	Value	Description
None	0	No audit privileges. This is the default value.
Config Audit	8	Can configure auditing.
Purge Audit	16	Can remove audit trail entries.
View Audit	32	Can view audit trail entries.

The repository owner, superusers, and users with the View Audit extended privilege can view all audit trail entries. Other users cannot view audit trail entries about ACLs, groups, and users.

Extended privileges are also combined by adding the corresponding integer values. For example, granting View Audit and Purge Audit results in the value 48 (=16+32).

User management

As mentioned earlier, a user is stored in the repository as an object of type `dm_user`. No user can be authenticated against a repository without the presence of the corresponding `dm_user` object. Some important attributes of `dm_user` are described as follows:

Property	Label	Description
user_state	State	Active or Inactive; only active users can connect to the Content Server.
		0 means that the user can log in.
		1 means that the user cannot log in.
		2 means that the user is locked.
		3 means that the user is locked and inactive.
user_name	Name	Display name.
user_login_name	User Login Name	Login ID or user account. This is the name used for authenticating the user.
user_login_domain	User Login Domain	Windows domain or LDAP config name. The usage depends on the value of user_ source.

Property	Label	Description
user_source	User Source	*As described earlier.*
description	Description	Any free-form information about the user.
user_address	E-mail Address	User's email address.
user_os_name	User OS Name	User's OS name, if any. This property is useful when the user source is OS.
user_os_domain	Windows Domain Name	Windows domain of the user.
home_docbase	Home Repository	Default repository for the user; useful when a user is a member of multiple repositories.
restricted_folder_ids	Restrict Folder Access To	This property is used to restrict access to only a certain set of locations (cabinets or folders) within the repository. Note that when a folder is included, its subfolders are implicitly included in the set.
default_folder	Default Folder	Default folder for objects created by this user.
user_db_name	DB Name	User's name in the underlying database.
user_privileges	Privileges	*As described earlier.*
user_xprivileges	Extended Privileges	*As described earlier.*
client_capability	Client Capability	*As described earlier.*
workflow_disabled	Workflow Disabled	This property can be used to prevent a user from participating in workflows.
failed_auth_attempt	Turn off authentication failure checking	Setting this property to -1 disables the counting of unsuccessful authentication attempts. If not disabled, this property is reset to 0 on a successful login.

User management involves creation and modification of dm_user objects. Sysadmin or Superuser privilege is required for creating a user in the repository. If the client application enforces client capabilities, then system administrator client capability is also required for this purpose. User administration also involves managing group memberships for users, which is discussed in *Chapter 6, Groups and Roles*.

Note that even though `user_source` identifies where a user is authenticated, the existence of the user at that source is not a prerequisite for the creation of the user in the repository.

For example, a user may be created in the repository with the default authentication set to OS, even though the user account does not exist on the OS. The user will be created in the repository although authentication attempts by such a user will fail until the corresponding user has been created at the specified source.

The users in a Documentum repository can be created in several ways:

- The easiest way to create individual users is through Documentum Administrator. The web-based interface provides friendly ways to specify values for various user properties. For example, repository locations can be browsed and suitable values for user sources can be selected from a drop-down interface. Webtop offers a similar interface.

- If the enterprise infrastructure already has an LDAP user directory, users can be created in the repository by using the LDAP directory as the user source. An **LDAP Sync** job is available that can read user information from the LDAP directory to create the corresponding user objects in the repository automatically.

- Users can be created by importing a file in the **LDIF (LDAP Data Interchange Format)** format, containing the information about the users being created. This file format is commonly used with LDAP servers.

- When users need to be created frequently or if the user information is available from sources other than an LDAP directory, user creation can be scripted using DQL or API.

- Custom application interfaces can be created using DFS, DFC, and WDK for user administration tasks. This approach can also be used for importing user information from external sources of such information.

User information can be modified as well using the preceding mechanisms.

User management with DA

Let's look at DA features for user management. Once the user logs into DA, the user management functionality can be accessed via the browser-tree on the left, as shown in the following screenshot:

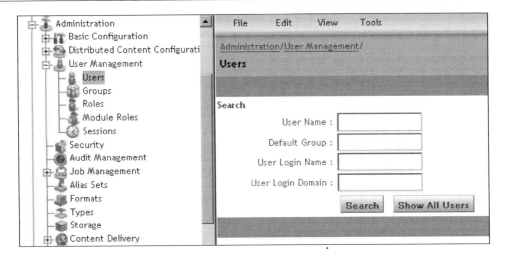

Managing existing users

The work area shows user search controls and a button for listing all existing users. These controls help locate an existing user and then the properties of the user can be viewed or modified. A user list is just like a document list, as shown in the following screenshot:

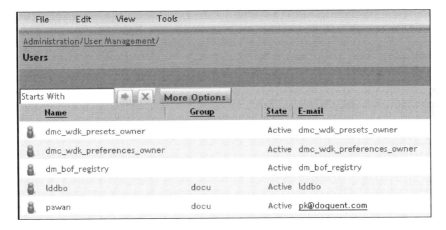

Note that there are some users with a name starting with dm. These are system accounts used internally by the Documentum platform. A few properties of each user are shown in the list view and the other properties can be accessed by viewing properties, just as we did for documents.

A user can also be deleted by selecting the user and then using **File |
Delete** menu item, **Delete** shortcut key, or with the right-click context
menu. In general, it is not a good idea to delete a user because a user
may have become associated with a large number of objects in the
repository. The user should be made inactive instead.

Creating users

A new user can be created with **File | New | User** menu item, which opens the
following screen. This screenshot shows a partial set of user attributes that were
discussed earlier:

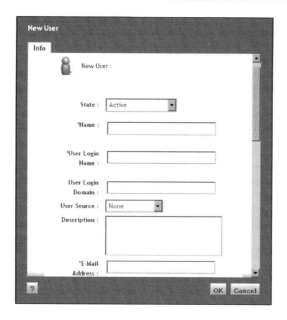

Help—some DQL queries

Here are some helpful queries related to users. These queries are based on the
information presented in this chapter.

The following query retrieves some basic information about a user with login
name jdoe:

```
SELECT user_name, user_login_name, user_address, description,
                                    home_docbase, user_state
FROM dm_user
WHERE user_login_name = 'jdoe'
```

The following queries set up a new user named Jane Doe. The first query creates the user object. The second query creates a folder in the repository and the third one sets this new folder as the home folder for the new user.

```
CREATE dm_user OBJECT
  SET user_name        =  'Jane Doe',
  SET user_login_name  =  'jdoe',
  SET user_address     =  'jdoe@doquent.com',
  SET user_group_name  =  'docu',
  SET user_source      =  'inline password',
  SET user_privileges  =  2,
  SET client_capability =  4


CREATE dm_folder OBJECT
  SET object_name      =  'jdoe',
  SET owner_name       =  'Jane Doe'
  LINK '/Home'

UPDATE dm_user OBJECT
  SET default_folder   =  '/Home/jdoe'
  WHERE user_login_name =  'jdoe'
```

The following query lists the inactive users in the repository:

```
SELECT user_name, user_login_name
FROM dm_user
WHERE user_state = 1
  OR user_state = 3
```

The following query lists the privileges for the same user. Recall that both the basic and extended privileges are stored as numbers that are sums of the component privileges. For example, a privilege value 6 (= 2 + 4) implies Create Cabinet and Create Group privileges.

```
SELECT user_name, user_privileges, user_xprivileges
FROM dm_user
WHERE user_login_name = 'jdoe'
```

The following query lists the LDAP configuration objects present in the repository:

```
SELECT object_name
FROM dm_ldap_config
```

Documentum product notes

Documentum uses the user's name rather than the login name as a key for the user in various scenarios. For example, the user name is used for identifying the owner, modifier, and creator for an object. This approach is unlike most other applications that use the login name or another identifier to uniquely identify a user. One practical problem that this approach raises is that changing a user's name is not a simple exercise. Users may want to modify the name when they get married or divorced, for example. Documentum provides a job for renaming users. However, it must be used with caution because any usage of user names in custom attributes will not be addressed by this job.

Documentum supports distributed architecture and a **federation** is a set of repositories that share user and security information. Recall that a user needs to be represented in each repository that needs to be accessed by that user. Federations facilitate user management for users that need to be present in all of the participating repositories. Such users are called **global users**. A **local user** is managed in the repository in which the user is defined. Global users are managed from a designated repository known as the federation's **governing repository**.

In addition to the usual scenario of logging into an application, users are also authenticated when they perform certain operations, such as:

- Change password.
- Assume an existing connection. This usually happens in programmatic applications utilizing session pooling capabilities.
- Sign off an object electronically

Content Server uses various passwords to connect to third-party products such as database and LDAP servers. Some internal jobs also use passwords to connect to the repository. These passwords are stored in files in an encrypted form. DFC automatically decrypts these passwords before passing them to the Content Server. The DFC client applications can also use the encryption capability using the `IDfClient.encryptPassword()` method. This feature avoids storing clear-text passwords in files, which is a security risk. Methods can be configured to run as server in which case a password is not needed for creating a valid session in these methods.

Many business processes require the performer of an activity to be verifiably recorded. In our example scenario, there can be a requirement for a signature by an approver before the loan amount can be disbursed. Content Server provides **signature** capabilities in the following ways:

- An **electronic signature** is a signature recorded in a formal signature page generated by Content Server and stored as part of the content of the object. Electronic signatures are generated and managed by Content Server when using TCS. This option is not available on Linux platforms.

- **Digital signatures** are generated by third-party products and are useful for supporting signatures in client applications.

- A **signoff** authenticates a user and creates an audit trail entry for the event. This is the least rigorous signature option.

Learn more

The topics discussed in this chapter can be further explored using the following resources:

- EMC Documentum Content Server 6.5 Fundamentals
- EMC Documentum Content Server 6.5 Administration Guide
- EMC Documentum System 6.5 Object Reference Manual
- EMC Documentum Webtop 6.5 SP2 User Guide
- EMC Documentum Documentum Administrator 6.5 SP2 User Guide
- (White Paper) EMC Documentum Security: A Comprehensive Review

Checkpoint

At this point you should be able to answer the following key questions:

1. What is user authentication? What are the different ways in which Documentum supports authentication?
2. What is authorization? What are the different ways in which Documentum supports authorization specifically for a user?
3. What is the difference between privileges and client capabilities?
4. What are the different ways of creating and managing users?

6

Groups and Roles

In this chapter, we will explore the following concepts:

- Groups
- Roles and Domains
- Module Roles and Privileged Groups
- Group management

Authorization

In the last chapter, we introduced the concepts of authentication and authorization. For correct authentication each user must be identified uniquely. However, it is very common that multiple users play the same business role in an organization and need similar levels of access. If access is granted to each user separately, it may become difficult to manage the access control due to the following reasons:

- There are a large number of users needing access and/or resources to be secured
- All the users with similar access levels need to be assigned new permissions

In our example scenario, suppose that the mortgage company is organized into geographical zones. All the zones follow the same processes but each zone controls the documents related to the loans processed by that zone. The zones are identified by numbers such as 1, 2, 3, and so on. Suppose that a zone has 60 loan officers, who perform the same kind of activities and need similar access levels to the loan applications initiated in their zone. Configuring the same access repeatedly for 60 users is inefficient. Further, if this access needs to be changed (or taken away) for all of these users, it requires the same laborious process again.

Both of these scenarios lead to repeated work of the same kind that deserves to be *automated* and *simplified*. A **group** provides this capability by representing a set of users who need to be treated as equals from some perspective of authorization. **Roles** and **domains** are special types of groups that can be used by client applications to restrict access to application features. We will use the notation illustrated in the following diagram for distinguishing among groups, roles, and domains:

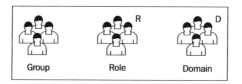

Groups

A **group** is a set of **members** where a member can be a user or another group. A group contained in another group is referred to as a **nested group** and it provides implicit membership to its direct members. Groups can be nested repeatedly and the implicit membership is transitive through the nested hierarchy.

In our example scenario, suppose that a group zone1_loanofficer is created to represent the loan officers from zone 1. It contains John as a member. Further, zone1_loanofficer is a member of another group zone1_all. Implicitly, John is a member of zone1_all as well. If zone1_all is a member of zone_all group, then John is also an implicit member of zone_all group. The following figure illustrates this example:

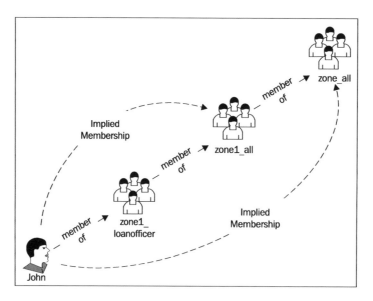

A group is represented as an object of type `dm_group` in the repository. There are five kinds of groups – **group, role, module role, privileged group** and **domain**. The kind of group is identified by `dm_group.group_class`.

Some important properties of `dm_group` are described in the following table:

Property	Label	Description
group_name	Name	Name of the group, at most 32 characters long.
Description	Group Description	Free-form description of the group.
is_private	Private Group	Indicates if the group is private or public; T means private, F means public. Public and private groups are discussed later in the section *Group Management*.
group_address	Group Email Address	Email address for the group.
group_class	Group Class	The type of group – `group`, `role`, `module role`, `privilege group`, or `domain`.
group_admin	Group Administrator	Name of user or group who can modify this group.
owner_name	Group Owner	Name of user or group who owns this group.
users_names	Individuals in Group	Names of the directly contained users in this group.
i_all_users_names		List of all users in this group, and indirect members via nested group membership.
groups_names	Groups in the Group	Names of groups that are members of this group.
i_supergroups_names		Name of the group and all groups that contain this group.
is_dynamic	Dynamic Group	Indicates if the group is dynamic; T means dynamic, F means standard.
is_dynamic_default	Dynamic Membership Default	Determines whether the members of the dynamic group are considered members by default; T means members, F means not members.
alias_set_id	Group Alias Set ID	Object ID of an alias set associated with this group. Alias sets are discussed in detail in *Chapter 14, Aliases*.

A group can be a **dynamic group** if the members of the group can be changed when the group is being used at run time. However, the membership changes cannot be arbitrary. The dynamic behavior only allows the membership to be changed within a set of pre-configured members. There are two additional options for dynamic groups—consider members to be *members by default* or consider them to be *non-members by default*. During run time, a client can programmatically add and remove members from a dynamic group.

An example will help clarify these concepts. Suppose that `Sam`, `John`, and `Jane` are members of `zone1_support`, which is a dynamic group. Also the members are to be considered non-members by default. When a client application checks membership of `zone1_support`, it appears to be an empty group. The client application can then add `Sam`, `John`, and `Jane` to `zone1_support` but no other user/group could be added. The dynamic membership of the group only lasts for the user session. In a new session, the same behavior repeats again.

A dynamic group is typically used as a variation of role-based security (roles are discussed in the next section). For example, it could be used to add or remove users from the dynamic group based on their geographical location. Such a solution may rely on Global Positioning System (GPS) for identifying the user's location and **multi-dimensional access control** (**MAC**) for specifying dynamic group assignment rules. MAC is a security feature provided by **Trusted Content Services** (**TCS**) and is discussed in *Chapter 7, Object Security*.

Recall that groups can have other groups as members. A dynamic group cannot be a member of a non-dynamic group but a dynamic group can have non-dynamic groups as members. When this happens the members of the non-dynamic group are considered as potential members of the dynamic group just like the users that are direct members of the dynamic group.

In *Chapter 5, Users and Privileges*, we learned about local and global users in the context of federations. Similarly, **global groups** are present in all the repositories in a federation but managed in the governing repository. A **local group** is managed in the repository in which it is defined.

Roles

Roles and domains can enable access to features within applications to a more granular and specific level than what client capability provides. For example, Webtop gives priority to roles over client capability. Further, custom roles can be created and used in Webtop via customization. Webtop recognizes roles named `consumer`, `contributor`, `coordinator`, and `administrator`. Custom roles can contain these roles and these

roles can contain custom roles as well. Web Publisher contains these roles, by default
– `wcm_content_author_role`, `wcm_content_manager_role`, `wcm_web_developer_role`, and `wcm_administrator_role`.

 As with client capability, roles and domains have meanings to client applications only and the Content Server does not assign any special meaning to them.

A **role** is a group with the `group_class` property set to `role`. Roles can form an **inheritance hierarchy** similar to an object-oriented inheritance hierarchy. When a role is added to another role, the member role is called a **sub-role** or **derived role**. The containing role is called the **parent role** or the **base role**. The sub-role is said to **inherit** from the parent role. In reality, inheritance is in terms of access to application features and is provided by the client application using the roles. From the Content Server perspective, this relationship is just a nested group membership relationship described earlier. The following figure illustrates a role hierarchy where the `loanofficer` role is a kind of `employee` role. For example, users in `loanofficer` role will also have access to features intended for the `employee` role in a client application.

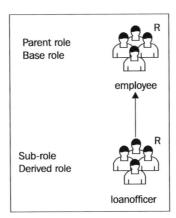

Domains

Agroup is identified as a **domain** when the value of the property `group_class` is `domain`. The purpose of a domain is to identify all the roles that apply to an application and, therefore, the members of a domain are roles. Once again, a domain only has meaning for client applications and not for the Content Server. Usually, one domain group is created per application. The client application should only use roles that are members of its domain.

Module roles

A group is identified as a **module role** when the value of the property `group_class` is `module role`. A module role is like a role except that it is used internally by an installed BOF module. It represents a role assigned to a module of code rather than to a particular user or group.

Privileged groups

A group is identified as a **privileged group** when the value of the property `group_class` is `privilege group`. A privileged group is a group whose members are allowed to perform privileged operations even though the members do not have those privileges as individuals.

Privileged groups are used in the context of **privileged DFC**, which is a DFC instance recognized by a Content Server as privileged to invoke higher privileges or permissions for a particular operation than it may have otherwise. Sometimes the user running an application may not have the privilege or permission to perform an operation, which the application needs the user to perform in that context. In such a situation, a privileged DFC instance can request to use a privileged role to perform that operation. The operation is encapsulated in a privileged module invoked by the DFC instance. For example, **Records Manager** and **Retention Policy Services** use privileged DFC.

Groups support privileged DFC through another attribute named `is_protected`. When a dynamic group is marked as protected using `is_protected`, it can only be manipulated via privileged DFC.

Group management

Group management involves creation, modification, and deletion of groups. The key considerations around group management are the following:

- Who can create groups?
- How can groups be created?
- What are the constraints on group creation?
- What is the default behavior on creation of a group?

Let's address these questions one by one.

The user performing group management requires Create Group privilege. The applications that enforce client capability (such as Documentum Administrator) require System Administrator capability for such a user.

A group can be created in one of several ways – manually through an application such as Documentum Administrator or Webtop, programmatically using DFC, using a DQL script, or by importing from an LDAP server. The LDAP Sync job, mentioned in *Chapter 5, Users and Privileges*, can import groups as well as users from an LDAP server. The job connects to the LDAP server and retrieves users and groups according to the specifications in the LDAP configuration object.

A group name needs to be unique in the repository just like a user name. However, users can share the same user login name if they belong to different domains and Content Server is using the domain-required mode.

In various contexts, a group name is acceptable where a user name can be used. For example, we just saw that dm_group.group_admin can be a user name or a group name. Therefore, a group name cannot be the same as a user name in the repository. Indeed, when a group is created a corresponding dm_user object is also created with the same name. This object has its r_is_group attribute set to 1. The uniqueness constraint works both ways—a new user cannot be given a name that is the same as an existing group name.

A group can be **private** or **public**. This property is available for client applications to utilize for showing or hiding groups appropriately for different users. When enforced, a public group is visible to all users and a private group only to the group owner and group administrator. Content Server does not use this property in any special way. When a sysadmin or superuser creates a group, it is public by default; otherwise, it is private by default.

The terms *sysadmin* and *superuser* will be used as a short-hand for users with Sysadmin and Supersuser privileges, respectively.

Two special users (or groups) are associated with a group – **group owner** (dm_group. owner_name) and **group administrator** (dm_group.group_admin). The group owner is a user or group that owns this group. Group administrator is a user other than owner and superuser who can modify this group. An owner or administrator for a group can be assigned by a superuser only. When a group is created, the creator becomes the group owner, by default. A group administrator is not assigned automatically.

Group management with DA

Let's look at DA features for group management. The group management functionality can be accessed via the browser-tree on the left as shown in the following screenshot. Note that roles and module roles are listed under separate nodes for ease of use.

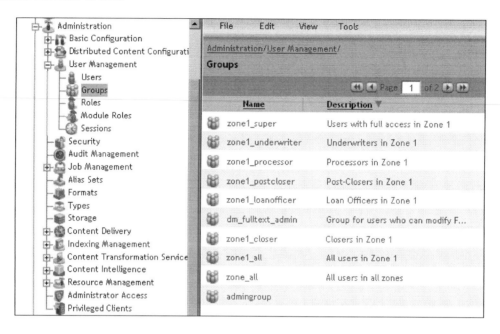

Managing existing groups

The work area lists all groups by default. Just like other lists, the group list may be paginated when there are more items in the list than the number shown on each page. The list can be filtered using the initial characters in the group name.

Note that some groups are named starting with dm. These are groups used internally by the Documentum platform. A few properties of each group are shown in the list view and the other properties can be accessed by viewing properties, just as we did for users.

A group can also be deleted by selecting the group and then using **File | Delete** menu item, **Delete** shortcut key, or with the right-click context menu. In general, it is not a good idea to delete a group without first analyzing the impact of this action. Deleting a group may impact its direct and indirect members even though the member users or groups are not deleted by this action.

Members can be added to an existing group by selecting the group and then using **File > Add Members** menu item or the right-click menu. Similarly, **File | Remove Member(s)** can be used for removing members. Existing memberships (other groups that this group is a direct member of) can be viewed by **View | View Current Group Memberships** menu item or the right-click menu.

Creating groups

Groups can be created using **File | New | Group** menu item, which opens the following screen. This screenshot shows a partial set of group attributes that were discussed earlier:

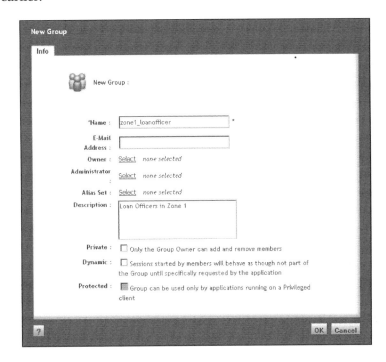

Help—some DQL queries

Some helpful queries related to groups are described in this section. These queries are based on the information presented in this chapter.

The following query retrieves information about a group named `zone1_all`:

```
SELECT group_name, group_address, owner_name, group_admin
FROM dm_group
WHERE group_name = 'zone1_all'
```

The following query retrieves the names of the groups that a user named John is a member of, directly or indirectly (through nested group memberships):

```
SELECT group_name
FROM dm_group
WHERE ANY i_all_users_names = 'John'
```

The following query retrieves the names of the users and groups that are direct members of a group named zone_all:

```
SELECT r_object_id, users_names, groups_names
FROM dm_group
WHERE group_name = 'zone_all'
```

The following query retrieves the names of all the roles present in the repository:

```
SELECT group_name
FROM dm_group
WHERE group_class = 'role'
```

The following query creates a group named zone1_all and adds two groups as its members:

```
CREATE PUBLIC GROUP 'zone1_all'
MEMBERS 'zone1_loanofficer', 'zone1_processor'
```

The following query adds two members to an existing group:

```
ALTER GROUP 'zone1_loanofficer'
ADD 'Sam','John'
```

Group members can be removed by using DROP instead of ADD in the preceding query.

The members in the CREATE GROUP and ALTER GROUP queries can also be specified via a SELECT query. For example:

```
ALTER GROUP 'zone1_loanofficer'
ADD (SELECT user_name from dm_user
     WHERE description = 'Loan Officer')
```

The following query deletes a group:

```
DROP GROUP 'zone1_loanofficer'
```

Documentum product notes

Group administration is typically done through Documentum Administrator. Repetitive or batch group administration activities can be scripted using DQL or API. Scripting group setup is especially useful when multiple environments such as development, testing, and production, need to be set up. User and group administration also involves managing group memberships where users and groups can be added to other groups or removed from them.

Privileged DFC is currently supported for internal use by Documentum client products. It is not supported for use by custom applications.

Learn more

The topics discussed in this chapter can be further explored using the following resources:

- EMC Documentum Content Server 6.5 Fundamentals
- EMC Documentum Content Server 6.5 Administration Guide
- EMC Documentum System 6.5 Object Reference Manual
- EMC Documentum Documentum Administrator 6.5 SP2 User Guide
- EMC Documentum Records Manager Administrator 6.5 SP1 User Guide
- (White Paper) EMC Documentum Security: A Comprehensive Review

Checkpoint

At this point you should be able to answer the following key questions:

1. What are groups? What purpose is served by groups?
2. What are dynamic groups? What are local and global groups?
3. What are roles and domains? What purpose do they serve?
4. What are module roles and privileged groups?
5. What are the different ways of creating and managing groups?

7
Object Security

In this chapter, we will explore the following concepts:

- Basic and extended object permissions
- Creation and assignment of ACLs
- Object owner and superusers
- Folders and object security
- Application-level control of sysobjects

Security—a recap

In previous chapters we studied various features of Documentum security, including users, groups, roles, domains, authentication, client capabilities, and basic and extended privileges. These features focus primarily on the identity of the user. The other side of security concerns is the resource being accessed,that is, an object. **Object security** defines access restrictions applied at the object level.

This chapter introduces the concepts associated with object security and their relations to other security parameters for specifying the overall access control configuration for Documentum.

Object security applies to sysobjects (objects of type `dm_sysobject` or one of its subtypes). All discussion in this chapter assumes the objects being secured to be of this type unless stated otherwise.

Repository security mode

Objects in a Documentum repository are secured using ACLs (discussed later in the chapter), by default. The configuration and behavior of this mechanism is the subject of this chapter.

Object security is controlled by the `dm_docbase_config.security_mode` property, which can have the following values:

Value	Description
acl	Secure respository using ACLs (default)
none	Turn repository security off

Object permissions

Each sysobject is associated with permission settings that grant specific permissions to certain users and groups. These permissions are categorized into **basic** and **extended permissions**.

Basic permissions

Basic permissions relate to accessing and manipulating an object's content and metadata and include the following levels:

Level	Value	Description
NONE	1	No access is allowed.
BROWSE	2	View object metadata (properties).
READ	3	View content associated with the object.
RELATE	4	Create relationships, such as between annotations and PDF files, documents, and lifecycles. Documentum uses various types of relationships to manage content effectively.
VERSION	5	Create new version.
WRITE	6	Modify without changing version (modify properties without checkout or modify and save as same version).
DELETE	7	Delete the object.

Basic permissions are hierarchical in nature, implying that a particular permission level includes all the lower permission levels as well. For example, granting VERSION permission to a user will implicitly grant RELATE, READ, and BROWSE permissions as well.

Extended permissions

Extended permissions allow specific actions against objects and support alias resolution, business rule enforcement, and the ability to purge without being able to read or modify content. As we will see later, the majority of the extended permissions are useful for enforcing business rules using lifecycles. The extended permissions are described in the following table:

Level	Description
Change Location	Move the object from one folder to another.
Change Owner	Change object owner (object owner is defined later in this chapter).
Change Permission	Change permission settings of the object (assigning ACL is described later in this chapter).
Run Procedure	Execute a Docbasic procedure. A Docbasic procedure is one way to execute code, which may be needed for a job, workflow, or an operation in a lifecycle.
Change State	Change an object's lifecycle state.
Extended Delete (Delete Object)	Only delete (separate from the basic DELETE permission and does not imply any other permissions).
Change Folder Links	Link an object to a folder or unlink an object from a folder. Applies to folders only.

Note that the extended permissions are independent of the basic permissions and must be granted separately and individually (that is, they are not hierarchical). These permissions are also optional. It is possible to have an object with no extended permission specified for it.

It is important to keep in mind that when multiple restrictions are in play all of them need to be satisfied to gain access. When working with objects, an extended permission may be insufficient on its own to perform the desired action and may also need additional basic permissions due to the effect that the action has on the object. The following table lists the dependencies of the extended permissions on the basic ones:

Extended permission	Additionally required basic permissions
Change Location	Moving from primary folder requires WRITE permission.
	Unlinking from non-primary folder or linking to additional folder requires BROWSE permission.
	Copying requires READ permission.
Change Owner	BROWSE
Change Permission	BROWSE
Run Procedure	BROWSE
Change State	WRITE
Extended Delete (Delete Object)	BROWSE

> The **primary folder** for an object is the first folder it was linked to. If the object is moved from this folder, the folder to which the object was linked earliest among the currently linked folders becomes the new primary folder. The primary folder object ID is present in i_folder_id[0] property. Concepts related to primary folder were discussed in *Chapter 2, Working with Content*.

ACLs

So far we have seen the basic and extended permission levels. When a permission level is assigned to an **accessor** (user or group) it is referred to as a **permission**. Permissions are created within an **ACL** (**Access Control List** also known as **permission set**). In other words, an ACL is simply a set of basic and extended permission levels associated with various accessors.

It is common to refer to permission levels as permissions and usually no distinction is made between the two terms.

An ACL is stored as an object of type dm_acl. ACLs are used for controlling access to sysobjects. The valid operations on renditions are controlled by the ACL on the associated sysobject. Recall that renditions cannot be edited or checked out.

There are four categories of accessors that can be granted permissions in an ACL – *owner*, *specific users*, *specific groups*, and *world*. These categories help resolve the permissions for any user who may attempt to access an object, using the following approach:

1. The user or group identified in the dm_sysobject.owner_name property is called the **object owner** for that object. The object owner is referred to as dm_owner in an ACL.

2. Specific users and groups can be granted basic and extended permissions using their names (dm_user.user_name and dm_group.group_name).

3. All users are considered to be a part of world, referred to as dm_world in the ACL.

A sample ACL is illustrated in the following figure. It shows permissions for a user accessor and a group accessor in addition to those for the owner and the world:

ACL		
Accessor	Basic Perm	Extended Permission
Owner	WRITE	Change State
John	VERSION	
zone1_loanofficer	READ	
World	NONE	

When a user attempts to access (perform an operation on) an object, Content Server evaluates the **effective permission** for that user before allowing or disallowing access. This evaluation begins with the ACL but it needs to account for some additional factors, such as whether the user is a special user and whether the user appears multiple times within the ACL. For example, the user may appear as a user accessor and as a member of a group accessor in the same ACL. When a user has multiple permissions on an object the most permissive (least restrictive) permission becomes the user's effective permission. These concerns and the exact approach for their resolution are discussed next.

Special users

There are two special kinds of users – object owners and superusers (users with Superuser privilege), who implicitly get certain permissions. Other users need explicit permissions for them to gain access to objects.

> Remember that the special nature of object owners and superusers is in terms of the permissions they are entitled to, irrespective of any explicit permissions specified in an ACL. Any discrepancies between the explicit and implicit permissions are resolved by Content Server, as discussed shortly.

Object owner

Each sysobject has an **object owner** identified by `dm_sysobject.owner_name`. The object owner is special as far as the particular object is concerned and gets the following permissions on this object automatically:

- READ permission
- All extended permissions except `Extended Delete` and `Change Folder Links`

The permission and extended permissions assigned to the owner in the ACL may be different from the previous **automatic permissions**. However, the previous permissions are automatic in the sense that they don't need to be explicitly assigned in an ACL. The following screenshot shows the automatic permissions for the object owner when no permissions have been granted to anyone in the ACL:

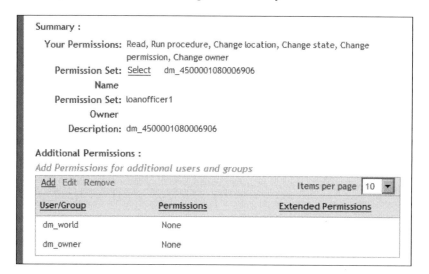

Let's look at another example. Suppose that the ACL on a document specifies NONE permission and no extended permissions for the owner. However, the object owner Jane also gets READ permission and all extended permissions except Extended Delete and Change Folder Links as automatic permissions. The ACL-assigned and the automatic permissions for the owner are illustrated in the following figure:

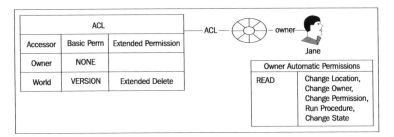

We will see shortly that the effective permissions for Jane on this object are resolved by considering each way Jane gets permissions on the object. Object ownership is only one way to get permissions. The other ways are as a user, a member of a group, and as a member of world.

 Automatic permissions should not be confused with default ACL, which is discussed later in the chapter. The easiest way to remember this distinction is that *automatic permissions are not dependent on ACLs.*

Managing object ownership

Since object ownership creates entitlement in terms of permissions, it is important to understand how object ownership is managed. An object can only have one specified owner (dm_sysobject.owner_name) at a time, which can be a user or a group. By default, the user creating the object becomes the owner of that object. Object ownership can be reassigned to another user or group. If a group is made the object owner, each member of that group (direct or nested) is treated as object owner.

We have already seen that changing ownership requires WRITE permission and Change Owner extended permission. Only a user satisfying at least one of the following requirements can change object ownership:

- Be the object owner (recall that the object owner automatically gets Change Owner extended permission) with WRITE permission

- Have the Superuser privilege (we will see that superusers are treated the same as object owners for resolving permissions) and WRITE permission

- Have WRITE permission and Change Owner extended permission on the object

Superusers

A **superuser** is a user with superuser privilege. A superuser is treated like an owner for *all* objects in the Documentum repository. Thus, a superuser gets the same permissions as those of the owner if no other permissions have been granted to the user directly or indirectly. If a specific superuser has explicit permissions on the ACL then these are considered along with the owner permissions for resolving the effective permissions, as discussed later.

Special groups

There are some built-in special groups that possess automatic permissions on every sysobject regardless of the ACL applied to the object. These groups are described in the following sections.

Browse-all group

Members of the group `dm_browse_all` get BROWSE permission on every sysobject regardless of the ACL associated with the object.

Read-all group

Members of the group `dm_read_all` get READ permission on every sysobject regardless of the ACL associated with the object.

Resolving permissions

It is possible for a user to be granted multiple permissions within an ACL. For example, a user may be the owner as well as a member of an accessor group in an ACL. Every user is implicitly a member of world as well. The permission levels assigned to the user via these accessor categories may be different. Further, as an object owner the user is entitled to the automatic permissions which may be different from what are assigned to the owner on the ACL. A user may also get automatic permissions via membership of `dm_browse_all` and `dm_read_all` groups. In this situation, what are the effective permissions for this user?

Content Server resolves the user's effective permissions on an object by taking the ACL, the special status of the user, and membership of special groups into account. In simpler terms, *the user gets all the implicit and explicit basic and extended permissions granted in different ways.*

What does this mean for the object owner and superusers? The object owner will always have the implicit (automatic) permissions mentioned earlier and these cannot be taken away via the owner permissions on the ACL. Let's look at the owner automatic permissions example again as reproduced in the following figure:

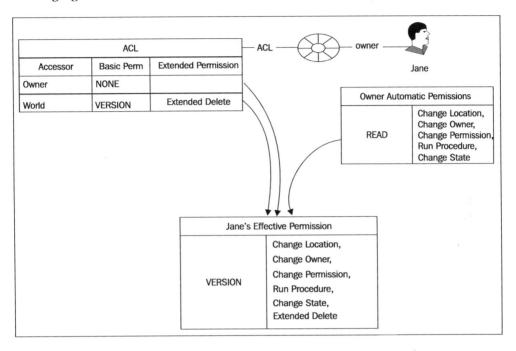

Jane is the object owner and also a member of world. So she gets NONE and VERSION from the ACL. She also gets the automatic permissions for the owner as shown. The basic permissions of NONE, READ, and VERSION resolve to VERSION. This is so because VERSION is the most permissive or least restrictive among these. Another way to look at it is that VERSION includes (implies) READ and NONE as well. Since there is no hierarchy for extended permissions each of these needs to be included individually. Jane gets Extended Delete as a member of world and Change Location, Change Owner, Change Permission, Run Procedure, and Change State from owner automatic permissions. The effective permissions for Jane on this object are shown in the figure. It should now be obvious that the effective permissions for an object owner cannot be more restrictive than the owner automatic permissions regardless of the ACL on the object.

Since a superuser is treated as object owner for all objects, the superuser gets at least the permissions resolved via ACL-assigned owner permissions, ACL-assigned world permissions, and owner automatic permissions. The superuser may get additional ACL-assigned permissions as an accessor user or a member of an accessor group.

Let's look at another example illustrating the mechanism for resolving effective permissions for a user. In the following figure, John gets permissions on the object in three ways – as the object owner, as a member of zone1_loanofficer, and as an implicit member of world. So what are his effective permissions?

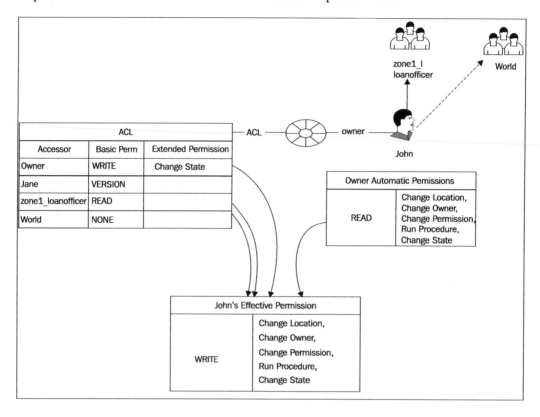

In basic permissions, he gets WRITE, READ, and NONE from the ACL. As an object owner, he gets READ automatically. The effective basic permission, therefore, is WRITE as it implies the other basic permissions. In extended permissions, he gets Change State from the ACL. As an owner he gets all the extended permissions other than Extended Delete and Change Folder Links automatically. Therefore, his effective extended permissions are all except Extended Delete and Change Folder Links.

Managing ACLs

An ACL is stored as an object of type dm_acl. It is uniquely identified by the combination of a name (dm_acl.object_name) and an owner name (dm_acl.owner_name). Of course, it can also be identified by its object ID.

The ACL owner should not be confused with object owner. ACLs are not sysobjects. The ACL owner provides a namespace or domain, within which ACL names must be unique.

ACL structure

Some key attributes of an ACL are described in the following table:

Attribute	Label	Description
r_is_internal	Is Internal	T indicates that this is an internal ACL (explained later in this chapter), F indicates otherwise.
acl_class	ACL Class	Regular (0) means private for the owner, Public (3) means available to everyone. The values 1 and 2 are used with **template ACLs**, which are discussed in *Chapter 14, Aliases*. If the ACL is owned by the repository owner it is available to everyone regardless of this property.
object_name	Permission Set Name	Name of the ACL.
owner_name	Permission Set Owner	Owner of the ACL.
r_accessor_name	Permission Set Members	Repeating accessor names.
r_accessor_permit	Assigned Permission	Repeating basic permissions.
r_accessor_xpermit	Extended Permissions	Repeating extended permissions.

The r_accessor_* properties describe the individual permissions in the ACL. These are repeating properties and their values at the same index correspond to each other. For example, r_accessor_name[3] = 'Joe', r_accessor_permit[3] = 4 means that Joe is being assigned RELATE permission. Refer to the basic permissions table, discussed earlier in the chapter, for the numeric values of basic permissions.

Extended permissions have an additional consideration that multiple extended permissions can be assigned to one accessor. Content Server translates the multiple extended permissions into a single internal integer code and this one integer value is stored per accessor. DFC provides programmatic means for working with extended permissions without dealing with their internal representation. However, if we are looking at a value retrieved from r_accessor_xpermit the following details can be helpful. This integer representation of extended permissions for an accessor is composed of bits (binary digit – 0 or 1), where each bit represents inclusion/ exclusion of one extended permission according to the following table:

Bit position	Extended permission	Values
0	Execute Procedure	0 means has permission 1 otherwise.
1	Change Location	0 means has permission 1 otherwise.
2-15	Reserved	
16	Change State	1 means has permission 0 otherwise.
17	Change Permission	1 means has permission 0 otherwise.
18	Change Ownership	1 means has permission 0 otherwise.
19	Extended Delete	1 means has permission 0 otherwise.
20	Change Folder Links	1 means has permission 0 otherwise.

Note that the meanings assigned to bits at position 0 and 1 are opposite of those in the other positions. As a result, "no extended permissions" translate to a value 3 (not 0) for r_accessor_xpermit.

Creating ACLs

ACLs can be created by Content Server as well as by users. ACLs created by users are called **external ACLs**. Content Server creates ACLs behind the scenes in certain situations related to ACL assignment and permission changes. ACLs created by Content Server are called **internal ACLs** (also known as **custom ACLs**).

External ACLs

ACLs created for a customization or solution development are external ACLs as they are created by users. Usually they are easy to identify since they are named in a human-friendly form such as `acl_zone1`. Any user can create an ACL, though applications (such as Webtop) honoring client capabilities would require System Administrator capability for this purpose. Typically, users create ACLs through DA though they could also use DFC or API for this purpose. In DA, ACLs can be searched, viewed, created, and modified using the **Security** node.

The creator of an ACL becomes its owner by default. However, the ACL owner can be changed afterwards. An ACL owned by the repository owner (`dm_dbo`) is called a **system ACL**. System ACLs are **public ACLs** — they are available to all repository users. System ACLs are managed by the object owner (repository owner), superusers, and sysadmins.

 Although `dm_acl.acl_class` specifies whether an ACL is public, system ACLs are always public regardless of this property.

ACLs owned by users other than the repository owner are called **user ACLs**. User ACLs can be public (`dm_acl.acl_class = 3`) or **private** (`dm_acl.acl_class = 0`). Private ACLs can only be used by the ACL owner. User ACLs are managed by the object owner (repository owner) or superusers.

To summarize, external ACLs can be further categorized as:

- External system ACLs — user-created, owned by `dm_dbo`, available to all users.

- External public user ACLs — user-created, owned by a user other than `dm_dbo`, available to all users.

- External private user ACLs — user-created, owned by a user other than `dm_dbo`, available only to ACL owner.

Assigning ACLs

ACLs are reusable and one ACL can be assigned to multiple objects. Objects sharing an ACL grant the same permissions to the same users, with the exception that the owner may be different for each of these objects.

Default ACL

When a sysobject is created and no ACL is applied explicitly during creation, Content Server automatically assigns it a **default ACL** according to certain rules. Each Content Server instance has a **default ACL mode** (`dm_server_config. default_acl`), which specifies the rules for assigning a default ACL, as described in the following table:

Default ACL	Value	Description
Folder	1	The primary folder's ACL (`dm_folder.acl_name`) is assigned to the object.
Type	2	The default ACL for the object's type (`dmi_type_info.acl_name`) is assigned to the object.
User	3	The default ACL for the creator of the object (`dm_user.acl_ name`) is assigned to the object. This is the default setting.

Since default ACL is copied from another object (folder, type, or user) when a new sysobject is created, the default ACL mechanism is also loosely referred to as **ACL inheritance**. The new sysobject is said to inherit its ACL from folder, type, or user. However, this is not true inheritance in the object-oriented sense.

> Note that the default ACL configuration is only used when an object is created. Changing the primary folder, object type, or owner of an existing object does not alter its association with an ACL.

ACL assignment

Content Server assigns the default ACL to a new object only if no permissions are set on the object explicitly. Permissions can be set for the object by assigning an ACL or by specifying explicit permissions. ACLs can be assigned to existing objects as well as new objects. When an ACL is assigned to an existing object, it replaces the existing ACL assignment for that object because only one ACL can be assigned to an object at any given time.

An object is associated with its assigned ACL via two attributes—`acl_name` and `acl_domain`. The following figure shows that the assigned ACL's `object_name` matches the object's `acl_name` and the ACL's `owner_name` matches the object's `acl_domain`.

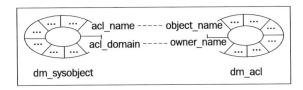

We have already seen that Content Server assigns the default ACL when no ACL is specified during object creation. If a non-default ACL needs to be assigned to a new object or if an ACL needs to be assigned to an existing object then it needs an explicit assignment. During ACL assignment, if a value for `acl_domain` is omitted Content Server first looks for the specified `acl_name` with the current user name as the ACL domain. If it finds a matching ACL that ACL is assigned. Otherwise, it looks for a public ACL, not owned by a group, with the specified ACL name. ACLs owned by groups can only be assigned if the `acl_domain` is explicitly specified during ACL assignment. Note that these considerations mostly apply to programmatic or script-based ACL assignment. When using an application such as Webtop for ACL assignment, the user selects a specific ACL for assignment and the values of `object_name` and `owner_name` from the ACL are copied to `acl_name` and `acl_domain` on the object respectively.

The user performing ACL assignment must belong to one of the following categories:

- Object owner
- Superuser
- A user with `Change Permission` extended permission on the object

Setting individual permissions

An external ACL provides a user-defined set of permissions that can be assigned to objects in a reusable manner. However, there are times when specific permissions need to be assigned to an object and there is no clear way for identifying an ACL that would provide those exact permissions. In such instances, Content Server creates an **internal ACL** with the desired permissions and assigns it to the object.

Internal ACLs

An **internal ACL** (also known as **custom ACL**) is created in an ad hoc manner to satisfy a specific situation and, therefore, is intended for a one-time assignment to an object. However, since it is an ACL it can be assigned to other objects within the constraints around ACL assignment in general. For example, an internal ACL assigned to a folder can serve as the default ACL for objects created within it if the default ACL mode is `Folder`. The easiest way to recognize an internal ACL is that its name begins with `dm_`. Internal ACLs are identified by `dm_acl.r_is_internal=1`.

Recall that Content Server creates an internal ACL when it cannot identify an existing ACL to assign to the object. Two kinds of situations lead to this requirement:

- Individual permissions are specified rather than the name of an ACL.
- A **template ACL** is assigned to an object.

Individual permissions can be specified on a new object with or without the default ACL during creation. Permissions can also be changed on an existing object, which may have an associated external or internal ACL. In all these cases, Content Server evaluates the resulting set of permissions and captures them in a new internal ACL, which is then assigned to the target object. Internal ACLs created in this manner are private ACLs owned by the user performing the changes.

When a **template ACL** is assigned to an object Content Server identifies the exact permissions based on the context. Even though a template ACL is an external ACL, it has one or more accessors specified as **aliases**. This means that the exact accessors are resolved by Content Server at the time of assignment. It needs to assign the resolved permissions, which must be captured in an internal ACL. Internal ACLs created from template ACLs are system ACLs (owned by the repository owner). Template ACLs are discussed in *Chapter 14, Aliases*.

To summarize, internal ACLs can be further categorized as:

- Internal system ACLs—owned by `dm_dbo`
- Internal private user ACLs—owned by users other than `dm_dbo`, available to the ACL owner only

ACL categories

We have seen various ways of categorization of ACLs—external or internal, public or private, and system or user. The following table summarizes these categories and how they interrelate with each other.

	ACL owner	External	Internal
		Created by user	**Created by Content Server Named dm_***
Public, for all users	dm_dbo	External system ACL	Internal system ACL
	Not dm_dbo	External public user ACL	
Private, for ACL owner only	Not dm_dbo	External private user ACL	Internal private user ACL

Note that Content Server does not create internal public user ACLs. An internal private user ACL can be made public though this is not useful, in general, since internal ACLs are intended for one-time use.

Folders and ACLs

Just like other sysobjects, folders (including cabinets) are also assigned ACLs. The ACL on a folder is used for three purposes:

- Controlling access to the folder object like any other sysobject
- Controlling operations on objects linked to the folder when **folder security** is enabled
- Assigning to new objects in the folder when the server's default ACL mode is set to `Folder`

Typical access control on folder objects relates to viewing and modifying their metadata and their deletion.

Folder security restricts operations on objects linked to a folder based on the ACL on the folder object. When folder security is enabled, object security is necessary, but not sufficient for adding objects to or removing them from a folder. The following table lists the permissions required on the folder for the corresponding operations to be allowed on the linked objects. Appropriate permissions are still required on the objects for operations to succeed.

Folder permission	Operations on linked objects
`WRITE` or `Change Folder Links`	Link (create, import, copy to, move to), Unlink (move from, delete)
`BROWSE`	Other operations

Note that folder security does not restrict the ability to search and view document metadata and content. These operations are only affected by object security.

Folder security is configured by setting dm_docbase_config.folder_security = 1. By default, folder security is enabled and it can be changed by users with Superuser or System Administrator privileges. Folder security can be configured using Documentum Administrator, DQL/API scripts, or via DFC.

We have already seen how default ACL assignment works. Even though the default ACL mode for a Content Server is User by default, it is common to use Folder as the default ACL mode. This approach places documents or objects requiring similar access control together in one folder or one folder tree. In our example scenario, the folder structure can be organized in the following manner. The documents can be grouped together by zones and within each zone by the loan account number. It is a convenient organization if permissions within a zone are similar by business function. Generally, documents related to a loan will be created and owned by the loan officer working on it. Therefore, the owner will need some elevated permissions compared to others. These needs can be achieved with the following setup:

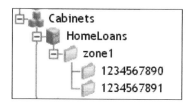

HomeLoans is the cabinet for holding loan-related documents. Recall that a top-level folder is called a cabinet. Each zone gets its own folder, such as zone1. Under the zone folder, each loan account gets its own folder with the account number as its name. ACLs assigned to the folders are shown in the following table:

Folder	ACL	Permissions	
HomeLoans	acl_home_loans	dm_world	NONE
		dm_owner	DELETE
		zone_all	BROWSE
zone1	acl_zone1	zone1_all	WRITE, Change Location
		dm_world	NONE
		dm_owner	DELETE
		zone_all	BROWSE

The other folders inherit the parent folder's ACL at the time of creation using the default ACL mode as `Folder`. Therefore, the loan account folder `1234567890` will also have `acl_zone1` as the default ACL. By default, the documents created within the loan account folder will also get the same ACL.

In Webtop, the ACL assigned to an object and its component permissions can be viewed in the **Permissions** tab of the properties page for an object, as shown in the following screenshot. Note that this page also shows the effective permissions for the current user.

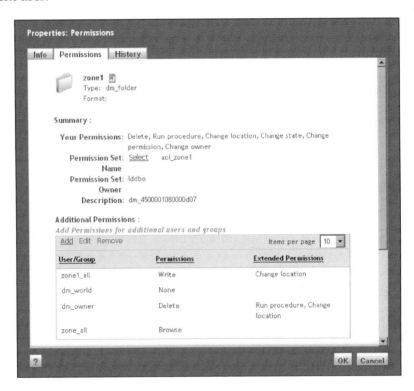

The preceding screenshot may also be used for assigning a different ACL to the object or for altering the permissions granted on the object. Another ACL can be assigned using the **Select** link for **Permission Set Name**. Permissions can be granted, revoked, or updated using the **Add**, **Remove**, and **Edit** links. If the permissions are modified here, an internal ACL will be created and assigned to the object.

Application-controlled sysobjects

Some business environments require certain documents or sysobjects to be manipulated only through approved client applications. Content Server supports **application-level control of sysobjects**, which enables client applications to "own" particular objects and restricts unapproved client applications from modifying these objects. Application-level control provides a restriction on top of the usual object security described earlier in this chapter and applies regardless of repository security. It is enforced for all users except superusers.

Application-level ownership is separate from object ownership by a user or group and is identified by dm_sysobject.a_controlling_app property. Each application that needs to assert application-level control has an application code that identifies it. The application sets this code on the objects it owns and then only that application or another one that knows the application code can change this code on the object. An application identifies itself via one or more application codes that are set in client configuration or in session configuration. If a superuser accesses an object, or the object does not have a_controlling_app set, or if the a_controlling_app matches one of the application codes for the client, the object's ACL is used for allowing access. Otherwise, dm_docbase_config.default_app_permit (READ by default) and the ACL are compared to grant the *more restrictive of the two*. When the application codes don't match, a non-superuser is never granted an extended permission.

An example of resolving effective permissions for application-controlled sysobjects is illustrated in the following figure. John is trying to access the shown object but is not using any application code. The target object has a_controlling_app set to '1234'. This means that dm_docbase_config.default_app_permit, which is set to READ, comes into play. The ACL-assigned permissions for John resolve to VERSION and Change State. Since John is not a superuser, he will not get any extended permissions. Further, READ is more restrictive than VERSION. As a result, John's effective permissions will only be READ.

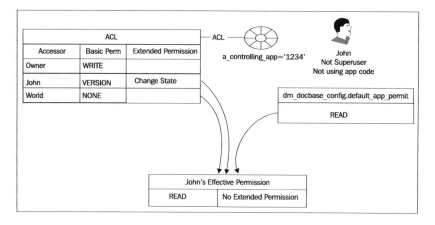

Help—some DQL queries

Some helpful queries related to object security are described in this section. These queries are based on the information presented in this chapter.

The following query retrieves basic permissions granted on a given object:

```
SELECT r_accessor_name, r_accessor_permit
FROM dm_acl
WHERE object_name =
  (SELECT acl_name
    FROM dm_document
    WHERE r_object_id = '0900006480000509')
AND owner_name =
  (SELECT acl_domain
    FROM dm_document
    WHERE r_object_id = '0900006480000509')
```

Note a few things in this query. DQL doesn't allow joins when retrieving repeating properties (accessor name and permit) – this query achieves the same effect using sub-queries. Also note that both `acl_name` and `acl_domain` should be checked when looking up the ACL for an object.

It is not straightforward to check extended permissions through queries since they return an integer value that needs to be decoded. However, this value can be decoded using the information provided in the chapter. It is best to view extended permissions through an application such as Webtop or Documentum Administrator.

The following query retrieves the default ACL for the type `dm_document`:

```
SELECT acl_name, acl_domain
FROM dmi_type_info
WHERE r_type_name = 'dm_document'
```

This ACL is assigned to new objects of `dm_document` when the default ACL mode is set to `Type`.

The following query retrieves the ACL assigned to a folder named `Temp`:

```
SELECT acl_name, acl_domain
FROM dm_folder
WHERE object_name = 'Temp'
```

The following query retrieves the default ACL for a user named `Jane`:

```
SELECT acl_name, acl_domain
FROM dm_user
WHERE user_name = 'Jane'
```

This ACL is assigned to new objects created by `Jane` when the default ACL mode is set to `User`.

Note that DQL cannot be used for creating ACLs but API may be used for this purpose.

Documentum product notes

The terms ACL and permission set are used interchangeably. Among internal artifact names, ACL is the preferred term. Within reference documentation the preference has shifted from ACL to permission set and back to ACL again over various product versions. Documentum Content Server 6.5 Fundamentals no longer refers to the term permission set. However, Documentum Composer 6.5 uses permission set as the preferred term for display labels. Currently, permission set is preferred in application display labels while ACL is preferred in technical discussion.

The **Administration** node in Webtop or Documentum Administrator can be used for creating and managing ACLs. The permissions tab on object properties can be used for reassigning an ACL or for modifying permissions. System Administrator client capability is needed for these operations.

Trusted Content Services (**TCS**) enhances security features of Content Server with an additional license. TCS features include encrypted communication (SSL) and storage, electronic signatures, and additional restrictions on top of the usual object security. One feature—**Multi-dimensional Access Control** (**MAC**, formerly known as **Mandatory Access Control**), is worth highlighting. Normal access control allows granting access to individuals or members of a group. It doesn't allow granting access to a subset of the members of a group based on additional constraints. MAC makes it possible to define sophisticated access control rules, based on a user's role, location, means of access, IP address, and other criteria that can be validated by an application. More commonly, it can combine memberships of certain groups and non-memberships of other groups to define access control. In our example scenario, suppose that all loan officers other than those in zone 1 need access to one set of standard operating procedures while those in zone 1use a different set of operating procedures due to differences in laws in zone 1. This access control can be defined using two groups such as `zone_loanofficer_all` and `zone1_loanofficer`. MAC will allow a rule based on a member of `zone_loanofficer_all` but not a member of `zone1_loanofficer`. TCS is required for specifying such a rule.

MAC is typically useful in conjunction with dynamic groups. For example, access for a user can be altered dynamically based on his/her geographical location. Such a solution would also use a mechanism such as GPS for identifying the user's location deterministically.

Learn more

The topics discussed in this chapter can be further explored using the following resources:

- EMC Documentum Content Server 6.5 Fundamentals
- EMC Documentum Content Server 6.5 Administration Guide
- EMC Documentum System 6.5 Object Reference Manual
- EMC Documentum Documentum Administrator 6.5 SP2 User Guide
- (White Paper) EMC Documentum Security: A Comprehensive Review
- DFC API Docs: `com.documentum.fc.client.IDfACL.getAccessorXPermit()` `com.documentum.fc.client.IDfSysObject.unlink()`
- Decoding xperms: `http://doquent.wordpress.com/2008/08/28/decoding-xperms/`

Checkpoint

At this point you should be able to answer the following key questions:

1. What is an ACL and how is it different from a permission?
2. What are basic permissions? What are extended permissions?
3. How is an ACL selected to be assigned to a new object?
4. What is an internal ACL? Who can create it and why is it needed?
5. How does folder security provide additional object security beyond the ACLs?
6. What are application-controlled sysobjects?
7. What kind of security is provided by Trusted Content Services?

Part 3

User Interface

Searching

Webtop Presets

8
Searching

In this chapter, we will explore the following concepts:

- Simple and advanced searching with Webtop
- Saving searches
- Full-text indexing
- Accessing known objects quickly

Locating objects

The previous chapters showed how to create and modify objects in the repository. We saw that various mechanisms could be used for this purpose, including programming and interactive scripts using IAPI or IDQL. However, the most common mechanisms of interacting with the repository are still applications, particularly Webtop.

The same can be said about locating documents or, more generally, objects within the repository. Webtop provides one of the easiest available interfaces for accessing content within the repository. Typically, business consumers of information prefer graphical user interfaces (GUI) and the alternatives to Webtop for searching documents are less desirable to them.

There are two key ways of locating objects within the repository:

- *Navigating* through the browser tree to a known path
- *Searching* using the words that may be found within the metadata or content

Faceted search, supported by **Documentum Search Services (DSS)**, will be a new way to search. It will allow searches to be progressively refined using facets. However, this product is not generally available in version 6.5 SP2.

The navigation mechanism is used when the user knows (or can guess) where an object is located within the folder hierarchy. This chapter is primarily about locating objects by searching for them without knowing where they may be linked within the folder tree. Since Webtop is the most common way to perform these searches, this chapter will focus on Webtop functionality related to searching.

Search process

Webtop enables searching for objects in two ways and there are some nuances to each approach that will be discussed in this chapter. However, there is a common underlying pattern to the search process as illustrated in the following figure:

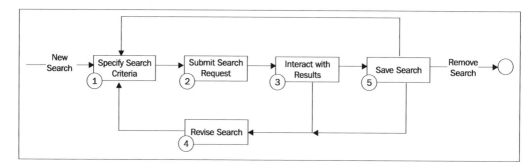

1. *Specify search criteria*: **Search criteria** define the conditions that an object has to satisfy to be a part of the results. Search criteria typically include words being searched for in metadata or in content and additional conditions (such as last modification date being later than a specified date) on the metadata. The criteria may be explicitly specified by the user, may be implicit, or could be retrieved from a previously saved search.

2. *Submit search request*: The search request is submitted once the desired criteria have been specified. Webtop passes on the search request to the Content Server where the search is performed. Searching includes matching criteria within content if full-text indexing (described later in this chapter) is enabled in the deployment.

3. *Receive results and interact with them*: Content Server always honors the configured security and only returns objects for which the current user has at least BROWSE permission. Webtop receives the results and presents them to the user in a paginated manner, if needed. The user can interact with the results by navigating through pages of results and can perform operations on individual objects by selecting them. Note that Webtop may hide the objects marked as hidden. Hidden objects may be revealed by using Advanced Search, which is discussed later in the hapter.

4. *Revise search*: If the user feels that the search criteria need to be altered to get better results, the search can be revised. Revising a search takes the user to the advanced search screen with the current criteria populated on the form. The user can alter the search criteria and can submit the request again.

5. *Save search*: Search criteria and, optionally, the results of the search can be saved for reuse. At a later time, the user can initiate step 1 from an existing saved search. The saved search can also be revised or removed.

This interaction pattern remains the same, though there are some variations with the two types of searches and optional features. The rest of this chapter explores these variations and details.

Simple search

Simple search is simple in terms of what the user has to do to perform the search. There is just one field to specify the search words (criteria) and a button to submit the search request. The biggest benefit of simple search is that the user just specifies the search words and gets to the results. The following screenshot shows the simple search control:

A simple search can be performed by entering the words being searched in the field and then clicking on the lens icon. Clicking on the inverted triangle icon reveals additional links. The advanced search screen can be accessed by clicking on **Advanced** or using *Shift+S* shortcut. Clicking on **Last Results** retrieves the results of the last search, if any, performed by the user.

It is possible to search multiple repositories for objects in one search operation. For a simple search, all repositories designated as *default* are searched. Multiple repositories can be set as default user preferences, as described later in this chapter.

A search operation can query full-text indexes as well as object properties. Full-text indexes capture information about the textual contents of documents and enable searching the content as well as the object properties. Full-text indexes are created by Index Server when it is present as a part of the Documentum installation.

Processing of the simple search request can vary depending on the presence of full-text indexes.

Simple search—without full-text indexing

When full-text indexing is not enabled, simple search is truly simple. The searches are *case sensitive*, meaning that the search words are matched exactly as specified. Words separated by spaces are *ANDed*, meaning that if two words are specified both must be present in the match. The search words are matched against the values of `object_name`, `title`, and `subject` properties.

Simple search—with full-text indexing

Full-text indexing makes simple search more powerful and a little bit more complex. With full-text indexing, simple search behavior changes as follows:

- The search is *case insensitive*, meaning lower-case letters are considered a match with upper-case letters as well.

- The space-separated search words are *ORed*, meaning that if any word is matched the target object is considered a match.

- All searchable properties are compared for a match. A property is searchable if `is_searchable` is set to 1 for this property in the data dictionary. The data dictionary is discussed in *Chapter 11, Custom Types*.

- The indexed content is also searched for matches for the search words.

- The search words can include * (called asterisk or star) as a **multiple-character wildcard**. A wildcard is a pattern that can match anything. The wildcard * matches any text of any length. For example, `te*` will match `ten`, `test`, and `temporary` as well. Similarly, `?` is a **single-character wildcard**.

> Note that with or without full-text indexing, a phrase can be searched by enclosing it in double quotes, as in "out of box".

Advanced search

Advanced search provides full flexibility to the user for specifying search criteria. The user can reach the advanced search screen when initiating a new search (as explained earlier) or when revising a search. The biggest benefit of advanced search is that the user can be very specific about the search criteria and is more likely to get relevant results, particularly when there are a large number of potential matches for the search words.

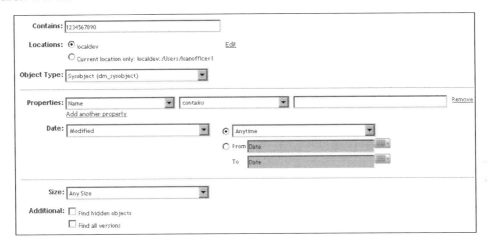

 Note that wildcards are only supported when indexing is enabled. In Advanced Search, wildcards can only be used in the **Contains** field. Wildcards are not supported for searching external sources.

Advanced search enables the user to be very specific about the search criteria in the following manner:

- Additional areas can be specified to be included in the search besides default repositories. Including additional areas may require re-authentication against the new areas, if the authentication credentials have not been saved. *Login preferences* can be used to cache login credentials to avoid re-authentication on such occasions.

- Specific locations—folder paths and cabinets can be used for the search rather than searching the entire repository.

- If **Federated Search Services (FSS)** is installed, external sources other than Documentum repositories can also be included in the search. FSS is described later in this chapter.

- The target object type can be specified for the search. For example, perform the search only against objects of type `dq_loan_document`, where `dq_loan_document` is a custom type.

- Multiple property conditions can be specified as a part of the criteria. Each property condition is of the form *name–operator–value*. For example, `subject-begins with-Mortgage`.The properties available to be used in these conditions are dependent on the selected object type. Various property conditions can be combined together using AND and OR operators.

- Date-based conditions can be included in search criteria. For example, search all documents that were last modified after 4th July, 2009.

- The file size can be used in the criteria. For example, find all documents with the content size larger than 2MB.

- Hidden objects can be included in searches. SysObjects can be marked as hidden using `a_is_hidden`.

- All versions can be searched rather than only the current ones.

Interacting with results

The results from a search request, simple or advanced, are shown in the work area described in *Chapter 1, ECM Basics*. The result objects are shown as a list and pagination is available if the result list size is more than the number of items displayed per page. When page navigation is visible, users can go from one page to an adjacent page, jump to a specific page, or jump to the first or the last page.

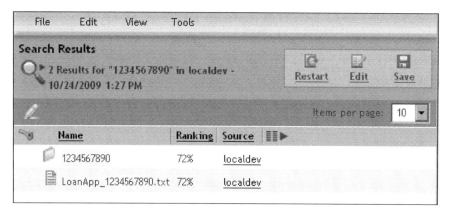

Lightweight Sysobjects (LwSO) are presented differently by simple and advanced searches. Simple search results display only the shared parent objects. Advanced search results display only the individual children. LwSO were introduced in *Chapter 3, Objects and Types*.

The **Restart** link enables the same search to be performed again. The **Edit** link takes the user back to the **Advanced Search** screen that displays the parameters for the current search. The user can update the search criteria and perform the search again. The **Save** link enables the user to save the current search for future reuse.

Saving searches

After performing a search, the user may want to save it for running again in future. Saving a search may be desirable when a particular search is performed frequently or when the search criteria contain several conditions. It is also possible to save the current results along with the search criteria.

One set of search criteria can return different results at different times because the repository contents may change over time. Therefore, a saved search can return different results when performed at different times. However, the results saved with the search can be viewed repeatedly without performing the search again.

In our example scenario, if a saved search lists all approved loan applications the result list will be different after additional loan applications have been approved. The search is saved as a *hidden* **smart list** (object of type `dm_smart_list`) in the `Saved Searches` folder under the user's default folder (also known as **home cabinet**). The type `dm_smart_list` is a subtype of `dm_sysobject` and has no properties of its own.

The following screenshot displays the **Save Your Search** screen:

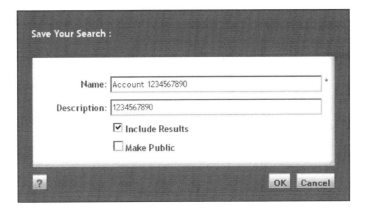

The user can provide a name and description for the saved search. Note that it is optional to save the results with the search criteria. Selecting **Public** makes it a **public saved search**, which makes it available to all repository users. Otherwise, it remains a **private saved search** — visible only to the user saving it.

In Webtop, saved searches can be accessed via the **Saved Searches** node in the browser tree, as shown in the following screenshot:

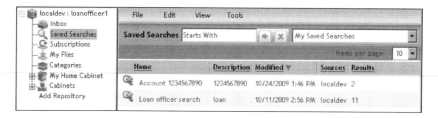

Saved searches are grouped into two categories:

- **My Saved Searches**: This includes only the private saved searches for the current user
- **All Saved Searches**: This includes all the public saved searches and the private saved searches for the current user

These categories can be selected using the previous dropdown control, the list of saved searches. The list of saved searches can be shortened by using the **Starts With** filter, also present above the list of saved searches.

The easiest way to use a saved search is by using the right-click context menu as shown in the following screenshot:

The saved search can be revised using **Edit**. It can be launched using **Run Search**. If the results were saved with the search criteria, they can be viewed using **View Saved Results**. The saved search can be removed using **Delete**.

While users can manually save the searches they perform, the **last search** performed and its results are both saved automatically in the user session. The simple search control shown earlier provides access to the results of the last search, which can be revised or re-launched from the results page.

Search preferences

Preferences in Webtop allow users to store their preferred ways of interacting with the application, so that they can avoid specifying these choices repeatedly. Essentially, preferences help users work efficiently. Preferences can be accessed using the **Tools | Preferences** menu item.

Search-related preferences affect search behavior for a user. These preferences are listed as follows:

- **Columns** specify the set of properties that are displayed in various object lists. The **Search Results** section in columns preferences identifies the columns displayed for search results. The list of columns can be modified using the **Edit** link. Column preferences can also be modified from any list view (including search results) via the last icon in the column header row.

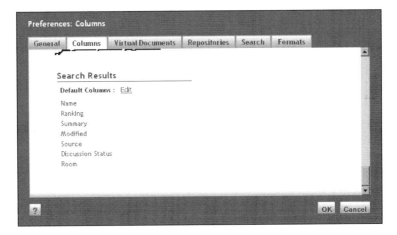

- **Default Search Locations** are included in searches without specifying them explicitly for each search. The default search location can be specified in search preferences as shown in the following screenshot. Favorite repositories are specified in the **Repositories** preferences.

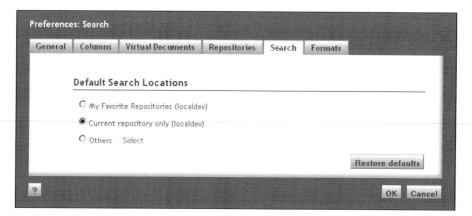

- Favorite repositories indicate the repositories that a user accesses frequently. Repositories can be selected as favorite by selecting them from the available list under **Repositories** preferences. Favorite repositories can be specified as default search locations as previously described.

Full-text indexing

We have already seen that full-text indexing affects search in significant ways. It is worth understanding the fundamental concepts of full-text indexing even though it is an optional component of the Documentum platform.

Full-text indexing is implemented by **Index Server**. One Index Server instance can provide indexing for multiple repositories and, thus, for multiple Content Servers. An **Index Agent** is associated with each Content Server instance and supports the indexing needs of the associated repository.

Index Server participates both in creation of and searching of full-text indexes. Full-text index creation is coordinated by the Index Agent through the FAST Index Plugin. Querying the indexes is coordinated by the Content Server using the FAST Query Plugin. This interaction is illustrated in the following figure:

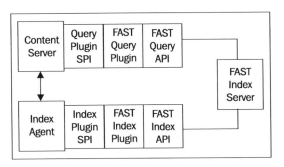

Note the presence of Query Plugin SPI and Index Plugin SPI in the preceding figure. **SPI** stands for **Service Provider Interface** and is a common architectural mechanism for supporting multiple implementations for a service. This implies that **FAST** is one of many engines that could be used by Index Server. Indeed, **Lucene** (an open-source text-search engine) has been used with the Index Server in the embeddable edition of Content Server.

Let's examine the indexing and querying interactions in some more detail. When a sysobject with `a_full_text`=TRUE is added to the repository, removed from the repository, or modified in a way that might affect the full-text index, Content Server adds an indexing task for the Index Agent. In response to this task, the Index Agent sends an indexing request to Index Server. The index server then fetches the content and metadata for the object and updates the full-text index. If the object has been removed from the repository then it removes the corresponding index entry.

Note that properties are always indexed while indexing enabled. Only content indexing is controlled by `a_full_text`.

The nature of this indexing process leads to a delay between the sysobject events and the update of full-text indexes. Therefore, there is a period for each sysobject change during which search results may not reflect that change. Once a modified object has been re-indexed, it starts showing up in search results appropriately.

Frequently accessed objects

Searching and navigation provide convenient ways to locate objects based on criteria or location, respectively. However, if there are certain documents that a user accesses frequently, these approaches are still somewhat inefficient. Webtop provides three mechanisms for accessing such objects quickly — my files, subscriptions, and hyperlinks.

My files

The **My Files** node in browser tree lists the files currently checked out by the user and the files that have been checked in recently by the user. In general, this is the fastest mechanism to access the files the user has been working with.

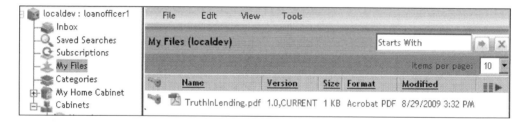

Subscriptions

Subscriptions represent bookmarks, favorite locations, or favorite documents. Users can subscribe to the objects or paths that they access frequently. All the subscribed objects show up under the **Subscriptions** node in Webtop.

Objects can be subscribed to or unsubscribed via the **Tools | Subscribe** and **Tools | Unsubscribe** menu items in Webtop.

A user can also subscribe to **read notifications** or **change notifications** for objects. Notifications can be subscribed to by using **Tools | Turn On Read Notification** and **Tools | Turn On Change Notification**. Similarly, notifications can be unsubscribed by using **Tools | Turn Off Read Notification** and **Tools | Turn Off Change Notification**. Notifications show up in the user's **Inbox** in Webtop.

Subscriptions and Inbox are shown in the following screenshot:

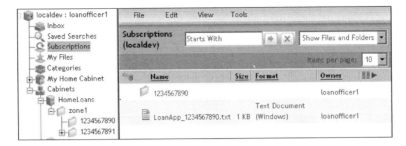

Hyperlinks

Hyperlinks provide quick access to specific objects via Webtop. Hyperlinks are also known as shortcuts, links, web links, bookmarks, URL (Uniform Resource Locator), and DRL (Document Resource Locator).

> DRL is a term specific to Documentum while the other terms previously mentioned are generally applicable.

A hyperlink can be created in one of the following ways:

- Using the menu item File | Email as Link. This creates an email message with the hyperlink to the item embedded in it.
- Using drag-and-drop on the bookmark icon from the properties tab. This approach can be used to create a shortcut on the Windows desktop. This mechanism only works with Internet Explorer when drag-and-drop has been enabled in Webtop.
- A hyperlink can also be stored as a bookmark in the browser by clicking on the bookmark icon on the properties.

The bookmark icon previously mentioned is indicated in the following screenshot:

Once a hyperlink has been created, it can be followed by selection or double-clicking to access the object. The object will be accessed via Webtop and the user may be required to authenticate again.

When accessing an object through the hyperlink, the user gets the option to *view* or *edit* the object. If the hyperlink was to a non-current version of the object, the user also gets the option to *access the current version* instead. As always, appropriate permissions are needed to access the object.

Help—some DQL queries

While this chapter focused on searching using Webtop, the DQL SELECT query is also used to perform searches. We have already seen SELECT queries in several chapters, so we will only look at the full-text support in DQL queries here. The following queries assume that an Index Server is present in the Documentum deployment.

In general, a SELECT query can be a standard SELECT query or an FTDQL SELECT query. The syntax for an FTDQL SELECT query is a subset of the syntax for a standard SELECT query. This means that every FTDQL SELECT query complies with the standard SELECT query format but the converse is not true. If the statement conforms to the FTDQL SELECT syntax, it is run against the full-text index only and the repository is not queried.

While various features of full-text searches are supported in DQL, we will look at the following key ones:

- The SEARCH clause enables searching the full-text index.
- The keywords SCORE, SUMMARY, and TEXT can be used in the selected values list:
  - The SCORE keyword returns the document's *relevance ranking* as determined by Index Server. A higher relevance ranking implies a better match. By default, the results are returned in descending order of SCORE.
  - The SUMMARY keyword returns a summary of each document as determined by the Index Server.
  - The TEXT keyword returns the various forms of the search word that were matched for a document. For example, 'pay' may have matched 'paid' and 'payment'.

The following query retrieves documents containing the word `contract` in their content or metadata:

```
SELECT object_name, SCORE
FROM dm_document
WHERE SEARCH DOCUMENT CONTAINS 'contract'
```

The following query retrieves documents containing the words `contract`, or `loan`, or both in their content or metadata:

```
SELECT object_name, SCORE
FROM dm_document
WHERE SEARCH DOCUMENT CONTAINS 'contract loan'
```

The following query retrieves documents containing the phrase `"loan approval process"` in their content or metadata:

```
SELECT object_name, SCORE
FROM dm_document
WHERE SEARCH DOCUMENT CONTAINS '"loan approval process"'
```

Note that * can also be used as a wildcard in the search string.

DQL supports the use of **hints**, which can alter query behavior. Hints appear at the end of a `SELECT` query. For example, when a `SELECT` query does not contain any of `SEARCH`, `SCORE`, `SUMMARY`, and `TEXT` keywords, it could still be run as FTDQL using the hint `ENABLE(FTDQL)`. Similarly, `ENABLE(NOFTDQL)` makes the query run as a standard `SELECT` query. `TRY_FTDQL_FIRST` causes the query be tried as FTDQL first. If the query times out, it is retried as a standard `SELECT` query. DQL also includes hints for behavior unrelated to full-text indexing.

Documentum product notes

Webtop stores the search criteria as XML in smart lists but other clients may use a different format. Therefore, the saved searches may be incompatible across different applications.

The search behavior can be altered by the presence of **Federated Search Services (FSS)**. FSS is an optional component of the Documentum platform and it allows external sources of information (such as databases, websites, or other enterprise applications) to be searched along with the Documentum repositories.

EMC provides adapters for various external data and content sources so that they can also be searched through FSS. For example, one search request can pull results from two repositories, a database, and Google and show all the results together. If FSS is not installed, the external source options are not available for searching.

The search capabilities can be enhanced by using the **Extended Search** option—a part of FSS, which adds the following features:

- *Smart navigation*: Search results are grouped into clusters of related results in the navigation pane.

- *Real-time monitoring*: Status of results from various sources is displayed in real time in graphical and tabular formats.

- *Search Templates*: A **search template** is like a saved search with part of the search criteria unspecified. The unspecified portion of the criteria is provided by the user while performing the search based on a template. Search templates are available under the Saved Searches node.

Full-text search behavior can be configured via the `dfc.properties` file, which is present in the `$DOCUMENTUM/config` (or `%DOCUMENTUM%\config` on Windows) directory. For example, the maximum number of results returned by any query can be restricted with the following entries:

```
dfc.search.maxresults=1000
dfc.search.maxresults_per_source=350
```

Documentum Search Services (**DSS**) will provide the next generation of search capabilities in the Documentum platform. It is expected to become generally available in late 2010. It is built upon **xDB** and uses **Apache Lucene** for indexing. It provides capabilities such as relevance sorting, advanced query processing, and native support for VMWare, NAS, and SAN. One of the key features it will enable is **faceted search**, which allows users to refine their search progressively using facets.

Learn more

The topics discussed in this chapter can be further explored using the following resources:

- EMC Documentum Documentum Webtop 6.5 SP2 User Guide

- EMC Documentum Content Server 6.5 SP2 Full-text Indexing Deployment and Administration Guide

- EMC Documentum Content Server 6.5 SP2 DQL Reference Manual

- EMC Documentum Content Server 6.5 Fundamentals

- EMC Documentum Content Server 6.5 Administration Guide

- EMC Documentum System 6.5 Object Reference Manual

- (White Paper) EMC Documentum Architecture: Delivering the Foundations and Services for Managing Content Across the Enterprise, A Detailed Review

- Next Generation Documentum Search—`http://momentum.conference-services.net/viewfile.asp?abstractID=346206&conferenceID=1754`

Checkpoint

At this point you should be able to answer the following key questions:

1. What is the difference between simple and advanced searches in Webtop?

2. What is full-text indexing? How is it enabled? What is the impact of full-text indexing on search behavior?

3. Which preferences affect search behavior?

4. How can sources other than Documentum repositories be searched from within Webtop?

5. How can searches be saved and reused?

6. What are the alternatives to search for locating frequently accessed objects within the repository?

9

Webtop Presets

In this chapter, we will explore the following concepts:

- Webtop presets
- Preset scope and rules
- Scope precedence
- Creating and managing presets
- Webtop Express preset

Configuration and customization

A Documentum environment with default out-of-box configuration has many features that are not applicable to specific situations, such as users belonging to a specific group or to documents linked to a particular folder. On the other hand, there are many requirements for the environment which are specific to the business and are not available in the out-of-box feature set. These challenges are not unique to Documentum and occur with anything that can be considered to be a framework or a platform. Like any good platform or framework, Documentum provides mechanisms for implementing such specific needs of the business.

In general terms, a Documentum environment can be adapted to meet specific requirements using **configuration** and/or **customization**. Configuration involves instantiating a prescribed model using the means provided in the platform to attain the desired behavior. Configuration does not involve writing code. While configuration is convenient and desirable, it is impossible to anticipate and model all the kinds of requirements that the platform may be used for. In order to support such needs, the platform provides hooks and mechanisms to extend and alter the behavior of the platform considerably. Usually, a combination of configuration and customization is needed while implementing Documentum solutions to meet the business requirements. **Webtop presets** place the ability to configure the user interface in the hands of end users and alleviate the need for customization for many common requirements.

Even with definitions such as the above, the boundary between configuration and customization is often blurry. In order to avoid such confusion, we will define configuration to include:

- Changes that are made through GUI tools for users and administrators. This chapter deals with Webtop presets, which belong to this category.

- Editing configuration files, usually in XML or properties format. Enabling drag-and-drop for IE by editing app.xml falls in this category.

All other changes will be considered to be customization. This distinction becomes more important when discussing long-term maintenance concerns for a solution.

Presets

The Webtop UI displays information about repository contents to the users and allows them to perform actions on it. We have already seen that such visibility is constrained by the client capability of the user. For example, a user with Consumer client capability does not get access to actions related to virtual documents. However, these restrictions are predefined and are not intended to be altered for specific deployments.

WDK configuration can be used to restrict access to WDK components by various scopes, such as roles and object types. However, this is a technical administration activity and is usually performed as a part of a wider application customization. It is a static configuration change and is not a part of the normal usage of the application.

Documentum solutions are commonly required to reveal only the information and actions that are relevant to the user's role or tasks. Before the introduction of Webtop presets, WDK customization was the primary means for implementing these restrictions. **Presets** enable business or technical administrators to specify such restrictions via the Webtop UI. Presets dynamically filter the selections and actions available to users in various functional areas of the Webtop UI.

Presets cannot be used to enforce security since they are not implemented by Content Server. Presets are implemented by Webtop and interactions with Content Server that do not go through Webtop are not affected by the presence of presets. For example, a user may use DQL to create an object using a type and ACL that may be restricted for him via presets when using Webtop.

Preset scope

Presets make the Webtop UI sensitive to a wide variety of contexts or situations defined in terms of folder paths (locations), users, groups and roles, and object types. A preset is applicable to precisely one set of contexts, which is called its **scope**. In our example scenario, suppose that only loan officers should be starting workflows. If John is a member of the group zone_loanofficer, John being the user is one context relevant to this example. The set of all the contexts where the logged in user is a member of zone_loanofficer is the scope that should be associated with the preset for implementing this restriction. For simplicity, we just say that the scope of the preset is the group zone_loanofficer.

A preset scope consists of a combination of one or more of the following items:

- A set of locations
- A set of users, groups, and roles
- A set of object types

 If a location is part of a preset scope, it doesn't imply that the subfolders of that location are in scope. However, any number of folders may be added to the same scope explicitly.

Each preset must have unique scope, that is, only one preset can be associated with one scope. Therefore, the scope of two presets must have at least one difference. For example, two presets cannot have the folder /HomeLoans/zone1 as their scope. However, it is possible to have the folder /HomeLoans/zone1 as the scope of preset A while the scope of the preset B is a combination of the folder /HomeLoans/zone1 and group zone1_loanofficer. These scopes are illustrated using the following Venn diagram:

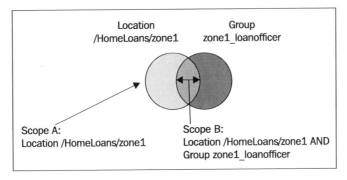

Scope precedence

It is possible for different scopes to overlap as we saw in the previous example. For another example, suppose that the scope for preset C is the combination of location /HomeLoans/zone1 and the type dq_loan_app. The scope for preset D is the group zone1_loanofficer. Now suppose that Jane, who is a loan officer in zone1, is working with a document of type dq_loan_app in the folder /HomeLoans/zone1. This context (situation) falls in both the scopes as previously described and, therefore, these scopes overlap as shown in the following figure:

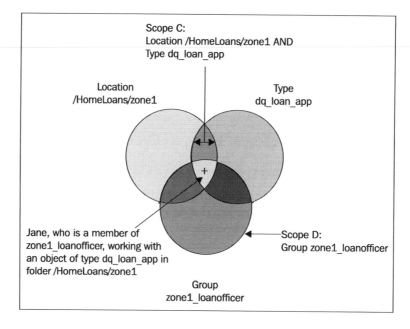

When a situation falls in multiple preset scopes, a mechanism called **scope precedence** is applied for ordering scopes (and the corresponding presets) for selection. Scope precedence orders scope **qualifiers** in a way that enables prioritization of one preset scope over another. There is a pre-defined (default, out-of-box) precedence as follows:

1. Location
2. User or group
3. Role
4. Object Type

Scope precedence is defined in the `webtop`-layer `app.xml` file in the Webtop application deployment using the `qualifiers` element. The qualifier precedence in the default `webtop app.xml` is shown in the following screenshot:

```
<?xml version="1.0" encoding="UTF-8" standalone="no" ?>
- <config>
  - <scope>
    - <application extends="webcomponent/app.xml">
      - <qualifiers>
          <!-- Location qualifier, scope="location", context="location"   -->
          <qualifier>com.documentum.webtop.app.ApplicationLocationQualifier</qualifier>
          <!-- User qualifier, scope="user", context="user"   -->
          <qualifier>com.documentum.web.formext.config.UserQualifier</qualifier>
          <!-- Role qualifier, scope="role", context="role"   -->
          <qualifier>com.documentum.web.formext.config.RoleQualifier</qualifier>
          <!-- Docbase type qualifier, scope="type", context="objectId" | "type"   -->
          <qualifier>com.documentum.web.formext.config.DocbaseTypeQualifier</qualifier>
```

Assuming default scope precedence for the last example, we can see that the relevant location (`/HomeLoans/zone1`) for the current situation is only associated with scope C. In this situation, location has the highest precedence and, as a result, preset C will also have higher precedence than preset D.

It is also possible to define an order among roles using the `roleprecedence` element in the same file. **Role precedence** is useful when a user belongs to multiple roles that are associated with different preset scopes. If precedence between two roles is not configured using this element then the following logic determines the precedence:

- If one role is a descendant of another in the role hierarchy, then the descendant role has precedence over the other
- Otherwise, the role that appears first in alphabetical order gets precedence

The complete logic for selecting one effective preset for a situation is discussed later in this chapter.

Preset rules

While the preset scope and precedence help select a preset to apply in a particular context, the preset **rules** specify what the preset does. Each rule specifies the selections or actions available within a particular functional area. For example, suppose that a preset includes a rule for permissions that allows only `acl_zone1`. If a user tries to assign a ACL and the previously mentioned preset applies, the UI will show only `acl_zone1` as the option even though the repository contains many other ACLs.

Preset rules define the options available in the following functional areas:

Functional area	Description
Navigation	Repository nodes in the browser-tree. The rule also specifies the default node to open after login. Nodes controlled by client capability/role may not be added via this rule. For example, a navigation rule may specify **Inbox** as the start node and **Inbox** and **Saved Searches** as allowed nodes.
Actions	Menu items, action links, action buttons, and tool buttons. Menu items are restricted in the context menu as well. For example, **Check Out** action may be excluded from the available ones.
Types	Object types for assigning to objects. For example, dq_loan_app may be selected as an available type.
Attributes	Default values for attributes. Constraints on attributes rules are discussed later. For example, dq_loan_app.keywords may get 'Application' added automatically on import.
Formats	Formats for assigning to an object. When file extension is available the formats associated with the file extensions are also shown in addition to those specified by the applicable preset. For example, pdf, doc, crtext may be the available formats.
Templates	Templates to use for creating new objects. Type and format of the object may disallow (and hide) some templates allowed by preset. For example, any of the existing templates may be selected as available.
Lifecycles	Lifecycles to assign to an object. For example, dq_loan_lifecycle may be selected as an available lifecycle.
Workflows	Workflow templates (process definitions) available for starting workflows. For example, dq_loan_approval may be selected as an available workflow template.
Groups	Groups or roles for an ACL of a quick-flow. Individual users are not filtered. For example, zone1_loanofficer can be added as an available group.
Permissions	ACLs for assigning to object. For example, acl_zone1 could be selected as an available ACL.

Rules for various functional areas follow certain constraints as mentioned in the following table:

Scope element	Rules not allowed
Location	Navigation
Type	Navigation, Types, Attributes

Additional constraints for an attributes rule are discussed separately to keep the preceding table succinct.

Attributes rules

An attributes rule provides values to be assigned to properties automatically. For example, all documents of type dq_loan_doc created in the folder /HomeLoans/ zone1 should get zone='zone1' as the default value. In this example, the scope may not include a type since attributes rules are not allowed when scope includes types.

An attributes rule may only be applied to attributes of type string, integer, or double. Aspect attributes are not included in presets. Further, object_name, a_ content_type, and read-only attributes cannot be included in the rule. If an attribute present in the applicable rule has been made read-only by the object's lifecycle state, that attribute is not set even if the rule specifies a value for it.

A single-valued attribute is not overwritten by a preset rule if it already has a value. If the property is multi-valued, the values specified in the preset rule are added to the existing list.

If the values in the preset rule conflict with the data dictionary values, the data dictionary prevails while showing the options to the user. In this case, the auto-attribute value is not set on the attribute.

If all the mandatory attributes during import are set via an auto-attribute preset, the user is not presented with the attributes screen and the import process is silent after a file has been selected for import.

Effective preset

Knowledge of preset terminology including context, scope, qualifiers, precedence, and rules helps us understand how presets are defined and how they might be applied in simple cases. However, we still need to understand how the effective preset is resolved in the general case, which can be complicated. This understanding is also important for designing presets to meet a coherent set of requirements.

When a user is trying to perform an action in a given context c in a functional area f, Webtop needs to know the effective preset rule, if one exists. It can be determined using the following logic:

1. Identify the presets whose scope includes the context c.
2. Order the presets from the previous step using scope precedence. If there are two scopes that cannot be ordered by precedence, the narrower scope has higher precedence.

3. Inspect presets in order from previous step, looking for a rule in the functional area f.

4. The first rule that is found in the previous step is the effective rule, and the preset containing that rule is the effective preset.

5. If no rule is found in the previous step then there is no effective preset rule to apply.

> Note that the preset with the highest precedence among applicable scopes doesn't always become the effective preset. A preset must have a rule in the relevant functional area in order to apply in a particular situation. For example, when the user is trying to assign an ACL a preset without a permissions rule cannot affect this interaction.

Let's look at an example to illustrate this algorithm. Suppose that there are three presets A, B, and C, whose scopes include the current user context. These presets are listed by scope precedence in the following table. An X in a column indicates that a rule in that functional area has been defined for the corresponding preset. There are no other rules defined for these presets.

Precedence	Preset	Lifecycles rule	Permissions rule	Actions rule
1	A	X	X	
2	B			X
3	C		X	X

If the user opens a menu, which menu items will be shown? Steps 1 and 2 in the algorithm have already been performed for creating the preceding table. Since the user is opening a menu, the functional area is Actions. According to step 3, we go down the Actions Rule column looking for the first X, which appears in the row for preset B. Therefore, the effective preset is B and its actions rule determines the enabled actions. The enabled actions that belong in the menu being opened will be displayed.

Managing presets

Webtop includes a **Presets Editor** UI for creating and managing presets. Presets can be managed by members of the group dmc_wdk_presets_coordinator or a Sysadmin (user with Sysadmin privilege). Presets can be accessed using the **Presets** node under **Administration** node in the browser-tree, as shown in the following screenshot:

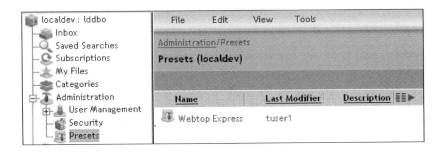

There is a predefined preset named `Webtop Express` as shown in the preceding figure. This preset is discussed later in this chapter.

 Note that Presets Editor is not available in DA.

Creating presets

Presets can be created using the menu option **File | New | Preset**, which opens the Presets Editor containing two tabs—**Setup** and **Rules**. On the **Setup** tab, the preset can be named and its scope can be defined.

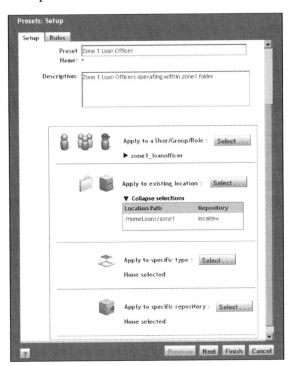

Preset rules can be defined on the **Rules** tab. It lists the functional areas on the left and allows creation of the corresponding rules on the right. As rules are created, they start showing in the **Preset Summary** at the bottom.

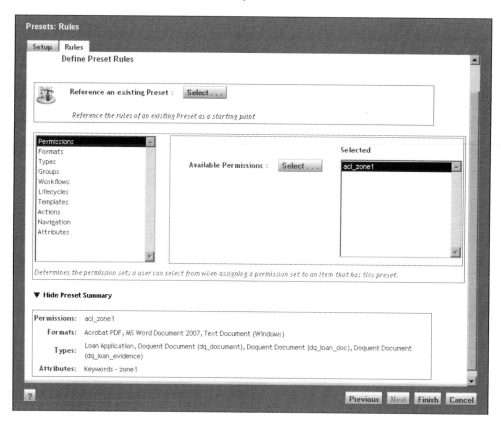

Preset templates

It is often convenient to base a new preset on an existing preset, in which case all the rules from the existing preset are copied over to the new one. The existing preset acts like a template. In fact, it is possible to create presets whose sole purpose is to serve as templates—just create a preset without a scope. The **Rules** tab enables the user to select an existing preset for copying the rules.

Editing presets

A preset can be edited using the context menu **Edit** option, which opens the Preset Editor populated with the preset details for editing.

Modifying a preset doesn't undo its effects on existing objects. The new scope and rules only affect future actions.

Deleting presets

A preset can be deleted using the context menu **Delete** option. Deleting a preset removes it from all scopes and doesn't alter any existing objects.

Webtop Express preset

There is a predefined preset named `Webtop Express` as mentioned earlier. The scope of this preset is `express_user`, which is a built-in role. The out-of-box rules in this preset give the user limited access as follows:

Functional area	Description
Navigation	**My Home Cabinet, Cabinets, Subscriptions, My Files, Inbox**
Actions	Document: content transfer, subscriptions, email, quickflow, properties, clipboard actions, create, delete
Types	`dm_document`, `dm_folder`, `dm_cabinet`
Formats	None, text, PDF, all MS Office formats
Templates	Templates corresponding to formats

A user can be assigned the user experience dictated by the `Webtop Express` preset simply by assigning the `express_user` role to the user. Further, this preset can be modified like any other preset to meet specific requirements.

Documentum product notes

WDK provides a model and framework for completely customizing components that support various functions. Roles are used for restricting access to these components via configuration in XML files. WDK customization can be used to meet the requirements that are too complex to be implemented via presets.

When a repository is created, the Presets DAR (Documentum Archive) is automatically installed in the repository. It installs artifacts such as types that store presets and scopes. Presets are also included with applications based on Webtop such as WebPublisher.

Learn more

The topics discussed in this chapter can be further explored using the following resources:

- EMC Documentum Documentum Webtop 6.5 SP2 User Guide
- EMC Documentum Web Development Kit 6.5 Development Guide
- EMC Documentum Web Development Kit and Webtop 6.5 Deployment Guide
- EMC Documentum Web Development Kit and Webtop 6.5 Reference Guide

Checkpoint

At this point you should be able to answer the following key questions:

1. What is the purpose of a Webtop preset?
2. What is meant by the scope of a preset?
3. What is the need for scope precedence? What is the default scope precedence?
4. How is an effective preset determined?
5. What are preset rules?
6. How are presets created and managed with Webtop? What is the effect of modifying or deleting a preset?
7. What is the Webtop Express preset?

Part 4

Application Development

Documentum Projects

Custom Types

Workflows

Lifecycles

10

Documentum Projects

In this chapter, we will explore the following concepts:

- Customizing Documentum
- Documentum Composer
- Creating and managing Documentum projects
- Building and installing Documentum projects

Documentum Customization

In *Chapter 9*, *Webtop Presets* , we saw how **configuration** could be used to implement business requirements for a Documentum solution. However, most solutions for specific business needs require **customization**, which goes beyond setting parameters and declaring rules. Documentum provides a model and framework for creating a business application, that can include customizations involving various areas such as object model, presentation, and security. In our example scenario we may need to capture loan-related metadata on documents. Some actions, such as import, may need to be customized. Access to various folders may need to be restricted to appropriate groups.

Documentum has a rich feature set and this richness brings complexity. As a result, customization of a Documentum deployment can touch multiple layers of Documentum architecture. Management of these customizations and their ongoing maintenance can easily become a daunting challenge.

 Typically, Documentum solution development includes Webtop configuration via presets, WDK customization, and repository customization. This book does not discuss WDK customization.

It becomes even more challenging when Documentum infrastructure is shared among multiple business units and each business unit has its own customizations. In this case, it is possible that multiple customizations are performed by different development teams but deployed within the same repository, as shown in the following figure:

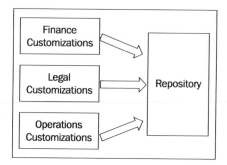

Another dimension of managing customizations is the number of environments in which a customization may need to be deployed. It is common to use at least two environments for Documentum deployments—*development* and *production* (also known as *live*). Ideally, a third environment called *QA* (or *staging*) should also be present.

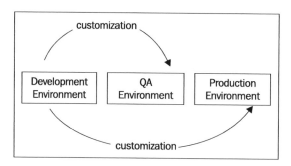

The development environment is used for developing the customizations and may allow uncontrolled changes. Normally, this environment is primarily used by the developers. Once the customizations are ready to be tested, they are deployed into QA. Testing can occur in QA while development and bug fixes are taking place in development. Once the customizations reach a level of quality that is passed in QA, the customizations are deployed to production. The concerns discussed earlier along with the need for managing customizations across multiple environments make a daunting challenge. **Documentum Projects** and **Documentum Archives (DAR files)** provide the means for overcoming this challenge.

Documentum version 6.0 introduced Documentum Projects and Documentum Archives to replace **DocApps** and **DocApp Archives**, respectively. DocApps are discussed in the Appendix *DocApps*.

This chapter discusses Documentum projects and key concepts related to customization. Some of these concepts are discussed in detail in later chapters and, therefore, receive only brief attention here.

Documentum Composer

Documentum Composer is the primary tool for developing repository customizations. It is an **Integrated Development Environment** (IDE) based on **Eclipse**, the popular open-source IDE and platform. We will not discuss general usage for Composer in this book since extensive and excellent documentation is available for both Composer and Eclipse. We will focus on Composer features specific to Documentum customizations.

Let's take a look at the general structure of the Composer UI—the **workbench**. The key widgets in the workbench are views and editors. A **view** is a tab that can be displayed on the workbench and can be positioned in one of multiple positions. A view usually focuses on one development aspect such as tasks, problems, or navigation. An **editor** is used to view and edit files in one or more formats. Multiple files may be open at the same time. A **perspective** is a set of views commonly used for working with certain types of projects or performing certain types of tasks within a project. Switching to a perspective opens the predefined set of views included in that perspective. Some examples of perspectives are Java Perspective, Debug Perspective, and Documentum Artifacts Perspective.

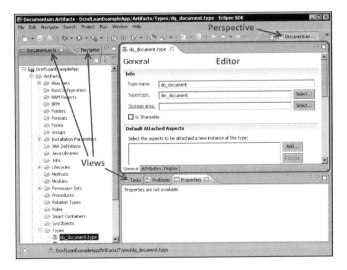

Installing Composer is a straightforward process though some post-install configuration is needed for using Composer. The JRE and Compiler preferences are used to configure a compatible Java version. Connection Broker preference enables Composer to connect to repositories for installing projects. Project installation is discussed later in this chapter.

Documentum projects

Composer organizes development artifacts into **projects** and a set of related projects constitutes a **workspace**. A running instance of workbench works with one workspace at a time. A **Documentum project** is a kind of Eclipse project, that is instantiated in Composer for developing a Documentum solution.

A Documentum project facilitates management of a set of **artifacts** together and these artifacts are typically related to customization for a set of related requirements. As a good practice, a project should be used to package only related artifacts. Unrelated customizations should be packaged in separate projects.

Projects address the challenges related to customizations mentioned earlier. Multiple artifacts related to the same customization can be managed (created, installed, modified, reinstalled) together. A project is created outside a repository and then installed into one or more repositories, thus facilitating portability across repositories and environments. One repository can contain objects corresponding to artifacts from multiple projects. Therefore, it is a good idea to only keep artifacts related to one business-level customization in one project. Since a project exists completely outside a repository, its contents are persisted as files on the file system, making it amenable to source code management just like any other source code. In particular, project contents can be put under version control.

In a typical development cycle, a project is installed into a development repository leading to creation/updates of objects corresponding to the artifacts in the project. When the customizations are ready to be tested, the project is built (also said to be *archived* or *serialized*) onto the file-system in a format known as **Documentum Archive (DAR)** . The DAR file is a binary version of the project and can be distributed and installed into multiple repositories. The DAR file is installed into a test repository and the customizations are tested. Changes are made to the project artifacts to correct the problems found during testing. The modified project is archived and installed again into the development repository.

This process is repeated until the customization is considered ready for prime time. At this point, the current DAR can be installed into a production repository. If the customization is a part of a product, the DAR is included in the product distribution.

Working with Documentum projects

Having looked at what Composer and Documentum projects are, we are ready to explore how to work with Documentum projects within Composer. Working with projects typically involves creating a new project, creating and modifying artifacts within the project, building the project, and installing the project into repositories.

Creating a new project

A new Documentum project can be created using the **File | New | Project...** menu item. This command starts a wizard that allows the user to select the kind of project to create. A Documentum project can be created as a blank new project, as shown in the following figure. For a blank new project, a **Project Name** is required and it should be unique within the workspace. Optionally, **Description** and **Referenced Projects** can also be specified. The ability to reference projects enables sharing of artifacts between projects without duplicating them. Referencing projects also facilitates organization of related projects.

 One key difference between **DocApps** (the means for packaging Documentum customizations prior to version 6.0) and Documentum projects is that a DocApp is created in a repository and requires a connection to a repository to get started. There is no such requirement for creating a Documentum project. As previously mentioned, this difference enables Documentum project artifacts to be managed in a common source control system.

It is also possible to convert a DocApp existing in a repository or a DocApp archive existing on the file system into a new Documentum project. These choices are also shown in the previous screenshot and provide ways for migrating old repository customizations into new environments.

The core project

Every workspace in Composer gets a project named `DocumentumCoreProject` when a Documentum project has been created in that workspace. This project is shown in the following screenshot. It is a read-only project; that is, artifacts cannot be added to this project and it cannot be installed into a repository. Why would we need a Documentum project that cannot be installed?

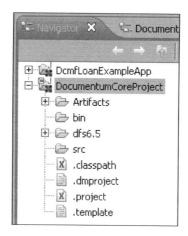

Recall that a project contains artifacts that correspond to objects in the repository. Further, artifacts exist outside a repository and can be manipulated without a connection to the repository. When a new repository is created it contains an initial set of objects such as object types, folders, and formats. While working with a Documentum project, we may need to refer to some of these initial objects (rather to the artifacts corresponding to these objects). For example, the custom type `dq_document` needs to specify `dm_document` as its supertype. The **core project** contains the artifacts corresponding to the initial objects in a repository. Every user-created Documentum project references the core project, by default, and has access to the artifacts corresponding to the initial objects in the repository.

Currently, the core project also includes the **DFS SDK** to support development of DFS services and clients. This feature makes it unnecessary to download and deploy the DFS SDK separately for developing Web services.

Artifacts

An **artifact** is a resource in a Documentum project and it corresponds to an object
in the repository in which it is installed. An artifact is created and managed outside
a repository and creates or modifies an object in the repository when it is installed
in that repository. The artifacts are placed under the **Artifacts** folder in the project.
The kinds of Documentum artifacts that can be created in a project are shown in
the following screenshot and are discussed afterwards. The new artifact wizard
shown here can be opened using the **File | New | Other…** menu item or the
Ctrl+N keyboard shortcut.

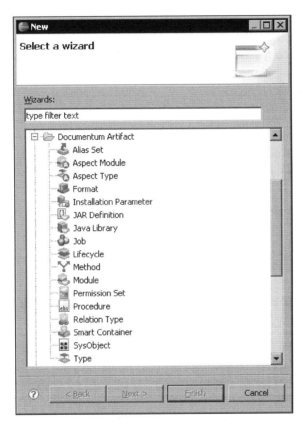

 Note that there are additional kinds of artifacts that must be imported
into a project from a repository as they cannot be created in Composer.
The process of importing artifacts is discussed later in the chapter.

Alias sets

Aliases act as placeholders for actual values representing users, groups, folders, or cabinets that can be inserted at an appropriate time before they are needed. Thus, aliases can make customizations portable across multiple contexts. Multiple aliases and their values are grouped together in an **alias set**. Alias sets are discussed in detail in *Chapter 14, Aliases*.

Aspects

Aspects extend attributes and behavior for objects, *independently of their object types*. The aspect attributes are specified by the **aspect type** artifact while the behavior for the aspect is specified by **aspect module**. An aspect module is made up of the aspect type, the implementation and interface of the aspect behavior, and any interface classes of the code that the implementation depends on. In terms of structure, an aspect module is similar to the module artifact discussed later. Aspects are discussed in detail in *Chapters 3, Objects and Types* and *Chapter 11, Custom Types*.

Formats

A **format** identifies a particular file format (organization of content within the file). The format is typically used to identify applications that can understand the contents of the document. Formats play a key role in terms of document renditions. Formats are discussed in detail in *Chapter 2, Working with Content*.

A new format artifact can be created by selecting **Format** in the new artifact wizard:

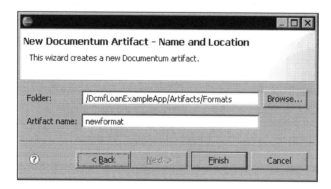

Once the format has been created, it can be updated with additional information such as the default file extension for the format and whether it can be indexed.

Installation parameters

An **installation parameter** applies to the whole project and specifies an option that is used at installation time. For example, installation parameters include pre-install and post-install procedures and upgrade options. Another use for an installation parameter is to provide a value at install time, such as an alias value in an alias set. Such an installation parameter is shown in the following screenshot:

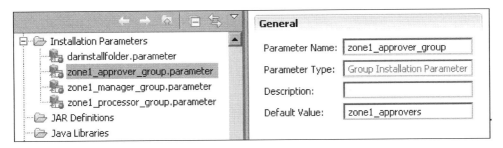

JAR definitions and Java libraries

A **JAR file** packages Java class files in a package convenient for distribution and deployment. Java classes are used for implementing behavior in Documentum customizations.

 The operation and usage of JAR definitions and Java libraries is governed by some technical Java concepts, primarily **class loading**. These details are beyond the scope of this book. However, some recommendations in this regard are included here. Readers interested in learning more about these concepts can use the resources listed at the end of this chapter.

A **JAR definition** is a wrapper that adds metadata to a JAR file and makes it available for use within a project. The metadata includes name, minimum JVM version, and the type of JAR, which can be `Implementation`, `Interface`, or `Interface and Implementation`.

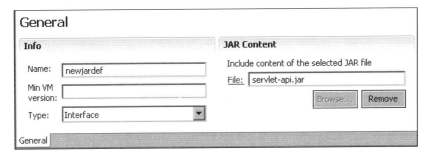

A Java library bundles multiple JAR definitions together for sharing across modules and for convenient administration in the form of one unit. Usually, third-party JARs and code shared among related modules are good candidates to be placed in a Java library.

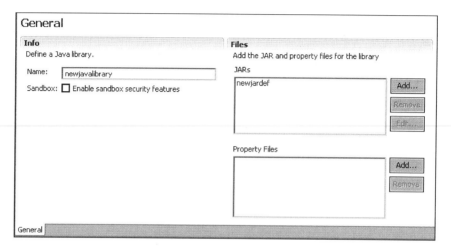

Modules

A **module** implements a behavior, that can be used with service-based objects (**SBO**), type-based objects (**TBO**), or aspects. It includes the interface classes for the behavior, implementation classes, any libraries that these classes use, and any supporting documentation.

A module consists of executable business logic and, therefore, may have dependencies and constraints for the code to run successfully. These dependencies can be specified in the module configuration. The key configuration elements are described as follows:

Attribute	Description
Name	Name of the module using up to 255 characters. For an SBO, provide the fully qualified primary interface name. For a TBO, enter the name of the object type.
Type	Module type as TBO, SBO, or Standard Module. The standard module represents a generic module.
Required Modules	Other modules required for correct operation of this module.
Implementation JARs	JAR definitions for implementation JAR files for the module.
Class Name	Primary Java implementation class for the module.

Attribute	Description
Interface JARs	JAR definitions for the interfaces that this module implements.
Java Libraries	Additional Java libraries used by the module.
Attachments	Javadocs and other resources to be attached to the module.
Min DFC Version	Minimum DFC version on the client for this module to work properly.
Min VM Version	Minimum JVM version on the client for this module to work properly.
Java System Properties	The Java system properties specified as name-value pairs. The values specified for the properties must match those present on the client.
Statically Deployed Classes	Classes that need to be present on the client for the module to function properly.
Local Resources	Files required on the client for this module to function properly. The files are specified as paths relative to the deployment.

A module can use both JAR definitions and Java libraries to include executable code. Some recommended practices for such usage are listed as follows:

- One JAR definition should not be shared across modules. Further, a JAR definition should be included in the same project that contains the module using the JAR definition.
- When a JAR needs to be shared across modules, its JAR definition should be included in a Java library.
- Usually, a Java library should enable sandbox security.
- If multiple modules communicate with each other and need to share JARs, then the shared interface JARs should be separated into a distinct non-sandboxed Java library.
- A Java library must exist only in one project. Modules in other projects should reference the project containing the Java library if they need to use the Java library.

Lifecycles

A **lifecycle** is a set of linearly connected **states** that define the stages in an object's life. It is used to specify business rules for changes in the properties of an object. Lifecycles are discussed in detail in *Chapter 13, Lifecycles*.

Methods and jobs

A **method** is an executable program, which maybe a Docbasic script or a program written in another language such as Java. A method object has properties specifying how to execute the underlying program.

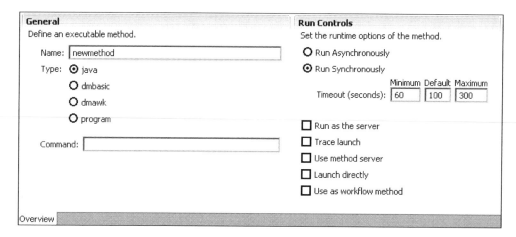

A **job** enables the execution of a method on a schedule or on demand. The properties of a job identify the method to run, the arguments to pass to the method, and the schedule for running the method.

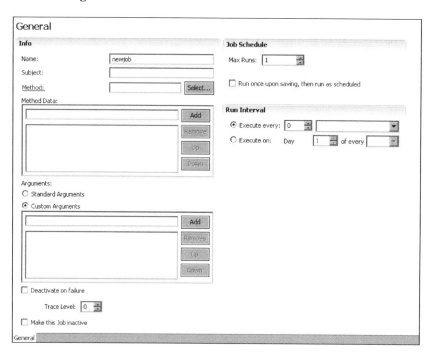

Permission sets

An **ACL** (**permission set**) grants permissions to accessors (users or groups) and is the fundamental means for providing object security. An **ACL template** (**permission set template**) is an ACL that uses one or more **alias references** as accessors. Both ACLs and ACL templates can be created in a project, as shown in the following screenshot:

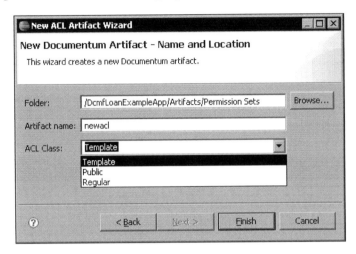

An ACL can be defined as shown in the following screenshot. The `dm_owner` and `dm_world` entries are present by default. These can be modified and other entries can be added.

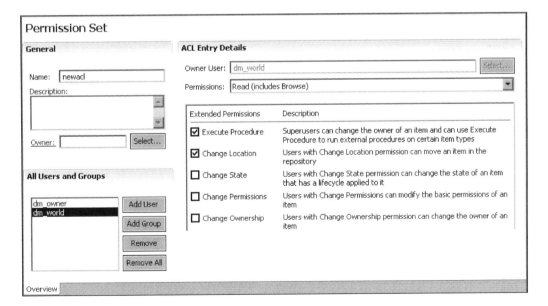

Note that actual users and groups cannot be selected since they are not represented by artifacts. Instead, the accessors are specified via user and group installation parameters.

Permission sets are discussed in detail in *Chapter 7, Object Security* and ACL templates are discussed in detail in *Chapter 14, Aliases*.

Procedures

A **procedure** is a **Docbasic** script used for modifying the behavior of Content Server or a client. Docbasic is a proprietary scripting language used with Documentum. A procedure can be defined by typing the script or loading it from an existing file.

Relation types

Let's take a look at relationships before discussing how to manage relation types with Composer.

Relationships

Two objects in a repository can be connected using a **relation**, where one of these objects is treated as a **child** while the other is treated as a **parent**. A **relation type** needs to be defined before relations of this type can be created.

System relation types are the predefined relation types that cannot be manipulated by users. For example, annotations are implemented using a relation type between sysobjects and notes. Another example is the translation relation type, which connects a document with its translations.

The relation types that can be added and managed by users are called **ad hoc relation types**. For example, a paystub image could be related to a loan application as a supporting document. In this case, the loan application could be treated as the parent. The relation type for this relation could be named dq_support_doc. The following figure illustrates a relation instance for this example:

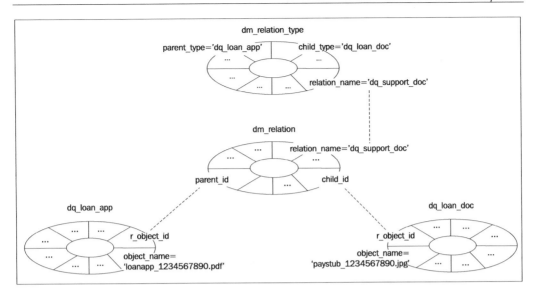

One object can refer to another using an attribute of type ID. So why would we want to use a relation type to formally relate two objects? Relationship instances can be secured when using relation types. Referential integrity can also be enforced for related objects. In some cases, we need to relate objects of existing types that cannot be modified to add an ID attribute. Sometimes we may even want to capture information about the relation instance. This can be achieved by creating a subtype of dm_relation_type with the desired attributes.

Managing relation types

A relation type has the following key properties.

Attribute	Description
Name	Name of the relation type.
Security type	Security type can be None, Parent, Child, or System. None means that this relation type is not secured. Parent means that the security for the relation is same as that for the parent object. Child means that the security for the relation is same as that for the child object. System means only sysadmins and superusers can create or manipulate relations of this relation type.
Referential integrity	Referential integrity specifies what happens to the relation when the parent is deleted. Allow delete (default) means that the parent can be deleted. Restrict delete means that parent cannot be deleted while a child is related to the parent. Cascade delete means the child is also deleted when the parent is deleted.

Attribute	Description
Parent type	Optional restriction on the object type of the parent
Child type	Optional restriction on the object type of the child
Relationship direction	Relationship direction can be `From Parent to Child`, `From Child to Parent`, or `Bidirectional`
Permanent link	Indicates whether the relationship is preserved when the parent is copied or versioned. When the relationship needs to be preserved the child and relation are copied.

Smart containers

A **smart container** models a set of objects and relationships as a template. It is usually parameterized for creating separate instances from the same template. Just like Webtop presets, smart containers provide a declarative mechanism for implementing a common customization need.

Smart containers are commonly used for setting up hierarchical structures. In our example scenario, consider the structure needed for each loan application. We need a folder for the loan application, which is has the loan account number as its name. The account folder contains the loan application, completed forms, communications about the account, and evidentiary documents. The following screenshot illustrates this example:

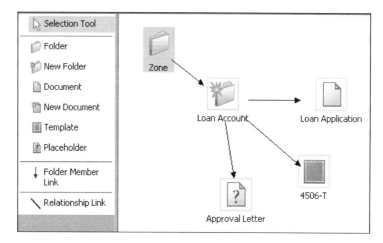

Within a smart container the object relations are either folder link relations or actual `dm_relation` instances. One object in a smart container is identified as the **primary object**. A smart container can include the following kinds of items:

- **Existing documents**: An existing document can be included in the instance of the smart container. Existing documents are included by passing their identity as a parameter during instantiation. This is often useful when creation of a document or an action on a document leads to the instantiation of the smart container. For example, importing a loan application may set up the structure for a loan account.

- **Existing folders**: An existing folder may be used in a manner similar to existing documents. For example, the loan application structure may need to be created under an existing folder, whose identity is passed as a parameter for the smart container.

- **New documents**: New documents can be created and their properties may be set based on values defined in the smart container.

- **New folders**: New folders can be created and their properties may be set based on values defined in the smart container.

- **Template objects**: These are existing objects which are copied into the smart container instance. For example, an existing blank form PDF could be automatically copied in each loan account folder.

- **Placeholders**: A placeholder specifies an object that is usually part of the structure but is not created automatically when a smart container is instantiated. For example, a loan approval letter may be added to loan account but may not exist in the structure until the letter has been issued.

As mentioned earlier, smart containers often use parameters, which are resolved at run time. Within the smart container a parameter named `param` is referred to as `${param}`. At run time, this expression resolves to the value provided for `param`.

A smart container is installed as an object of `dm_class` in the repository. The content associated with this object is an XML representation of the smart container. The object also has an attached aspect, which has the logic for interpreting and instantiating composite objects using the template.

A smart container is usually instantiated programmatically. The DFC interfaces make it very simple to instantiate a smart container. Such code could be used in WDK customization, workflow activities, or lifecycle actions to meet specific requirements.

Sysobjects

It is also possible to include documents, folders, or, in general, sysobjects (objects of `dm_sysobject` type or its subtypes) in a project. These are the objects that need to be created once for the set of customizations included in the project. For each sysobject, its object type, content file, format, lifecycle, and alias set can be specified. Aspects may also be attached to the object. Depending upon the specified object type, available properties can be set on the object. In our example scenario, the `HomeLoans` cabinet and the zone folders under it can be included in the project.

Types

Object types are probably the most important and most common artifact in customizations. Types are discussed in detail in *Chapters 3, Objects and Types* and *Chapter 11, Custom Types*. Composer allows the creation of both standard and lightweight object types, as shown in the following screenshot:

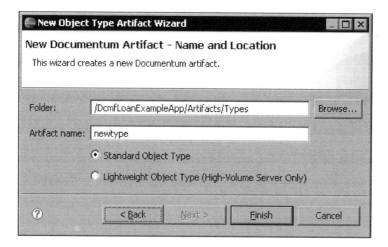

Importing artifacts from a repository

Most of the preceding discussion deals with creating new artifacts. However, it is also possible to add an artifact to a project by importing the artifact from a repository. This is a useful approach if the object representing the desired artifact already exists in a repository. For certain artifacts, such as **process templates** (also known as **workflow template** or **process definition**), this is a necessity since they cannot be created in a project directly. Process templates are developed using Workflow Manager or Process Builder, neither of which is integrated with Composer. The following screenshot shows artifact selection for import:

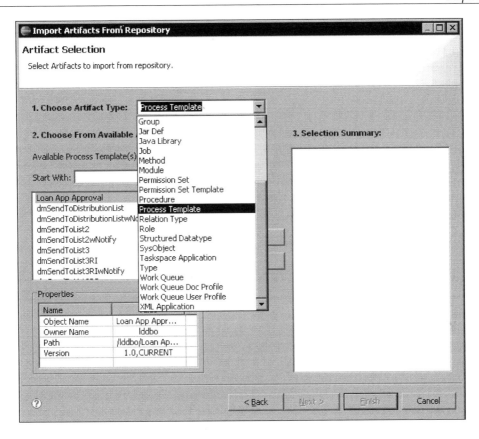

When importing an artifact it is important to reference relevant projects that the artifact would depend upon. Otherwise, Composer will attempt to import all the dependencies in the project along with the desired artifact.

 Artifacts cannot be imported from one project into another. They can only be imported from a repository to a project.

XML applications

XML applications customize and automate the storage and management of XML objects in the repository. For example, an XML application can specify whether to chunk XML objects and how to extract and apply metadata from XML. Due to its hierarchical structure, an XML document can be divided into chunks and the chunks can be organized as nodes in a virtual document. This approach offers all the benefits of virtual documents, such as independent and concurrent management of chunks by multiple users. XML chunks could also be used to assign metadata to other documents.

Currently, XML applications cannot be created in Composer. However, the configuration file for an XML application can be imported and edited in Composer. Each XML application has a configuration file (in XML) which specifies rules for processing XML during content transfer to and from the repository.

Web services

Composer supports development and testing of DFS-based **Web services** and **Web-service clients** in a project. It includes a DFS registry plugin, which enables connection to a Web service registry, import of WSDL file to create the client library, create services, and export the services into an **EAR** (Enterprise ARchive)) file. An EAR file is a standard packaging mechanism for deployment to **JEE** (**Java Enterprise Edition**)) compliant application servers.

Building and installing a project

A Documentum project is created and managed outside the repository. It includes artifacts and also supports Web service development. However, project contents just remain as specifications until the project is installed into a repository. A project can be installed into a repository in the following ways:

- Composer User Interface: If the project source is available, it can be opened in Composer and installed into a target repository. However, projects are rarely distributed with source, just like software that is not open source. For distribution, a project is converted into an executable and portable form called the DAR file for the project. The DAR file cannot be imported into Composer for installation.

- **DAR Installer**: The DAR Installer requires Composer to be installed but it does not launch the full Composer IDE. It provides a GUI for only installing a DAR file.

- ANT tasks and **Headless Composer**: ANT tasks and Headless Composer provide a command-line mechanism for installing a DAR file into a repository. This alternative is useful for scripting the DAR installation task. This is also the preferred option when an organization does not want to install full Composer just for installing DARs.

Installation options

Project installation into a repository is governed by two sets of options—project installation options and artifact installation options.

Project installation options

Project installation options affect the whole project and are specified in the project properties. These options also act as defaults where similar options could be specified for artifacts individually. Project installation options are accessed by selecting the project node in the **Documentum Navigator** view, selecting the **Project | Properties** menu option, and then selecting the **Documentum Project** node.

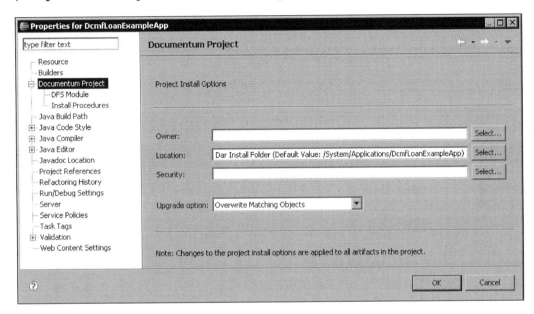

Upgrade option specifies installation behavior when objects matching project artifacts are found in the target repository. Matching objects are likely to be found when the project is installed more than once in a repository. This option can have one of the following values:

- Overwrite matching objects: Matching objects are overwritten and when no matching objects are found new ones are created.

- Ignore matching objects: Matching objects are ignored and when no matching objects are found new ones are created.

- Create new version of matching objects: Matching objects are versioned and objects are installed as new versions. When no matching objects are found new ones are created.

How does Composer match objects in the target repository to the project artifacts? Each artifact has a **Uniform Resource Name** (URN) for identifying it. When a DAR is installed into a repository, an object of dm_dar is created to record the details of the installation. This object records a mapping of URNs to repository object IDs in its content. When the same DAR is installed again, this map is used for identifying objects matching project artifacts.

Pre-installation procedures and **Post-installation procedures** are scripts that can be run before and after the installation of the project, respectively. **DFS module options** apply when the project is used for developing DFS-based services.

Artifact installation options

Artifact installation options affect how an individual artifact is installed. When a similar project option is set at the project level the value at the artifact level prevails (overrides). Artifact installation options are accessed by selecting the artifact in the **Documentum Navigator** view, selecting **File | Properties** menu option, and then selecting the **Documentum Artifact** node.

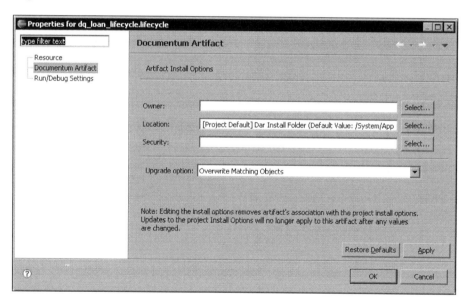

 The upgrade option for a smart container should be set to **Create New Version of Matching Objects**. Choosing **Overwrite Matching Objects** would lead to broken model-instance associations for existing instantiations of the smart container.

Installing a project

A project can be installed by right-clicking on the project in the **Documentum Navigator** view and selecting the **Install Documentum Project...** option. The project installation wizard is shown in the following screenshot. The installation settings essentially include repository connection information and some optional parameters for overriding some project options.

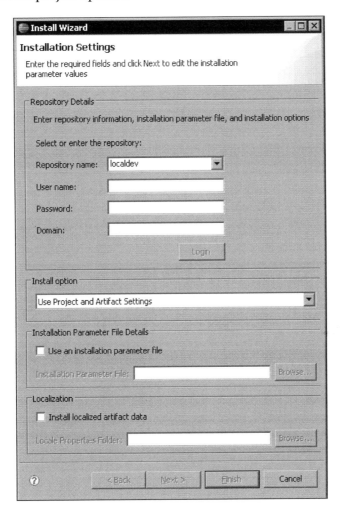

 A repository must be available via DFC configuration before the project installation wizard can start.

Creating the DAR file

The project DAR file can be created by building the project. If the **Project | Build Automatically** menu option is set then the project can be rebuilt by using **Project | Clean...** option and selecting the project. Otherwise, **Project | Build Project** menu item can be used to build the project. The DAR file is created under the `bin-dar` folder in the project, as shown in the following screenshot:

Installing a DAR file

A DAR file can be installed using the DAR Installer or using Headless Composer as discussed in the following section.

DAR Installer

DAR Installer works as a plugin for Composer but it only launches the GUI for installing DARs as shown in the following screenshot:

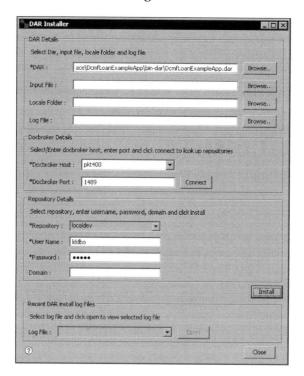

Note that the required parameters consist of the **DAR** file absolute path and the repository connectivity information (**Docbroker Host**, **Docbroker Port**, **Repository**, **User Name**, and **Password**). The optional parameters include an **Input File** for installation parameters, a **Locale Folder** containing localized properties, and a location for a **Log File** for installation.

 There are additional constraints when the DAR being installed depends on other DARs. If DAR B depends on DAR A then A must be installed before B. When B is being installed, A must also be present in the same folder as B.

Headless Composer

A DAR file can be installed into a repository using **Headless Composer**, which is a non-GUI command-line version of Composer. In addition, Headless Composer can also import, build, and install a project—these are useful capabilities for scripting when the source project is available. Headless Composer includes an ANT task named `emc.install`, which is used for installing a DAR file into a repository.

Documentum product notes

Workflow Manager is bundled with Composer even though they are not integrated.

Documentum supports conversion of DocApps and **TaskSpace** applications to projects. These capabilities facilitate migration of customizations from previous versions to the current one.

Even though Composer allows creation of **Lightweight SysObjects (LwSO)**, only applications designed for the High Volume Server can make proper use of LwSOs currently.

The Headless Composer ANT tasks must be run through Eclipse AntRunner due to the way they leverage the Composer and Eclipse infrastructure.

Documentum **xCelerated Composition Platform (xCP)** provides a rapid development and deployment framework for case-based solutions. Loan processing, claims processing, and police case processing are some examples of case management since each of them deals with cases. In our example scenario, a case is centered on a loan application. xCP includes a set of prebuilt software components for case management, tools, and best practices for configuring and deploying xCP solutions. As a result, solutions built using xCP can replace most customization needs with configuration. Typically, this approach can lower customization costs while improving quality of the solution.

Learn more

The topics discussed in this chapter can be further explored using the following resources:

- EMC Documentum Documentum Composer 6.5 SP2 User Guide
- EMC Documentum Documentum Composer 6.5 SP2 Introduction to Documentum Composer for DAB Users
- EMC Documentum Documentum Composer 6.5 SP2 Building a Documentum Application Tutorial
- (White Paper) Introduction to XML Applications — Umair Nauman
- (White Paper) The EMC Documentum Composition Platform — A Detailed Review
- Introduction to Documentum Composer — `http://www.bluefishgroup.com/library/2008/an-introduction-to-documentum-composer/`
- ECN: Build Your First Application — `https://community.emc.com/docs/DOC-3557`
- Documentum Composer: The Core Project — `http://paulcwarren.wordpress.com/2009/10/26/documentum-composer-the-core-project/`
- Documentum Development: Past, Present, and Future — `http://paulcwarren.wordpress.com/2009/06/30/documentum-development-past-present-and-future/`
- Jar defs and Java libraries — `http://donr7n.wordpress.com/2009/01/20/jar-defs-and-java-libraries/`
- What's a Smart Container — `http://donr7n.wordpress.com/2008/11/19/whats-a-smart-container/`
- Documentum Composer: Smart Containers — `http://paulcwarren.wordpress.com/2009/01/16/documentum-composer-smart-containers/`
- Documentum Composer: What's in an install? — `http://paulcwarren.wordpress.com/2009/01/09/documentum-composer-whats-in-an-install/`
- ECN: Documentum Composer 6.5: Smart Container Demo — `https://community.emc.com/docs/DOC-2489`
- Composer 6.5: Smart Container Demo — `https://community.emc.com/docs/DOC-248920/the-elements-of-a-smart-container/`
- Creating DFS Services using Documentum Composer — `http://paulcwarren.wordpress.com/2008/08/11/creating-dfs-services-using-documentum-composer/`
- Eclipse Documentation — `http://eclipse.org/documentation/`

Checkpoint

At this point you should be able to answer the following key questions:

1. What is Documentum Composer?

2. What is a Documentum project? What is its purpose?

3. What are Documentum artifacts? What kind of artifacts can be managed in a Documentum project?

4. What is a DAR file? What is its purpose?

5. What are the options for installing a project into a repository?

11
Custom Types

In this chapter, we will explore the following concepts:

- Managing custom types
- Data dictionary
- Aspect types

Custom types

A Documentum repository contains many built-in object types that support the functionality of the platform. Some other object types are for general use and can be used for business purposes as well. However, all possible business needs can neither be anticipated nor be supported out-of-box. Therefore, Documentum allows creation of new object types, which are called **custom types** or **custom object types**.

Before reading this chapter, it would be helpful to revisit *Chapter 3, Objects and Types,* since the majority of the concepts pertaining to object types apply here as well. The concepts repeated here are explained in more detail in that chapter.

In our example scenario, a *loan application* has metadata such as *loan type, amortization type,* and *loan program.* If we import the loan application as an object of dm_document, we will not find adequate attributes for storing the metadata previously mentioned. However, we can create a custom type, say dq_loan_app, containing custom attributes for the metadata previously mentioned. Thus, we can extend the default object model for implementing business requirements. This chapter examines the details of creating and managing custom types.

Documentum Composer, Documentum Administrator (DA), and DQL provide support for managing custom types. However, Composer is the most commonly used application for creating custom types since it fully supports the **data dictionary** (see *Data Dictionary* section later in this chapter) and it has a Graphical User Interface (GUI) specifically designed for creating and managing custom types. All serious solution development efforts should employ Composer for managing custom types. We will primarily use Composer interface for discussion while DA and DQL examples will be shown for illustration only.

 Recall that Composer manipulates **artifacts** outside a repository. Artifacts create or update corresponding objects in a repository when the artifacts are installed into the repository. Therefore, all discussion pertaining to actions in Composer will imply actions on artifacts. For details about Composer and artifacts, see *Chapter 10, Documentum Projects*.

Managing custom types

A user-defined object type is called a **custom type** and the user-defined attributes are called **custom attributes**.Attributes are also known as **properties**. Custom types can be created, modified, and removed as long as certain rules are followed. These rules and other details related to managing custom types are discussed in this section.

Creating a custom type

A custom type can only be created by a user with Create Type privilege. Recall that Sysadmin and Superuser privileges implicitly include this privilege. The user creating a type becomes its **owner**.

A custom type can extend an existing type through **inheritance**, which facilitates reuse, organization, and management of types (see *Chapter 3, Objects and Types*). A new custom type can have an existing custom type or one of the predefined Documentum object types as its **supertype**. For our example scenario, we can create a type hierarchy as shown in the following figure. Other types in the overall type hierarchy are not shown here.

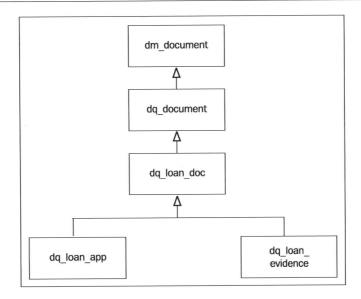

Type hierarchy is one of the core concerns in designing a solution on the Documentum platform. Further, altering a type hierarchy may require dropping types, which is a non-trivial change. Therefore, sufficient care and forethought must be invested into the design of the type hierarchy. Let's examine the example type hierarchy illustrated in the preceding figure.

The most common supertype for a custom type for representing documents (in general, content types with associated content) is dm_document. The majority of the content management operations act on sysobjects, and dm_document is a subtype of dm_sysobject for representing documents. It is also an appropriate choice for the supertype of our document types. Why would we want to create multiple custom types? Why can't we create just one custom type for our solution with dm_document as its supertype? The answers are similar to the reasons for having object types in the first place. Reuse, storage efficiency, and grouping objects in query scopes are some of the reasons. Let's explore the specific reasoning behind the design of the type hierarchy shown in the preceding figure.

It is a common practice to create a base custom type for an organization. All custom types for the organization are subtypes of this base type. It provides a central place to define attributes that apply to all custom types for that organization. It also provides a convenient way to refer to all the custom types for the organization. In our example, dq_document is this base type. It is fairly common for the base type to not define any attributes of its own initially.

The first application of Documentum within this organization is for storing loan documents. However, it is possible that the organization may need to store other kinds of documents in future. Therefore, we define `dq_loan_doc` to represent loan-related documents. It is still a kind of base document, just not at the organization level. It has `dq_document` as its supertype.

> Adding base types makes the type hierarchy deeper, which leads to more tables in joins and adds to the complexity of the object model. While performance is less of an issue with modern RDBMS implementations, we should scrutinize each custom type in the hierarchy to prevent the model from becoming unnecessarily complex.

Next, we inspect the kind of loan-related documents and the corresponding metadata that need to be stored. At one extreme, we could create one custom type for each kind of document we want to store—loan application, pre-approval letter, Preliminary Underwriting Finding, paystub, bank statements, and so on. This is usually an impractical approach and it can lead to a plethora of custom types. At the other extreme, we could just add all the relevant attributes to `dq_loan_doc` and not create additional custom types. In practice, a realistic solution lies somewhere between the two extremes. We do want to create specific custom types but only to the extent that they facilitate the implementation of the overall solution. In our scenario everything is tied to a loan application so we should create a custom type `dq_loan_app` for it. There are several documents that support the loan application and are part of the application package. Usually, these documents provide evidence for the information entered in the loan application. We can create a custom type called `dq_loan_evidence` for such documents. Loan-related documents such as a pre-approval letter are neither an application nor evidence. All such documents can be stored using `dq_loan_doc`.

Our design approach makes it possible for different kinds of documents to be stored using the same type. If we need to know the exact kind of document it can be stored as metadata. For example, we can add an attribute called `biz_doc_type` (for business document type) on `dq_document` so that it is available on all our custom types. For example, a paystub may have this property set to `Paystub` while a bank statement may have it as `Bank Statement`, even though both use the object type `dq_loan_evidence`.

While type hierarchies have their benefits, it is also possible to create a custom type without a supertype. Such a type is called a **null type**. Only a superuser can create a null type. A null type is useful for storing data that does not need the usual object management features such as versioning. There are several built-in types that are null types such as `dm_user`, `dm_session`, and `dm_alias_set`. If a custom type is intended to only store non-versionable data, a null type may be appropriate for this purpose.

By default, custom null types are not visible in Webtop. Also note that Composer does not provide a way for creating or importing objects of custom null types into a project. If we need a set of objects of custom null types to be a part of the solution, we can write DQL scripts for creating these objects in the initial setup. Some organizations may consider this to be a disadvantage of using custom null types and may just use `dm_sysobject` as the supertype of the concerned custom type.

Composer uses type artifacts for managing types. Type artifacts are listed under the **Artifacts/Types** node in the **Documentum Navigator** view, as follows:

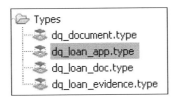

A type artifact is opened in a **Type Editor**, which is shown in the following screenshot. Various details of the type specification are grouped into sections which are organized on three tabs—**General**, **Attributes**, and **Display**.

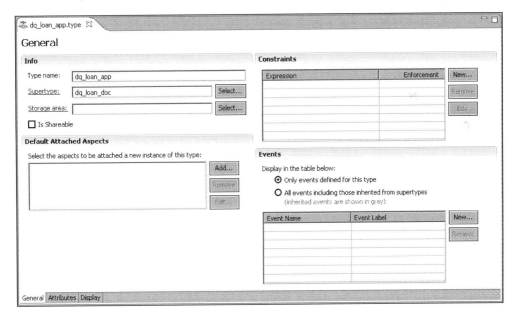

The **General** tab shows type-level information organized into **Info**, **Default Attached Aspects**, **Constraints**, and **Events** sections. These sections are discussed next.

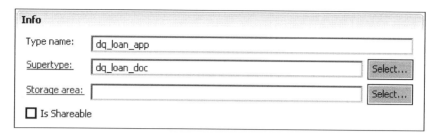

The **Info** section is shown in the preceding screenshot and captures the following details:

Field	Description
Type name	Name of the type. A type name must be unique (case-insensitive) in the repository and can be up to 27 characters long—all lower case.
	It should begin with a letter and should not end with an underscore. In between, it can contain letters, digits, and underscores. It cannot contain a space or punctuation nor can it be same as any DQL reserved word, such as SELECT or WHERE.
	Further, it cannot start with dm_, dmi_, dmr_. Prefixes used by Documentum applications (for example dcm_ is used by DCM) should also be avoided. It is recommended that a custom prefix (such as dq_ in our example) be used for custom type names to distinguish them from the other types. Any of the common approaches for defining a unique namespace could be used for this purpose.
Supertype	The supertype of the new type. An existing type can be selected as a supertype. This should be left empty when creating a null type.
Storage area	A **storage area** identifies where the content files are stored for objects. The default storage area identifies where the content files for objects of this type will be stored by default.
Is Shareable	Specifies whether the type is a **shareable type**. See *Chapter 3, Objects and Types* for details of shareable types.

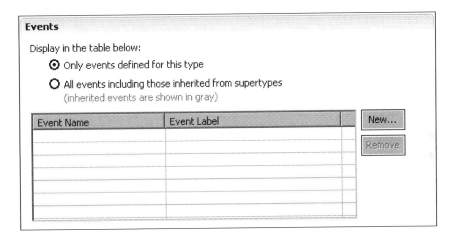

Constraints are conditions that must be met by objects and properties to be valid. In Composer, constraints can be specified as checks. A **check constraint** is a condition expressed as a Docbasic expression or a routine that evaluates to `true` or `false`. Check constraints for objects can be specified in **Constraints** section, as shown in the preceding screenshot.

> Custom types can also have **key constraints** which specify uniqueness of objects or their relationships with other objects. Key constraints can be specified via DQL and are discussed later in this chapter.

An **event** is something that happens in an application, for example, an operation on an object. A **system event** is an event that is recognized by and is auditable by Content Server. For example, checkin on a particular document is a system event. Promoting and demoting an object in a lifecycle are also system events.

On the other hand, an **application event** is recognized and is auditable only by the application. For example, an application event can be used to hold off workflow activities based on external dependencies such as conditions in other systems. Suppose that a workflow activity requires a performer to review a loan application. However, the performer needs access to borrower background data in another system in order to complete the review. An application event can be sent to the performer's inbox to trigger the activity once the required data is available in the other system.

Application events for custom types can be configured in the **Events** section as shown in the preceding screenshot. Note that events are also inherited from supertypes just like attributes.

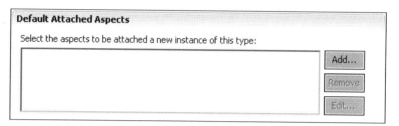

Aspects can attach properties and behavior to individual objects irrespective of the object type. Sometimes it is desirable to attach an aspect to all objects of a type. One or more aspects can be specified in the **Default Attached Aspects** section for a type, as shown in the previous screenshot. These aspects are automatically attached to the new objects of this type. An aspect is added by selecting its aspect module artifact, as shown in the following screenshot. Note that aspects can be selected from other projects as well.

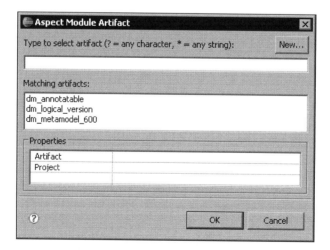

Attributes for the custom type being created are specified via the **Attributes** tab. The left half of this tab lists the attributes and is shown in the following screenshot. The right half of this tab changes depending on the selection in the attribute list.

The custom attributes for the type are listed as shown in the previous screenshot. Attributes can be added and removed using the **New** and **Remove** buttons. For each attribute, two additional nodes are listed—**Application Interface Display** and **Value mapping**. Attribute specifications can be made after selecting a node in the list as follows:

Node	Options
Attribute name	Selecting an attribute name exposes **Structure** and **Constraints** sections, which essentially affect storage of the attribute value.
Application Interface Display	Selecting this node exposes **General** and **Search** sections, which essentially affect the display of the attribute in a client application.
Value mapping	Selecting this node exposes **Conditional Assistance** and **Value Mapping Table** sections. These sections essentially guide the specification of values for the attribute in the client application interface by providing a list of values for selection.

This table suggests that there are numerous details that can be specified for each attribute. However, two key points make it easy to comprehend and to specify these details:

- Most of these details are optional and needed only when mandated by requirements
- These details can be categorized into structural and display-oriented information

Let's look at these sections one by one:

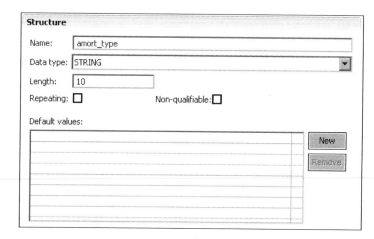

The **Structure** section contains the fundamental information about the attribute as listed in the following table:

Field	Description
Name	Attribute name must be unique within the type, including inherited attributes. The name must use all lower case letters and `'select'`, `'from'`, and `'where'` are not valid names. Further, an attribute name cannot start with dm_, a_, i_, r_, a number, a space, or a single quote.
Data type	Data type constrains the types of values this attribute can take. The allowed data types are `integer`, `boolean`, `string`, `double`, `time`, and `ID`. A `time` value can represent both date and time. An `ID` value represents an object ID.
Length	Length of the attribute if the data type is `string`.
Repeating	Whether this is a repeating attribute or single-valued.
Non-qualifiable	Whether this is a **non-qualifiable** attribute. Non-qualifiable attributes are stored in a serialized form and don't have columns of their own in the database. Non-qualifiable attributes cannot be used queries. Most attributes are qualifiable.
Default values	Default value for this attribute. For repeating attribute, multiple values can be specified.

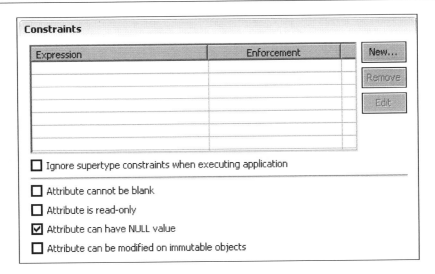

The **Constraints** section specifies check constraints at the attribute-level. Attribute constraints are inherited but can be ignored optionally. In addition to the Docbasic expression checks, there are some checks about missing value and modifiability that can be specified via checkboxes:

- Blank
- Read-only
- Nullable
- Modifiable on immutable objects

The **General** section specifies user interface support for this attribute other than search-related specifications.

Field	Description
Label	User-friendly name, for display as the default label in client applications.
Input mask	The **input mask** is used for validation and provides a pattern for valid values for this attribute. The mask is specified using the following characters with special meaning in addition to the regular characters:
	#: A numeric digit 0-9
	A: An alphanumeric character including a-z A-Z 0-9
	&: Any ASCII character
	?: Any alphabetical character a-z A-Z
	U: Similar to ? but automatically converted to upper case before saving
	L: Similar to ? but automatically converted to lower case before saving
	For example, suppose that an account number consists of eight characters where the first three characters must be alphabetic and the remainder can be alphanumeric. An input mask for this property can be specified as ???AAAAA.
Category	Name of custom tab in Documentum Desktop only.
User help	Help description for the attribute.
Comment for developers	Comments for developers.

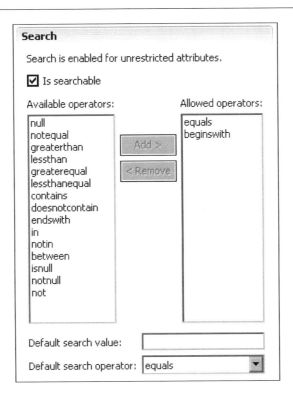

The **Search** section specifies search user interface support for this attribute when this custom type is specified in the criteria. The configuration includes the following information:

Field	Description
Is Searchable	Whether this attribute will be listed in search criteria.
Allowed operators	Types of matching that can be done on this attribute for searching, such as `equals`, `notequal`, `beginswith`, and so on. These are selected from the set of **Available operators**.
Default search value	Default value for the search field for this attribute.
Default search operator	Search operator among the allowed ones to be selected by default.

The preceding figure shows search configuration for `dq_document.biz_doc_type`. The resulting behavior in Webtop is shown in the following figure. Note that `dq_loan_app` is a subtype of `dq_document` and the data dictionary for `biz_doc_type` is inherited with the attribute. However, it is possible to override the inherited data dictionary in the subtypes. This capability is useful when the user interface for an attribute needs to behave differently for different types.

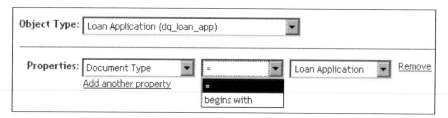

The **Conditional Assistance** section specifies lists of values that could be used for populating this attribute on objects:

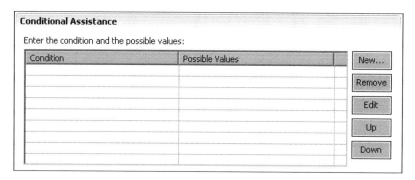

When users need to specify values for object attributes through client applications it may be desirable, for business reasons, to limit the values that can be specified for a property. For example, if an attribute represents a country name its underlying data type is string but only the country names are meaningful values for this attribute. When the user needs to specify a country name, the application can limit the value to one of the actual country names. This ability is supported by a feature known as **value assistance**.

 Value assistance cannot be specified for Boolean attributes, which can only have `true` or `false` as their values.

Value assistance specifies a list of valid values that can be used by client applications to facilitate valid user input for an attribute. The list of valid values can be an explicitly fixed list or a DQL query that returns a list of appropriate values from a data source, such as objects or database tables. The following screenshot shows value assistance for `dq_document.biz_doc_type`:

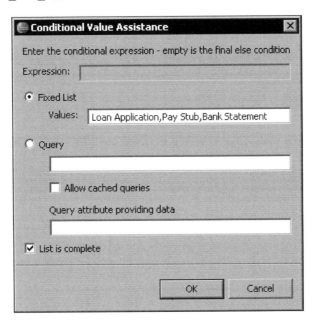

Webtop restricts the values for `biz_doc_type` to those provided by the value assistance, as shown in the following figure:

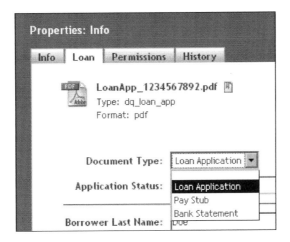

There are two other options that affect the behavior of these lists. One—**Allow cached queries**, specifies whether the queries are allowed to be *cached*. Caching queries improves performance by storing the lists retrieved for value assistance. However, if the data being queried is modified, the changes are not available in the application until the cache has been refreshed.

Type cache refreshing can be controlled using the `dfc.search.typecache.refresh_interval` property in `dfc.properties`. This property specifies the number of milliseconds between refreshes of type cache.

The other option—**List is complete**, specifies whether the list of values is complete. This option essentially specifies whether the user can enter a value other than those present in the list; for example, using a combo list or box. This option is useful when a set of initial or most frequently used values is known, but there may be cases when other values are acceptable but not known beforehand. In such a scenario, the manually entered value for an object property does not necessarily become a part of the value assistance list for future interactions. If the new value needs to be included in value assistance then the value assistance query needs to ensure that.

It is also possible to use one of many lists for value assistance on an attribute, depending on the situation. The list to use is decided dynamically based on certain conditions and this feature is referred to as **conditional value assistance**. One of these lists is identified as the *default* list and the others are identified as *conditional*. Each conditional list is associated with a condition and the list is used when the corresponding condition is true. The default list is used when none of the specified conditions is true. Note that regular value assistance is a special case of conditional value assistance when only the default list is specified.

Value Mapping Table

Enter the data value, the display string to be shown in the UI, and an optional description:

Attribute Value	Display String	Description	
dataValue	displayValue		New
			Remove

The **Value Mapping Table** section configures another useful feature for client applications—**value mapping**. A value mapping defines a correspondence between *stored values* and *labels to display* for those values. For example, a value mapping can be useful for showing the expansion for an abbreviation that is the stored value. A stored value ARM may be mapped to `Adjustable Rate Mortgage`, which will be displayed to the users.

> A keyword named `$value` can capture and utilize user-specified single values in a validation error message or in a value assistance query at run time. For example, `SELECT title from book WHERE author = $value(user_author) and category = $value(user_category)`. This query retrieves book titles where the author and category of the books are provided by the user.

User interface support for the type is specified via the **Display** tab, which includes **Application Interface Display** and **Display Configuration** sections as shown in the following screenshot:

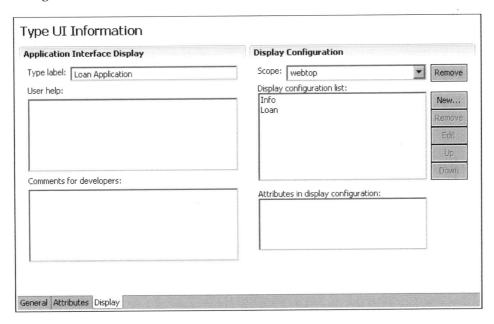

The **Application Interface Display** section specifies information for displaying the type in the UI and includes the following information:

Field	Description
Label	User-friendly name, used as default display label in client applications.
User help	Help description for the type.
Comments for developers	Comments for developers.

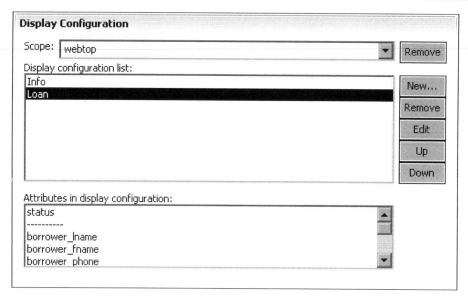

The **Display Configuration** section specifies how to display the type attributes in client applications using **display configurations**. Each display configuration is defined as follows:

- **Display configuration scope** determines the application, which will use this display configuration
- For each scope, multiple configurations can be defined
- For each configuration, an ordered list of properties is specified that constitutes the configuration

WDK applications utilize display configurations extensively. For example, Webtop uses display configurations to include custom attributes in the standard interface without writing any additional user interface code. Webtop displays attributes in one display configuration together on one tab on the properties page.

The following screenshot shows a **display configuration** named Loan:

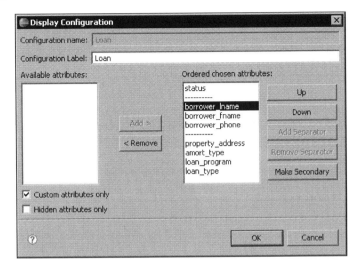

When the properties of an object of type dq_loan_app are viewed in Webtop, a separate tab named Loan displays the attributes included in this display configuration, as shown in the following figure. Note that the display order of the tabs can be altered by altering the order of the display configurations in Composer:

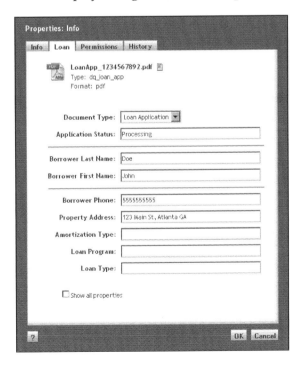

Note that, implicitly, the attributes not included in display configurations are not displayed on the application interface. Thus, display configurations can be considered as a way of exposing or hiding custom attributes.

When the information specified previously is saved, it is saved as an artifact in a Documentum project. It is persisted as an XML file on the file system. Recall that the project needs to be installed into a repository to create the corresponding custom type with these details.

Modifying a custom type

Sometimes we need to alter a custom type after it has been created. For example, an unforeseen need may arise or the requirements may change. A custom type artifact can be modified using Composer, in which case the *Documentum project needs to be reinstalled into the repository to update the type.* Changes made through DA or DQL affect the type in the repository directly.

Modifying a custom type is a privileged operation and only the type owner or a superuser can modify a custom type. The built-in Documentum types cannot be modified. Further, custom type modifications are restricted in the following ways:

- The type can be dropped (removed) only when there are no objects of this type and there are no subtypes of this type. In other words, before a custom type can be dropped its subtypes need to be dropped and its objects need to be deleted.

- Structural changes to a type are restricted to the following:
    - A new attribute can be added to the type
    - A non-inherited attribute can be dropped (removed) from the type
    - The length of a non-inherited string attribute can be increased

- Non-structural changes, such as those related to UI support or defaults, are not restricted.

Structural changes to a custom type automatically affect its objects, its subtypes, and objects of its subtypes. Non-structural changes do not affect existing objects. For example, adding an aspect to the default attached aspects for the type will not affect the existing objects of the type. As another example, changing value assistance on an attribute doesn't affect existing objects. Similarly, changing a display configuration will not change the objects though it will alter the presentation of all objects of this type in the UI.

Note that these restrictions are for making changes to types and not to type artifacts in a Documentum project. A type artifact can be freely modified using Composer and the screens for editing a type artifact are the same as those used for creating a new type artifact. If the artifact is installed into a repository for the first time these restrictions do not apply since a new custom type is being created. If the artifact is installed into a repository where it has been installed before the change restrictions do apply.

> Note that there is no uninstall or rollback support for type changes in the repository. However, it is possible to drop a type completely from the repository.

Remember that a type cannot be versioned and no history of type changes is retained (other than potentially through audit trails) in the repository. The type exists only in its most recent form. A history of project installations is maintained via versions of a `dmc_dar` object corresponding to the project but this only tracks mapping of artifacts (including types) to repository objects.

It is possible to change the type of an object, though that does not alter the type itself. The type of an object can only be changed to the immediate supertype or an immediate subtype of the existing type. For example:

```
change dq_loan_app objects to dq_loan_doc
WHERE object_name = '1234567890.pdf'
```

> Changing type for an object to its supertype can result in data loss if there are custom attributes on the current type of the object, since these attributes will be removed from the object.

Data dictionary

The **data dictionary** for a type consists of the non-structural information discussed earlier and includes constraints for properties, default property values, value assistance, and mapping information.

Data dictionary is stored in internal objects and is made visible to users and applications via the process of **publishing**. If there are any new changes to the data dictionary, publishing it creates or modifies objects of three types—dmi_dd_type_info, dmi_dd_attr_info, dmi_dd_common_info, which are visible and accessible to the client applications.

Data dictionary can be published using the built-in data dictionary publisher job. The API method publish_dd can also be used to publish the data dictionary. It can be used with arguments to selectively publish parts of the data dictionary such as the data dictionary for one type only. Note that Content Server clients may see the data dictionary changes only after the local cache has been refreshed. Refer to our earlier discussion regarding cache refreshing.

Data dictionary is available for client applications and Content Server uses only the following parts of data dictionary for its operation—default property values and whether to allow changes to properties on immutable objects.

Data dictionary can support multiple languages using locales. A locale is used to present the user interface taking into account the local conventions and language for a geographic location. For example, es_MX represents Spanish language and Mexican conventions and en_US represents English language and US conventions. The locales available in a repository are listed in dm_docbase_config.dd_locales.

Managing types with DA

DA provides only basic support for managing custom types and Composer should be used for full-fledged custom type management. However, DA exposes some additional type specifications that are currently not available in the Composer UI.

In DA, types are managed under the **Types** node in the browser tree. The **File | New | Type** menu option starts the **New Type** wizard, which is shown in the following screenshot:

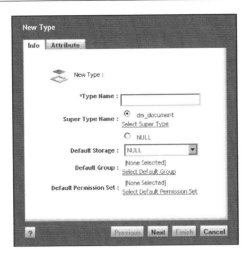

This wizard has two tabs—**Info** and **Attribute**. The **Info** tab specifies type-level details and it shows two specifications that were not present on the Composer UI:

- Default Group—a default group can be associated with the type
- Default Permission Set—a default ACL can be associated with the type

These defaults are useful when Content Server is using `Type` as its default ACL mode (`dm_server_config.default_acl=2`). In this case, a new object of this type gets this ACL assigned by default. See *Chapter 7, Object Security* for more details regarding the ACL mode.

The **Attribute** tab lists the attributes in the type as shown in the following screenshot:

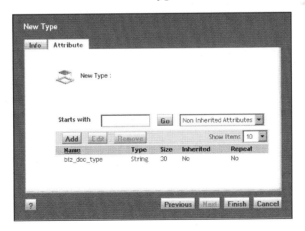

The preceding screenshots are also used for editing an existing type. However, changes to types are restricted as described earlier.

Managing types with DQL

Although types are best managed using Composer, DQL may be the only option for certain needs, such as defining key constraints for a type. Types can be manipulated with DQL using CREATE TYPE, ALTER TYPE, and DROP TYPE statements. These statements are discussed briefly in this section.

CREATE TYPE

The CREATE TYPE statement creates a new custom type. For example, the following DQL query creates a custom type named dq_loan_doc, which has dq_document as its supertype:

```
CREATE TYPE dq_loan_doc
(account_id STRING(10))
WITH SUPERTYPE dq_document
```

It is also possible to specify data dictionary information in the CREATE TYPE statement including value assistance, mapping table, default values for attributes, and type-level and attribute-level constraints.

We have already discussed check constraints earlier. DQL syntax allows specification of key constraints as well. Constraints for custom types can occur in the following forms:

Constraint type	Description
Primary Key	The primary key uniquely identifies an object of that type within the repository. There can only be one primary key constraint for a type.
Unique Key	A unique key is unique among all the objects of this type in the repository. There can be multiple unique key constraints for a type.
Foreign Key	A foreign key establishes a constraint between properties of two types. A Sysadmin privilege is required to create a foreign key constraint.
Check	A check constraint is a condition expressed as a Docbasic expression or a routine that evaluates to true or false.

An error message can be specified for each constraint and it can be displayed to the user when the corresponding constraint is violated. Optionally, each constraint can be flagged to be enforced, in which case the client application should enforce the constraint.

ALTER TYPE

The `ALTER TYPE` statement modifies an existing custom type. For example, the following DQL query adds an attribute named `status` to the custom type `dq_loan_app`:

```
ALTER TYPE dq_loan_app
ADD status STRING(20)
```

Type changes are privileged operations and the following changes can only be performed by superusers:

Modification	Applicable types
Add read-only attributes	Custom type
Allow aspects	Custom null type
Add, set, or remove default aspects	Any type that is not lightweight and allows aspects

The following changes can be performed by superusers or the type owner:

Modification	Applicable types
Set defaults	Any type
Change data dictionary	Any type; value assistance and constraints cannot be added to built-in types
Add or drop read-write attribute	Custom type
Increase size of string attribute	Custom type
Make type shareable	Custom type

One important default value that can be associated with a type is the **default lifecycle**. The default lifecycle for a type can be attached to an object of this type without identifying the lifecycle explicitly. *A default lifecycle does not get automatically attached to an object of this type.* The following DQL syntax is used for this purpose:

```
ALTER TYPE type_name
SET DEFAULT BUSINESS POLICY[=]chronicle_id
[VERSION version_label]
```

Here, `chronicle_id` is the chronicle ID of the lifecycle. The `VERSION` clause identifies the version of the lifecycle to be applied. The default version is `CURRENT`.

DROP TYPE

The DROP TYPE statement drops an existing custom type. For example, the following DQL query drops the custom type dq_loan_app:

    DROP TYPE dq_loan_app

Recall that an attempt to drop a type will fail if any subtypes or objects of this type exist in the repository.

Aspect types

Recall from *Chapter 3, Objects and Types* that aspects are similar to object types in the sense that they specify attributes and behavior. An aspect is defined in Composer using two artifacts—**aspect type** for attributes and **aspect module** for behavior.

An aspect type is created by creating a new aspect type artifact, as shown in the following figure. We will use the aspect example from *Chapter 3, Objects and Types*. Recall that the aspect named Exemplary was intended to tag documents that served as good examples for handling specific loan processing scenarios.

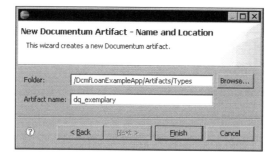

Attributes for the aspect type can be defined as shown in the following figure:

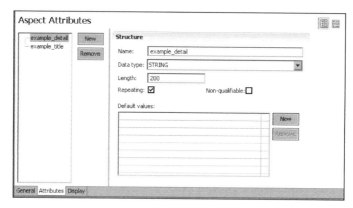

An aspect module is created like other modules except that **Aspect Module** is selected instead of **Module**. Module creation is discussed in *Chapter 10, Documentum Projects*.

There are two important things to remember when defining an aspect. *The aspect module and the aspect type for an aspect must have the same name.* Further, the *aspect module must reference the corresponding aspect type*, as shown in the following figure:

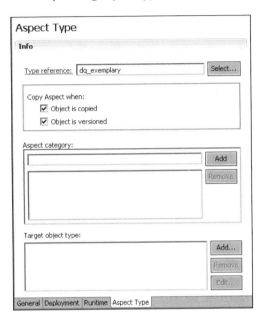

Help—some DQL Queries

Some helpful queries related to object types are provided in this section.

The following query retrieves the types of sysobjects matching a condition:

```
SELECT r_object_id, object_name, r_object_type
FROM dm_sysobject
WHERE object_name = 'loan_app.pdf'
```

The following query retrieves all the null types:

```
SELECT name
FROM dm_type
WHERE super_name = ' '
```

The following query retrieves the supertype of a given type:

```
SELECT super_name
FROM dm_type
WHERE name = 'dm_document'
```

The following query retrieves the names and labels for attributes of a given type:

```
SELECT attr_name, label_text
FROM dmi_dd_attr_info
WHERE type_name = 'dm_sysobject'
```

Documentum product notes

Some databases may disallow adding an attribute with the same name after it has been dropped from a custom type. Usually, this problem can be rectified by dropping the corresponding column in the underlying table. In general, extra care must be exercised in dropping attributes or types.

DFC provides `com.documentum.fc.client.aspect.IDfAspects` interface for attaching, detaching, and listing aspects attached to an object.

Recall that a type uses up to two tables (one for single-valued properties and one for repeating) of its own for storing non-inherited properties of its objects. There are additional database views available for retrieving all the attributes in the type together.

Note that it is possible to create a subtype of `dm_user` if we need to capture custom attributes for users. However, DA does not display custom user attributes by default. If a custom attribute is required it may become impossible to manage users in DA without customization.

Learn more

The topics discussed in this chapter can be further explored using the following resources:

- EMC Documentum Content Server 6.5 Fundamentals
- EMC Documentum System 6.5 Object Reference Manual
- EMC Documentum System 6.5 SP2 DQL Reference Manual
- EMC Documentum Documentum Composer 6.5 SP2 User Guide
- EMC Documentum Documentum Composer 6.5 SP2 Building a Documentum Application Tutorial
- ECN: Build Your First Application—`https://community.emc.com/docs/DOC-3557`
- DFC Javadocs for `com.documentum.fc.client.aspect.IDfAspects`
- Eclipse Documentation—`http://eclipse.org/documentation/`

Checkpoint

At this point you should be able to answer the following key questions:

1. What are custom types? How are they different from built-in Documentum object types?

2. What privileges are required for managing custom types? What changes are allowed to an existing custom type?

3. What is the data dictionary? What benefits does it provide? Why do we need to publish the data dictionary?

12
Workflows

In this chapter, we will explore the following concepts:

- Designing workflows
- Using workflows

Business processes

A **business process** is a set of linked activities that create value by transforming an input into a more valuable output. Both input and output can be documents and/or information and the activities can be performed by humans, machines, or both. The processes can serve the purpose of the core business operations (manufacturing, sales, and so on), management (strategy, planning, tracking, and so on), or support (hiring, accounting, and so on) of the core business operations.

The example scenario of a home loan application process was described in the *Introduction*. For the purpose of discussion in this chapter, we will examine automation of a portion of this process. In real life situations, multiple factors may influence the decision regarding what to automate. Do the relevant users have access to the repository? If there are external users involved, is the cost of infrastructure to include them in the automated process justified? Are the activities being automated manual, tedious, or error-prone?

The portion of the process illustrated in the following figure will be used for our discussion. It has been adapted from the original description to facilitate illustration and discussion:

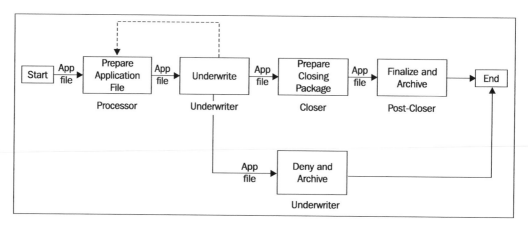

The process illustrated in the preceding figure takes an application file through the underwriting, closing, and archival activities. In this process, a *processor* packages the forms and documents into an *application file* and validates it for completeness and accuracy. The file is then handed off to an *underwriter* in the lending department. The underwriter reviews the file for guideline compliance and for completeness. If there are any problems the underwriter *suspends* the file and sends it back to the processor (the dotted backward path in the figure). The processor corrects the problems and sends the file back to the underwriter. Once everything is in order, the underwriter issues a *commitment letter* and adds it to the application file. The file is then forwarded to *closer* in the closing department. The closer prepares the *closing package* for closing the sale. At closing, the loan is funded and the file comes to *post-closer* with the closing documents. The post-closer performs quality control and then *archives* the file. It is also possible for the application to be denied during underwriting. In this case, the application is archived and doesn't go through closing activities.

Technology offers a great potential to serve businesses by making business processes more efficient or by providing capabilities that were infeasible without the use of technology. For example, automated business processes can make key information available faster and facilitate important decision making. Efficient execution of processes can reduce costs and improve cash flow. Since almost all business processes rely on some sorts of documents, enterprise content management has a key role to play in business process management. In our example, loan application is the key document that affects decision making, flow, and the outcome of the process.

Documentum supports process automation via workflows, which is the subject of this chapter.

Workflow concepts

It is very important to understand the difference between design and execution of a workflow and it can be generalized in terms of the following considerations:

- *Design-time*: Design-time considerations apply when the process is being designed and modeled
- *Run-time*: Run-time considerations apply when the process definition is in place and the workflow is being executed

These differences are important for disambiguating certain terms even though some of these terms may be used interchangeably. The terms *template* or *definition* are associated with design-time considerations and are used synonymously.

A **process definition** is the description (or design or definition) of a process in terms of the tasks in the process, the performers, the information it manipulates, and the overall behavior during execution. A process definition may also be referred to as **process template**, **workflow definition**, or **workflow template**. When a specific piece of information is acted upon by specific performers (humans or programs) according to a process definition, this execution is known as a **process** or **workflow**. In other words, a process/workflow is an instance of a process/workflow definition/template. Multiple processes, created from the same process definition, can execute simultaneously with each process operating on different content items.

> Even though multiple synonymous terms are available for this discussion, we will prefer to use the terms *process definition*, *workflow*, *activity definition*, and *task*. These terms provide a clear distinction and minimize confusion. They are also close to the internal representation of the corresponding objects in the repository.

A process definition consists of **activity definitions** linked together via **flows**. An activity definition describes a task that can be performed in a workflow. A flow describes the movement of information from one activity to another. Often this information consists of documents that are wrapped in **packages**. **Performers** specified in activity definitions carry out the corresponding tasks.

The business process example described earlier can be modeled in Documentum as the process definition shown in the following figure. Note that while it looks similar to the business process it's modeling, it deviates from that description in some ways—the package contains loan application rather than loan application file and the **Finalize and Archive** task has been split into two separate activity definitions. In practice, the modeling details depend on the exact business requirements, priorities, and the Documentum framework for implementing workflows. It is not uncommon to adapt the business process to some extent to make the best use of the available technology. This template will be used as an example in the rest of this chapter. The figure is annotated to illustrate some terms related to process definition.

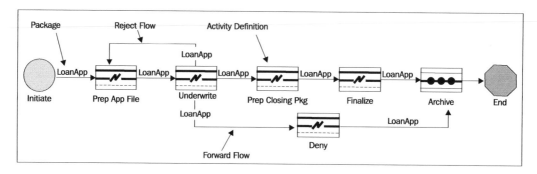

When a workflow is created from a process definition, specific objects are **packaged** and passed to the **tasks** (or **work items**) corresponding to the definition of the initial activities. As performers carry out tasks, they may alter existing objects or create new objects. These objects are passed on as packages to the following tasks. Workflows, tasks, and packages are *run-time* instances.

To illustrate these concepts further, consider the scenario where two borrowers—John Doe and Jane Doe, are separately applying for loans. Each loan application gets packaged separately and gets passed into a separate workflow instance. Each instance creates a task for the **Prep App File** activity definition. The two applications may be prepared by different processors. However, the workflows are based on the same process definition and the **Prep App File** tasks are based on the **Prep App File** activity definition. This example is illustrated in the following figure:

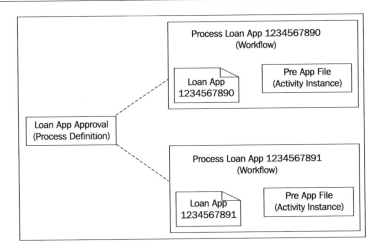

The relationships between various terms can be summarized using the following figure. Note that this is a simplified representation. Please refer to *EMC Documentum System Object Reference Manual* for exact object and attribute relationships.

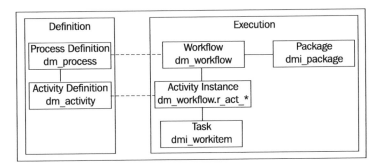

A *business process* is defined in the repository using a *process definition* (dm_process) which refers to one or more *activity definitions* (dm_activity). The business process is executed by Content Server by creating a *workflow instance* (dm_workflow) based on the process definition. The workflow instance includes one or more *activity instances* (dm_workflow.r_act_*) referring to the corresponding activity definitions. Each activity instance generates one or more *work items* (dmi_workitem), which are tasks corresponding to the activity. Each workflow instance is associated with one or more *packages* (dmi_package), which are routed to various activity instances as they execute. Thus, a task provides access to the packages that need to be processed via the task.

Workflows and customization

Workflows form a key component of Documentum solutions. Process definitions are packaged with other artifacts in Documentum projects. However, process definitions are managed outside Composer unlike most other artifacts. A process definition is developed in a repository using **Workflow Manager** or **Process Builder** and then it is imported as an artifact into a Documentum project using Composer. The following Composer screen shows the artifact import dialog, which can be launched using **File | Import… | Documentum | Artifacts From Repository**:

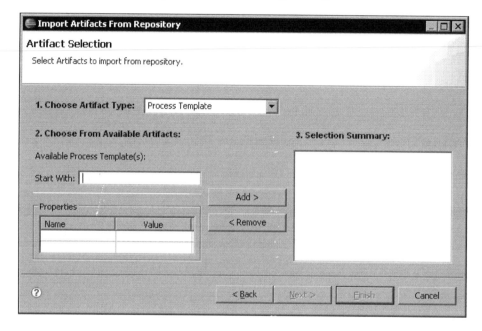

 Workflow Manager is a desktop tool for visually designing workflows and is bundled with Composer. It can be found within the Composer installation folders on file-system. Process Builder is a separate product that offers enhanced features for designing workflow templates. Process definitions designed with Process Builder execute in the Process Engine, which can scale to a large number of workflows.

A business process can be automated using Documentum in the following manner:

- **Analyze**: Gather information about the business process to be automated.
- **Model**: Model the process in terms of activities, performers, flows, and packages.

- **Define**: Formalize the model as a process definition using Workflow Manager or Process Builder. The template is validated and installed into the desired repository.

- **Use**: Start creating workflow instances from the process definition. Various performers participate in these workflows. Performers need appropriate access to perform these tasks.

- **Modify**: If the process definition needs to be modified, uninstall, modify, validate, and install the workflow template again.

These steps are described in detail in the following sections.

Analysis

Analysis of a business process involves gathering information regarding the activities involved, sequence of activities, whether there are any special situations and how they are handled, performers of activities and if the performers can be referred to in terms of business roles, and information and documents that are passed through activities, and if they can be modified by activities. The information gathered via analysis is used for modeling the process in a form suitable for implementation on Documentum.

Identifying reporting requirements is another key component of analysis for business process management. Reports can provide an insight in to the state of individual workflows as well as business intelligence based on aggregate workflow information. Reporting capabilities require appropriate metadata (out-of-box and custom) to be managed within the system. This chapter only discusses the out-of-box reporting capability in Webtop. **Documentum Business Activity Monitor** provides a dynamic dashboard in **TaskSpace** for managing business process performance.

In our loan application process example, analysis may require talking to the processors, underwriters, closers, and post-closers at the mortgage company to understand details such as what documents support the loan application, how the business roles are organized, if there are timing constraints between activities, who needs to be notified if there are any problems, and so on.

Modeling and definition

Modeling and definition of processes share several concepts and are discussed together in this section to avoid repetition. Modeling maps the requirements for the business process to Documentum terminology to facilitate definition. The model is defined in a Documentum repository as a process definition using Workflow Manager or Process Builder.

A process definition is saved as an object of type dm_process in the repository. Creating a process definition is a privileged operation and requires coordinator client capability and Sysadmin/Superuser privileges. Saving, installation, and uninstallation of a template require write permission on the template or Sysadmin/Superuser privileges.

While process definition mostly involves details about activities, performers, and flows, some details are specified at the process definition level:

- **Name** *and* **Description**: Name and description of the process definition identify it.

- **Instructions**: The instructions are displayed to the user during the execution of a workflow instance created from this process definition.

- **State**: Current state of the process definition. The states of a process definition are discussed next.

- **Owner**: Initially, the creator of the process definition is the owner but the owner can be reassigned later.

- **Default alias set**: The set of aliases that can be used for resolution during workflow execution. See *Chapter 14, Aliases* for more details about alias sets.

- **Auditing**: Turning on auditing for the process definition enables completed workflows to be shown in workflow reports.

The process definition (workflow template) properties are shown in the following screenshot:

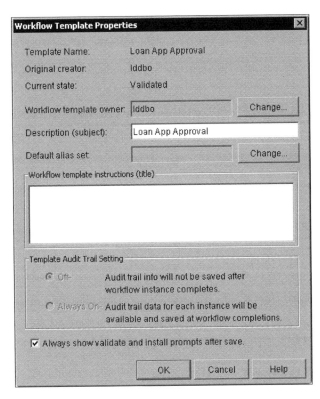

Each process definition has an associated **state**, which identifies where it is in the development process. A process definition can be in one of the following states:

- *Draft*: The process definition is under development
- *Validated*: No process definition errors present
- *Installed*: The process definition is available for instantiation (creating workflows from it)

A newly created process definition is in the *draft* state. When the developer validates it successfully, its state changes to *validated*. A validated process definition can be installed and its state changes to *installed*. The process definition needs to be uninstalled before any changes could be made to it. Uninstalling a process definition puts it back in the validated state. As soon as a change is made to the process definition it moves into the draft state. Thus, a process definition can move back and forth between these states but workflows can be created and be operational only while the corresponding process definition is in the installed state.

Activities

An **activity** is a step in a business process and a **process** consists of a set of interconnected activities. The characteristics of an activity are specified in an **activity definition**. Further, a process definition refers to activity definitions for defining its structure. An activity definition has draft, validated, and installed states, which have the same semantics as the process definition states. When a process definition is being created, it can only use the installed activity definitions.

Two activity definitions in a process definition can be connected in the following two ways, directly or indirectly:

- **Serial** (in sequence): If one activity must be completed before the second can begin, they are considered to be connected serially
- **Parallel**: If the two activities can be carried out simultaneously, they are considered to be connected in parallel

In our example, *Underwrite* and *Prep Closing Pkg* are serial activities. If there was an additional activity called *Schedule Closing* and it could be performed between *Underwrite* and *Finalize* but either before, after, or at the same time as *Prep Closing Pkg*, then it could be placed in parallel to *Prep Closing Pkg*, as follows:

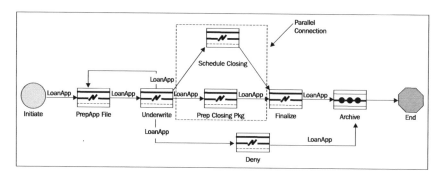

In the preceding figure, note that *Deny* seems to be in parallel to *Prep Closing Pkg* and *Finalize*. However, the business logic requires that only one of these paths is taken—either deny the application or prepare the closing package (if application is being approved). So these paths are not truly parallel paths. However, if the application is approved both *Prep Closing Pkg* and *Schedule Closing* need to execute, so they are truly connected in parallel.

 Each activity definition is stored as an instance of dm_activity. An activity definition can be reused across multiple process definitions and even within the same process definition. However, activity definitions must be uniquely named in a process definition.

An activity definition can be configured as **manual** or **automatic**. A manual task is performed by a human user while an automatic task is performed by a program on behalf of a user. In our example, *Underwrite* is configured as manual and *Archive* as automatic.

The following screenshot shows the interface for configuring an activity definition in Workflow Manager:

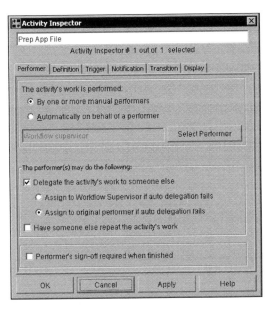

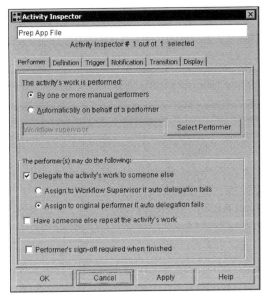

Configuration for an activity definition is grouped into **Performer, Definition, Trigger, Notification, Transition**, and **Display** sections with a separate tab for each section. The **Display** tab only affects the display of activity definition within Workflow Manager and is not discussed here any further. The configuration pertains to either *execution* of the activity or *transition* from/to the activity. The **Definition** and **Performer** tabs relate to execution and **Trigger, Notification**, and **Transition** pertain to transitions. The execution related configuration is discussed here while the configuration related to activity transitions is discussed in the next section.

Performer

A **performer** for an activity definition is a user who performs the corresponding task (recall that a task is a run-time manifestation of an activity definition). Performer specification for an activity definition depends on whether it is manual or automatic.

Manual activity

An activity is indicated as manual by selecting **By one or more manual performers** on the **Performer** tab as shown in the previous figure. A manual activity can be assigned performers via the **Select Perfomer** button on the **Performer** tab, which launches the following screen:

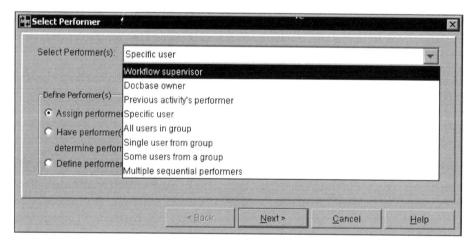

The following performer options are available for a manual activity:

- **Workflow supervisor** (the user who initiates the workflow)
- **Repository owner**
- **Previous activity's performer**

- **Specific user**
    - explicitly selected at design time
    - resolved at run-time by performer of another activity or via an alias

- **All users in a group**: All users in the performer group must complete the task for the workflow to move forward
    - explicitly selected at design time
    - resolved at run-time by performer of another activity or via an alias

- **Single user from a group**: All users in the group are notified and it can be specified which one user will perform the task:
    - first one to acquire the task from his/her *Inbox*
    - user with fewest unfinished tasks in his/her *Inbox*
    - The group itself can be selected the same way as for **All users in a group**

- **Some users from a group**: It is similar to **Specific user** except that multiple users or groups could be specified and they all perform the activity in parallel.

- **Multiple sequential performers**: Multiple performers can be selected and ordered. They perform the task one after another in the specified order. Optionally, each performer can be allowed to reject the task to the previous performer.

A good practice for designing process definitions is *not* to specify performers explicitly. Explicit specification of performers at design time limits the applicability of the process definition in different situations or across multiple repositories. The performers can be left to be identified at run time—the workflow initiator can pick performers, the performer of an activity can pick performers for other activities, or Content Server can determine performers by resolving aliases.

Note that this strategy is not always the most suitable one. If there is no need to use a workflow in diverse situations, this approach leads to inefficient execution and/or unnecessary complexity in design and configuration. In such situations, it may be preferable to specify performers at design time.

In our example, the processor could be allowed to select the underwriter. Alternatively, aliases could be set by zones. Recall that the mortgage business operation in our example is organized by geographic zones. This configuration will allow the task to be sent to all the underwriters in the correct zone (for example group `zone1_underwriter` for zone 1) and could be picked by anyone among them for underwriting.

A manual performer can be allowed to **delegate/forward** his/her task—the task is reassigned to another user or group without the intended performer completing the task. If delegation fails for any reason, the task can be sent to the workflow supervisor or to the original performer who delegated the task. This feature is useful when another user may be more suitable than the intended performer for completing the task in a special situation.

A performer can also be allowed to request the task to be **repeated**. Repeating a task is similar to delegation but the intended performer completes the task before reassigning it to others.

The configuration options for delegating and repeating a task are shown in the following screenshot:

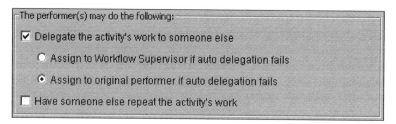

A manual activity can require **electronic sign-off** from the performer for completing the activity. Electronic sign-off is performed by providing the password used for user authentication.

Automatic activity

Automatic tasks are performed on the performer's behalf, which means that the security constraints used by the program are those of this user and any changes made by the automatic task are recorded in the performer's name.

An activity is indicated as automatic by selecting **Automatically on behalf of a performer** on the **Performer** tab. An automatic activity can be assigned performers via the **Select Perfomer** button on the **Performer** tab. Automatic activities have limited options for performer specification and these options are a subset of those described earlier for manual activities. The available options are the following:

- **Workflow supervisor**
- **Repository owner**
- **Previous activity's performer**
- **Specified user**

An automatic activity uses performer parameters as shown in the following screenshot:

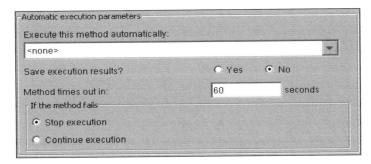

An automatic task is performed by a **method**, which is a program conforming to certain requirements. Only a valid workflow method can be selected for an automatic activity. A method is indicated as a workflow method by selecting **Use as workflow method** in Composer, which sets dm_method.a_special_app='Workflow' on the method object.

One of the available methods needs to be selected for an automatic activity. The method can be configured to save execution results. It can also be configured to halt the workflow on method failure.

Definition

The **Definition** tab specifies the basic information about the activity as shown in the following screenshot:

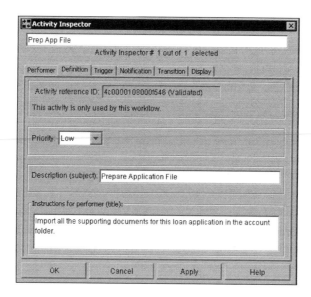

The **Activity Reference ID** is the object ID of the activity definition.

A **priority** can be set for an activity and is useful for automated tasks. The priority can be set to *low, medium, high,* or *dynamic.* Automatic activities are executed by the **workflow agent**. When the workflow agent executes automatic tasks, it executes them in the order of decreasing priorities—among the activities ready to be executed, an activity with a higher priority is executed before an activity with a lower priority. Dynamic priority allows applications to set the priority at run time.

The **Description** and **Instructions** are displayed to the manual performer.

Activity transitions

A **flow** connects two activities in a workflow as **outgoing flow** from one activity and **input flow** for the other. It carries one or more **packages** from one activity to another when the first activity completes. A package is the medium for carrying documents through a workflow and enables various performers to work on these documents.

A flow is created by selecting two activities so its end points are specified automatically. The only configuration needed for a flow is the packages it carries, as shown in the following figure:

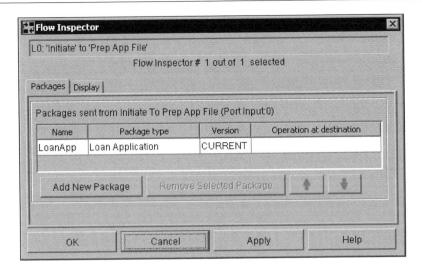

The activities connected by the flow are listed on the **Packages** tab. Packages can be added to or removed from the list. Each package is identified by **Name**, **Package Type** (type of the object packaged), and **Version** of the object. In our example, the package is called LoanApp, is of type dq_loan_app (labeled Loan Application), and uses CURRENT version. The same package is carried between activities throughout the workflow. If the loan application is modified and versioned in **Prep App File** task and the new version becomes the CURRENT version, the **Underwrite** task will get the new version in the package.

The object type for a given package name must remain the same on all flows in a workflow template.

When a task completes, it attempts to transition the workflow into the next task or tasks. These transitions happen along the outgoing flows from the corresponding activity definition in the process definition. The flows can include multiple **forward paths** and one **reject path**. Usually, the forward paths indicate normal progress and the reject path signifies an exceptional situation. In our example, most of the paths are forward and there is only one reject path—from *Underwrite* to *Prep App File*.

There can be multiple flows going out of an activity definition and, therefore, it is possible to trigger multiple following tasks. The outgoing flows to select are specified on the **Transition** tab on the activity definition configuration.

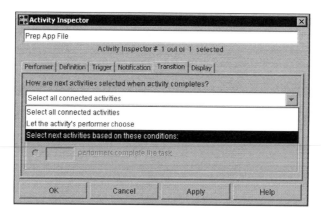

The outgoing flows can be selected as follows:

- **Select all connected activities**: All outgoing flows are selected
- **Let the activity's performer choose**: The performer of the current task will choose the next tasks that should be executed
- **Select the next activities based on these conditions:** Conditions can be specified in terms of the running workflow, the last completed task, or properties of the objects in packages

After a task completes, one or more other activity definitions may be ready to instantiate tasks. The readiness for an activity definition to execute is configured on its **Trigger** tab as shown in the following screenshot:

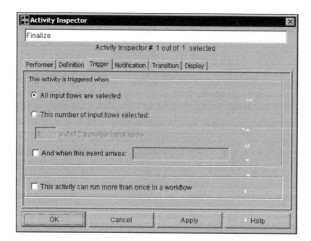

An activity definition can be configured to trigger when:

- A combination of prior tasks has completed (corresponding flows are selected) in one of the following ways:
  - All of the incoming flows are selected
  - A specified number of the incoming flows are selected

- An event (system or user-defined), if specified, is sent to performer inbox programmatically

Activity definitions can also be configured to *notify* the **workflow supervisor** about the progress of the corresponding task. Notifications can be sent to the supervisor's inbox for delays in both beginning and completing tasks, as shown in the following screenshot:

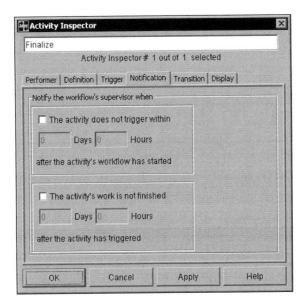

Once the process definition has been configured it needs to be validated and installed before it can be used for creating workflows.

Usage

At run time, a workflow is created from a process definition. Activity definitions in the process definition are instantiated as tasks. Notifications for manual tasks are delivered to performers' inboxes and automatic tasks are executed when they are triggered. Webtop provides workflow reports containing information about the current states of the existing workflows.

For starting a workflow via Webtop, the user needs to have contributor client capability.

There are two basic ways of starting a workflow in Webtop:

- **Start Workflow**: User selects a process definition first and adds packages afterwards. Only the process definitions accessible to the current user are visible for selection.

- **Start Attachments**: User selects the objects/documents first and then chooses a process definition to instantiate. Only the process definitions accessible to the current user and applicable to the type of the object are visible for selection.

The following screen shows the menu options for starting a workflow on a selected document:

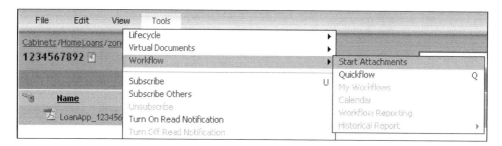

Next an installed process definition is selected for starting a workflow, as shown in the following screenshot:

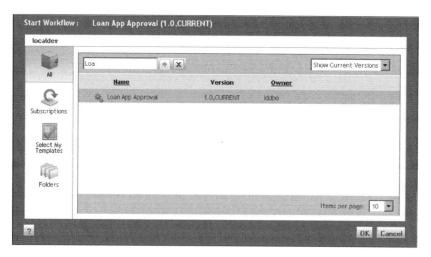

With either approach, the following actions need to be taken:

- Provide a description for the workflow instance
- Add comments
- Select activity performers, if needed

The following screenshot shows this interaction for starting a workflow. The user can name the workflow and add or inspect the attachments:

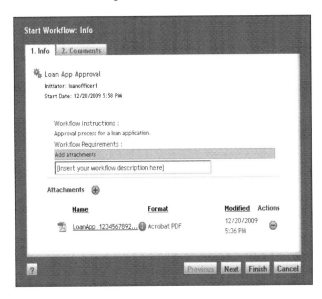

Additionally, the user can add or modify comments as shown in the following figure. These comments can be seen by performers of later tasks:

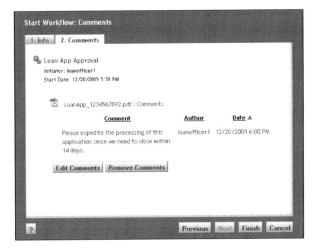

Once the workflow has been created, a task shows up in the inbox of the performer of the initial task—**Prep App File**:

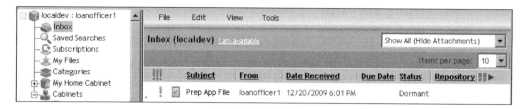

 Note the **I am available** link in the user's inbox. If a user is not going to be available for a period of time, this user can mark himself/herself as unavailable by identifying a **proxy**—someone who can act on this user's behalf. All *new* tasks intended for this user are forwarded to the user's proxy automatically. Existing tasks already assigned to this user are not automatically reassigned by this selection. When this user is available again to participate in workflows, the availability can be reset.

Double-clicking the task in inbox opens it in the **Task Manager** component of Webtop, as shown in the following screenshot:

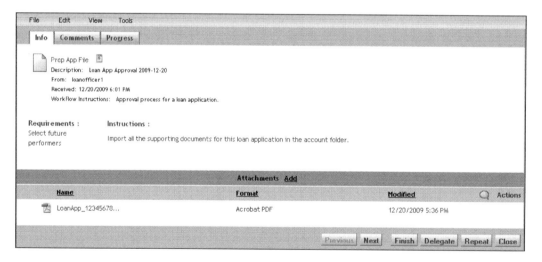

The loan application going through the workflow is accessible in the task view. The usual document management operations can be performed on it. The instructions configured on the activity definition are also visible here. Note the **Delegate** and **Repeat** actions are also available according to the activity definition. Once the actions required for the task have been performed, the performer can click **Next** repeatedly to complete the task.

The performer can add comments as shown in the following screenshot:

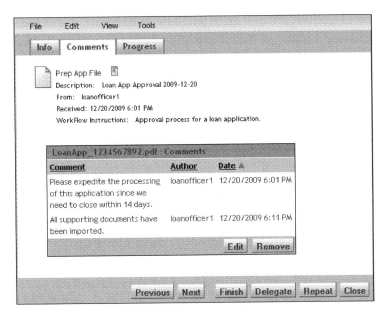

Clicking **Next** opens the **Progress** tab as shown in the following screenshot:

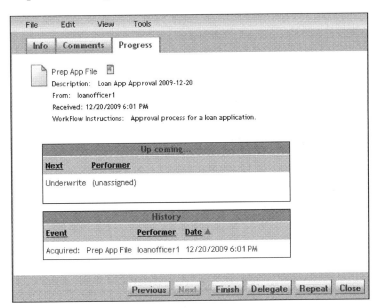

The **Progress** tab shows what has happened so far in the workflow and the tasks coming up. Note that the upcoming task Underwrite doesn't have a performer assigned because the performer of the current task is supposed to select the underwriter. Clicking on **Finish** prompts the performer to select a performer for the next task, as shown in the following screenshot:

Since the loan officer (performer of this task) belongs to zone 1, she selects the group zone1_underwriter as the performer for the Underwrite task. According to the activity definition the Underwrite task will go to the inboxes of all members of zone1_underwriter and will be assigned to the first performer who acquires it. Completing the task removes it from the current performer's inbox.

This also leads to an activity transition and tasks corresponding to the next activity definition will be created. The workflow moves forward as tasks are created and completed.

Quick flows

The details discussed in the previous section show how a process definition is created and instantiated. Another way to start a workflow is to use a **quick flow**. A quick flow is an *ad hoc* workflow (no custom process definition needs to be designed for it), which is also known as a **send to distribution list** workflow. A quick flow has one activity per performer and can be structured in sequential or parallel form.

Note that quick flows are implemented using out-of-box process definitions named `dmSendTo*`, which are present in a new Documentum repository.

If the activities are arranged sequentially, there is also a reject flow from each activity. The reject flow can go to the previous activity performer or to the initiator, but it is the same for all the activities in the quick flow (each can go to previous or each goes to the initiator). If the activities are in parallel, all the performers get their tasks simultaneously. The screen for starting a quick flow is shown in the following screenshot. It can be launched using the menu option **Tools | Workflow | Quickflow** or the shortcut key *q*.

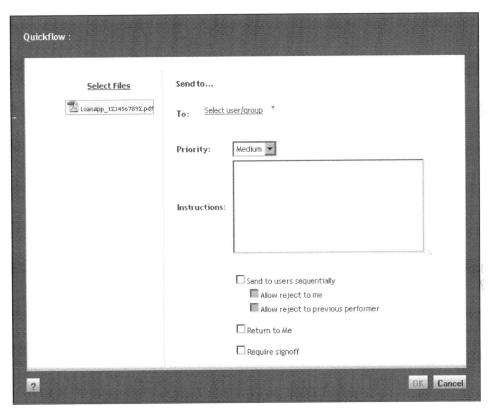

When starting a quick flow, the following information can be specified:

- Files being sent in the quick flow
- Performers
- Structure of the quick flow — sequential or parallel
  - For sequential, whether rejects to previous performer and/or to supervisor are allowed
- Instructions for completing the task
- Whether the initiator needs to be notified on task completion
- Whether sign-off is required
- Priority (low, medium, or high)

The execution of a quick flow is similar to a regular workflow where tasks appear in inboxes and are managed through Task Manager.

Workflow reporting

Workflow reporting can be used to monitor current and overdue tasks in various workflows and manage them. The report can be launched using the **Tools | Workflow | Workflow Reporting** menu item and looks like the following screenshot:

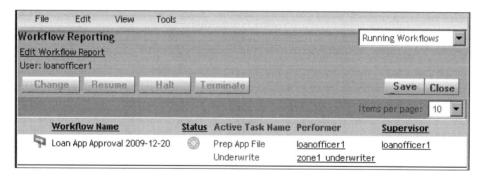

 Recall that completed workflows can be listed only for the process definitions that have auditing enabled.

From the workflow report, a user can select a workflow and can change supervisor, or halt, resume, or terminate the workflow. A summary view of a selected workflow shows its past and future tasks and also allows changing performers for future tasks. The audit trail entries for the workflow and progress for each task can also be viewed.

The report can also be saved as a Microsoft Excel file in the repository using the **Save** button. For example, the Excel file for the previous report looks like the following:

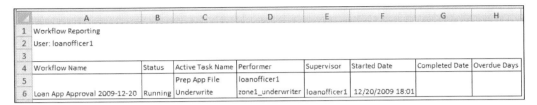

	A	B	C	D	E	F	G	H
1	Workflow Reporting							
2	User: loanofficer1							
3								
4	Workflow Name	Status	Active Task Name	Performer	Supervisor	Started Date	Completed Date	Overdue Days
5			Prep App File	loanofficer1				
6	Loan App Approval 2009-12-20	Running	Underwrite	zone1_underwriter	loanofficer1	12/20/2009 18:01		

Workflow states

- The workflow reporting discussion in the previous section mentions halting, terminating, and resuming workflows. These actions need some elaboration. A workflow instance can be in any of the following states:

- **Dormant**: A workflow is dormant when it has just been created or if it has been restarted from a halted state

- **Running**: A workflow is running when it has started execution from a dormant state or has been resumed from a halted state

- **Halted**: Halting a running workflow moves it to the halted state

- **Terminated**: Aborting a running or halted workflow moves it to terminated state

- **Finished**: Normal completion of a running workflow moves it to the finished state

These details can be summarized in a state transition diagram for workflows as shown in the following figure:

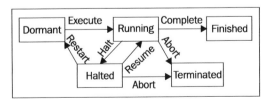

Activities and tasks also go through states during workflow execution. However, these details will not be discussed here. See *EMC Documentum Content Server Fundamentals* for further information.

Modification

If there is a need to modify the process definition, it needs to be uninstalled. Uninstalling a process definition halts its existing workflow instances. The process definition needs to be validated and installed again for the halted workflows to resume and for new workflows to be created from that process definition.

Help—some DQL Queries

The queries in this section are based on the information presented in this chapter.

The following query lists the process definitions present in the repository:

```
SELECT object_name
FROM dm_process
```

The following query lists the workflows for a process definition named 'Loan App Approval':

```
SELECT w.object_name, w.supervisor_name, w.r_runtime_state
FROM dm_workflow w, dm_process p
WHERE w.process_id = p.r_object_id
  AND p.object_name = 'Loan App Approval'
```

Note that dm_workflow.r_runtime_state can have the following values:

Value	Description
0	Dormant
1	Running
2	Finished
3	Halted
4	Terminated

The following query lists the packages using a document (by its object ID), along with the workflow name and process definition name:

```
SELECT DISTINCT pkg.r_package_name, w.object_name, p.object_name AS
process_name
FROM dmi_package pkg, dm_workflow w, dm_process p
WHERE w.process_id = p.r_object_id
 AND pkg.r_workflow_id = w.r_object_id
 AND ANY pkg.r_component_id = '090000108001052d'
```

Documentum product notes

Workflow Manager allows reuse of existing process definitions and activity definitions within a new process definition. Within Workflow Manager, existing definitions can be searched by cabinet or folder path, owner, name, and state. They can also be located using DQL queries. The existing definitions and activities can be added to the palette and then they can be utilized for creating new definitions.

Process Builder is a part of EMC Documentum Process Suite. Process Builder builds upon the core workflow capability to extend the workflows beyond the enterprise. A business process modeled through Process Builder can interact with email, web services, HTTP (web), FTP (file transfer), and XForms (XML forms) in tasks. It can also manage high volume tasks through work queues.

Activities in Process Builder are more configurable than in Workflow Manager. The data mapping capability in Process Builder is a powerful feature for passing data among workflow components during workflow execution. It provides a visual interface for mapping data such as workflow method arguments, process variables, parameters and return values for services such as HTTP and JMS. For example, if our loan approval workflow needed to fetch a credit score for the applicant from a web service, it could pass the required information from the application metadata and save the returned credit score on application metadata as well. In Process Builder, this data movement could be defined simply using the visual data mapping tool.

While Process Builder can be used to design business processes, Process Integrator enables integration for incoming information over various channels. For example, it can receive information and content over email (SMTP), the web (HTTP), or message queues (JMS) and process it in various ways, including automatic interaction with an existing workflow. Usually, Process Builder and Process Integrator are used together when the process management requirements include automated integration with incoming information over the channels previously listed. Process Builders is the design tool while process execution is managed by Process Engine.

Learn more

The topics discussed in this chapter can be further explored using the following resources:

- EMC Documentum Content Server 6.5 Fundamentals
- EMC Documentum Content Server 6.5 Administration Guide
- EMC Documentum Webtop 6.5 SP2 User Guide
- EMC Documentum System 6.5 Object Reference Manual
- (White Paper) EMC Documentum Process Suite: A Detailed Review

Checkpoint

At this point you should be able to answer the following key questions:

1. What is a workflow? What purpose does it serve?
2. What are process definitions, activity definitions, performers, flows, and packages? How are they related?
3. How can one execute and monitor workflow instances?
4. What states does a workflow go through during its lifetime?

13
Lifecycles

In this chapter, we will explore the following concepts:

- Designing lifecycles
- Using lifecycles

Business process and content management

Workflows enable content-centric business process automation on Documentum. Workflows carry one or more objects through various activities performed by different performers. *Lifecycles* add a powerful dimension to this mix by enabling documents to move through states according to business rules.

Documentum not only automates business processes but also automates movement of content through various phases of its life—enforcing and automating business rules through both mechanisms. Lifecycles can also be used independently of workflows but the combination of the two opens up the possibilities for satisfying complex requirements.

Lifecycles offer two key benefits for business content. They enable management and reporting by lifecycle state of content. This capability is further supported by capturing desired metadata as the content moves through lifecycle states. Lifecycles also enable acting on content with change in lifecycle state. For example, the location of the document or its permissions may be changed when its state changes. Lifecycles enable these capabilities in most part via configuration, and reduce the need for customization.

The simplified, but fundamental, difference between workflows and lifecycles is that a workflow is what people do and a lifecycle is what happens to a document. Let's examine our example scenario from the perspective of document lifecycle. Recall that the key document moving through the approval process is a loan application. For designing a lifecycle, we need to focus on what happens to this document after it has been imported into the repository.

Initially, there is the *new* loan application while the application file is being prepared. When it goes to underwriting it is under *review*. Finally, a decision is made and the application is either approved or denied. In either case, the application is finally *closed*. Based on this information, a lifecycle can be defined by simply mimicking this description. We can define three normal states—**NEW, REVIEW,** and **CLOSED** for this lifecycle. An exception state **HOLD** can be used for temporarily suspending application review pending more information. This lifecycle is illustrated in the following figure:

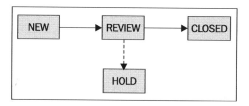

Note that this is just one way to model this lifecycle. Here states are not tied to the particular decision on the loan application. In general, the states may or may not correspond directly with activities in a workflow; indeed, lifecycles can be used without involving any workflows at all. For example, a lifecycle can be used to remove WRITE permissions when a document moves into a published state after editing and updates have been completed. This can be implemented without using any workflows.

In practice, lifecycle design depends on the automation needs, since transitions between lifecycle states can be controlled with conditions and can trigger actions automatically. These capabilities are discussed in detail in this chapter.

The differences between workflows and lifecycles are easy to highlight. A workflow is instantiated from a workflow template (process definition) and typically advances one or more objects through a network of activities. A lifecycle, on the other hand, changes the state of an object in a linear fashion. There are no templates or run-time instances for a lifecycle; there is just the lifecycle object.

Lifecycle concepts

A **lifecycle** is a set of linearly connected **states** that define the stages in an object's life. A state can be a **normal state** or an **exception state**. Normal states are used for normal progress through the stages and exception states help deal with the less frequent situations.

A lifecycle is associated with a set of object types and this lifecycle can be applied only to the objects of these types. An object can be associated with at most one lifecycle at a time, and it is in exactly one of the states present in the lifecycle. The object can move back and forth between the lifecycle states when specified conditions permit and can trigger changes durng the process.

A state can have **entry criteria** that must be satisfied for an object to enter that state. When an object is about to enter a state, **entry actions** specified for that state are executed. Once an object has entered a state, any specified **post-entry (post-change) actions** are executed. Actions can be predefined actions or custom ones.

These concepts are discussed in detail in the rest of the chapter.

Lifecycles and customization

It should be obvious that documents don't have to be associated with a lifecycle. The examples discussed in previous chapters did not use any lifecycles. However, lifecycles provide a key capability for Documentum customization. Lifecycles are usually bundled with other customization components in Documentum projects (see the *Chapter 11, Documentum Projects* for details).

A document lifecycle can be developed in the following manner:

- **Analyze**: Gather information about relevant document types (or object types, in general) and the stages a document will need to go through. Also consider the triggers for state changes, conditions for state changes, and the actions that may be associated with them. If it is difficult to identify actions associated with state changes, question the need for this lifecycle.

- **Model**: Model the lifecycle in terms of states, entry criteria, entry actions, and post-entry actions.

- **Define**: Formalize the model as a lifecycle using Composer. Install the lifecycle into the desired repository as a part of the Documentum project. The lifecycle will be validated as well.

- **Use**: Start applying the lifecycle to objects. Objects can progress through lifecycle states via workflows, manual actions, or scheduled actions.
- **Modify**: If the lifecycle needs to be modified, alter the corresponding artifact in the Documentum project and reinstall the project.

The following sections describe the previously-mentioned steps in more detail.

Analysis

Document lifecycle analysis involves gathering information regarding important stages in the life of a document of a certain type and the details around transitions between these stages. Some additional information may also be captured about how the documents need to be managed within Documentum as they progress through these stages. For example, it may be desirable to move the document to a new location and restrict access after a certain point in the document's lifecycle.

In our example, analysis may require talking to the processor, underwriter, closer, and post-closer about the loan approval process and how it affects the loan application document. It may be desired that a status attribute is set to a user-friendly description of the application status, such as `'Processing'`, `'Under Review'`, `'Approved'`, or `'Denied'`. It may also be desirable to change permissions on the loan application as it progresses through its lifecycle, and to move the approved and denied applications to an archival area.

Modeling and definition

Modeling and definition of lifecycles share several aspects and are discussed together in this section to avoid repetition. Modeling maps the requirements for the lifecycles to Documentum terminology to facilitate definition. The model is defined as a lifecycle artifact using Lifecycle Editor in Composer. The artifact creates or updates a lifecycle object of type `dm_policy` in a repository when it is installed there.

The following screenshot shows Lifecycle Editor in Composer. The graphical area at the top enables the developer to visually design the lifecycle. This interaction consists of creating normal and exception states and then connecting them. The **Properties** view at the bottom displays the properties of the selected state. When no state is selected it shows the properties of the lifecycle.

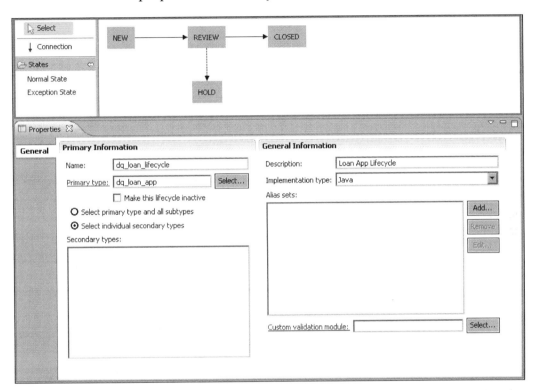

Lifecycle properties

A lifecycle has a unique name in the repository and a user-friendly label can be specified as description. It is also possible to deactivate a lifecycle, in which case it cannot be applied to objects. In the preceding figure, the lifecycle has been named dq_loan_lifecycle, it has the description Loan App Lifecycle, and is active.

A lifecycle is associated with a set of object types and it can only be applied to objects of these types. This set of object types is specified as one primary type and any number of secondary types, which must be subtypes of the primary type. Further, the primary type must be dm_syobject or one of its subtypes other than dm_policy. In the preceding figure, the lifecycle is applicable only to dq_loan_app.

Internally, the applicable types for the lifecycle are recorded on `dm_policy.inlcuded_type` (repeating string) and `dm_policy.include_subtypes` (repeating Boolean). These are repeating properties and correspond by indexes. The type at index 0 represents the primary type.

Lifecycle states can have associated actions which are implemented in either Java or Docbasic. This choice is specified as the **implementation type**, which is set to Java in the preceding figure.

A lifecycle can use custom validation logic, which can be specified as a custom validation module. This module can handle any business requirements for custom validation.

As in the case of workflows, aliases can be used to make lifecycles portable across multiple repositories and business situations. Multiple alias sets can be specified for a lifecycle and the aliases referenced in the lifecycle are resolved at run time. The alias resolution for objects with lifecycles is discussed in *Chapter 14, Aliases*.

States

A **state** in a lifecycle represents a stage in the life of an object. There are two types of states:

- **Normal**: Each lifecycle has **normal states** (`dm_policy.state_class=0`), which include a **start state** or **base state**, some intermediate **step states**, and a final **end state**. Each state can define behavior such as change of location, permissions, and ownership for the object. This capability facilitates automated management of content as it moves through the lifecycle.

- **Exceptional**: Optionally, a lifecycle can also have **exception states** (`dm_policy.state_class=1`) to represent unusual situations. One lifecycle can have multiple exception states but there can be no more than one exception state connected to a normal state. However, several normal states can use the same exception state. An object can be **suspended** in its lifecycle by moving from a normal state to an exception state and this suspension can be temporary or permanent. A suspended object can only be **resumed** to the last normal state (also referred to as **resume state**) or back to the base state. In our example lifecycle, **HOLD** is an exception state associated with **REVIEW**. If the loan application is put on hold during underwriting, it will be suspended to the **HOLD** state.

The following figure illustrates these concepts using the example lifecycle:

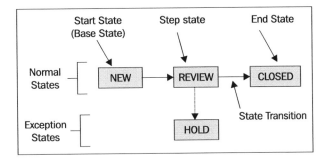

State properties

In Composer, properties for a state can be viewed by selecting a state. The state properties are grouped into **Overview**, **Entry Criteria**, **Actions**, **Post Change**, and **Attributes**. The state properties also include a **General** tab that is the same as the lifecycle properties discussed earlier.

Overview

The **Overview** tab of state properties is shown as follows:

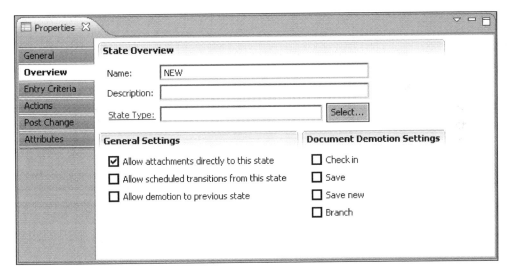

Name and **Description** identify the state. **State Type** is generally not used. It is used with certain client applications that have their own state types.

Other than these basic properties, all properties pertain to **state transitions**. The sole purpose of a lifecycle is to move objects through the states in the lifecycle and everything of interest happens during or right after a state transition. State transitions are governed by business rules.

When an object changes state from a normal state to another normal state it is called **promotion** or **demotion**. Promotion moves an object from one normal state to the *next* normal state within its lifecycle. Demotion can move the object from one normal state to the *previous* normal state (configured in `dm_policy.allow_demote`) or to the base state (configured in `dm_policy.return_to_base`). It should be obvious that promotion is not possible from the final state and demotion is not possible from the base state.

In the preceding figure, demotion is not allowed to the previous state since **NEW** is the base state and there is no previous state. Direct attachment to this state is allowed. While this is to be expected for the base state, *other states can also allow direct attachment*. It can be useful in scenarios where the business process may allow documents to be imported into the repository in different states.

The demotion settings indicate whether the object should be checked in, saved, saved as new, or branched on demotion from this state. These are the few settings which perform some actions at the time of leaving a state. Most actions during state transition are performed on entry into a state.

When an object changes state between a normal state and an exception state it is called **suspension** or **resumption**. An object can be suspended from a normal state to the associated exception state only. From an exception state, the object can be resumed only to the **resume state**, the state from which it was suspended.

 It is possible for an object to move from an exception state to the base state if so configured.

It is also possible to *schedule* a transition out of a state at a predefined date and time if scheduled transitions are allowed for that state. This feature can be used to prevent objects from getting stuck in a state indefinitely. Only one scheduled transition may exist for an object at any one time.

A permitted transition from state A to state B is illustrated in the following figure:

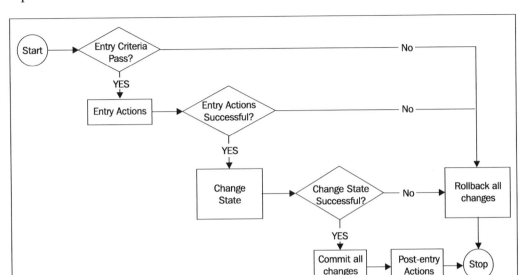

Now, let's examine these steps and the corresponding configuration in more detail.

Entry criteria

Entry criteria for a state are the conditions that must be met before promote, suspend, or resume operations can move an object to that state. Entry criteria are also checked when a lifecycle is attached to an object, since the object enters the initial state at this point. The criteria can be specified as Docbasic Boolean expressions on object properties or as Java or Docbasic procedures. For one lifecycle either all entry criteria procedures are Java or all are Docbasic; they cannot be mixed. However, Docbasic Boolean expressions are allowed irrespective of the implementation type for the lifecycle.

 A demote operation does not check for entry criteria. Entry criteria can also be bypassed when the state change operation is being performed by the lifecycle owner or a superuser.

The following screen shows the **Entry Criteria** tab for state properties. Custom logic can be specified via modules.

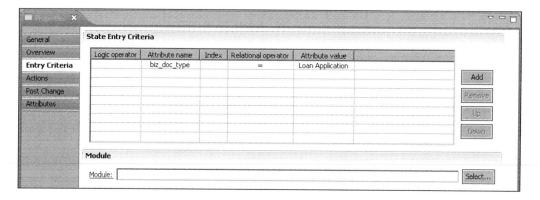

The preceding figure shows `biz_doc_type='Loan Application'` as a condition. This means that a document of type `dq_loan_app` cannot enter the state **NEW** unless its `biz_doc_type` attribute is set to `'Loan Application'`.

Actions

During a state transition, **entry actions** are performed if the entry criteria evaluate to `true`. The **Actions** tab for state properties is shown as follows:

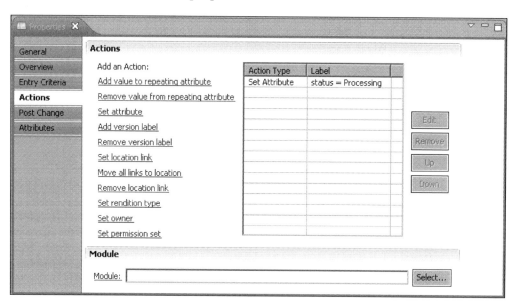

Entry actions can be standard system-defined or custom user-defined ones. At run time, system-defined actions are performed prior to user-defined actions. User-defined actions are specified by selecting a module. The standard system-defined actions include the following:

- Attributes
    - **Set attribute**: Set a value for a specified attribute.
    - **Add value to repeating attribute**: Add a value to a repeating attribute.
    - **Remove value from repeating attribute**: Remove a value from a repeating attribute.

- Version labels
    - **Add version label**: Add a version label.
    - **Remove version label**: Remove a version label.

- Security
    - **Set owner**: Set owner name (change owner).
    - **Set permission set**: Assign an ACL (change permission).

- Location
    - **Set location link**: Link the object to another folder/cabinet using a folder path or a location alias. The `$value()` keyword can be used to utilize property values in specifying location. `$value()` was discussed in *Chapter 11, Custom Types*.
    - **Remove location link**: Remove a link to the object from a folder/cabinet.
    - **Move all links to location**: Move all the links to the object to another folder/cabinet.

- Content
    - **Set rendition type**: Request a rendition of the object.

For the requested rendition to be created successfully, appropriate components of Content Transformation Services (CTS) must be installed and the requested transformation must be configured and supported. See *Chapter 4, Architecture* for CTS features.

Post change

Post-entry actions (**post-change actions**) are performed right after entering the new state. In our example, a post-entry action on the NEW state could start the loan approval workflow on the loan application document. Post-entry actions can also be implemented in Java or Docbasic.

The following screen shows the **Post Change** tab for state properties. Custom post-change code can be configured as a module:

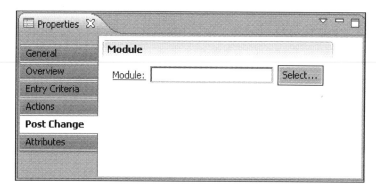

Attributes

A state can specify how object attributes behave while an object is in this state. We have already seen that object attributes may be assigned new values using entry actions while entering a state. Some data dictionary items may also be modified for object attributes using the **Attributes** tab, as shown in the following screenshot:

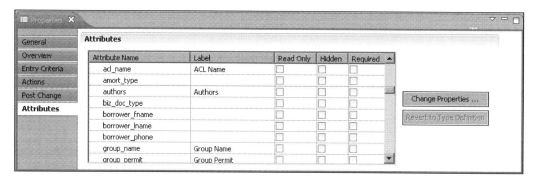

An attribute can be selected from the list to change its properties. Clicking on **Change Properties** opens the dialog for editing the attribute data dictionary as shown here:

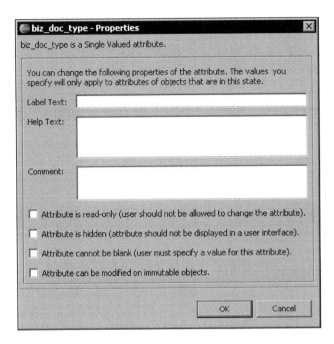

The data dictionary items that could be set for an attribute include label, help text, comment, read-only, hidden, nullable, and modifiable while the object is immutable.

Note that state transition only sets the data dictionary values and does not enforce them (with a couple of exceptions highlighted in the box) because data dictionary is used by client applications. For example, suppose a loan application has `amort_type` attribute set to blank. It enters a lifecycle state that sets **Attribute cannot be blank** for `amort_type`. There is no evaluation of `amort_type` being blank at this moment. However, Webtop may not allow its properties to be saved while `amort_type` is blank. In such a situation, it is also important that Webtop displays this attribute so that the user can enter a value for this attribute. This is achieved via display configurations as discussed in *Chapter 11, Custom Types*.

 Recall that Content Server does use the following data dictionary items—default property values and whether to allow changes to properties on immutable objects.

Security for state transitions

Lifecycle execution involves various actions as previously discussed. Since these actions can modify the attached objects they are subject to the usual security requirements for these operations to succeed. A key configuration related to these concerns is `dm_docbase_config.a_bpaction_run_as`. This property can be set to one of the following values:

- `session_user`: Current user (default value)
- `superuser`: Superuser
- `lifecycle_owner`: Lifecycle owner
- Specific username

This configuration can be inspected or modified in DA using the **Administration | Basic Configuration | Repository** node in the browser tree. The relevant portion of the configuration is shown in the following screenshot:

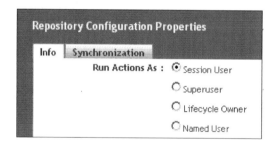

Promote, demote, suspend, and resume operations on an object require `WRITE` permission along with `Change State` extended permission on the object. However, granting `WRITE` permission just for allowing state change may not be a good security design. Therefore, there may be users who will have `Change State` extended permission but not `WRITE` permission. When such a user tries to change state for an object, Content Server tries to use the user set up in `dm_docbase_config.a_bpaction_run_as`. This user, if configured, needs to pass both the permission checks—`WRITE` and `Change State` for the action to be performed.

> Recall that object owners and superusers automatically (implicitly) have all extended permissions other than `Extended Delete` and `Change Folder Links`. Therefore, they only need explicit `WRITE` permission on the object for performing a state change operation.

State transition methods (scheduled or otherwise) are run as the user set up in `dm_docbase_config.a_bpaction_run_as`. If this property is not set, these methods are run as the user performing the state transition operation.

In addition to the state change security requirements discussed previously, the security requirements for other operations performed via lifecycle actions also need to be met. For example, if an action changes the location of the object the effective user (current user or `dm_docbase_config.a_bpaction_run_as`) must have `Change Location` extended permission.

Lifecycle definition states

Each lifecycle can be in one of three **definition states**—*draft*, *validated*, and *installed*. The definition states are related to the development and deployment of lifecycles to repositories. Recall that workflow templates (process definitions) also have these states. The difference is that a workflow template is created and refined in a repository. A lifecycle is created and refined as an artifact in a Documentum project. So the lifecycle definition state changes typically take place during installation of the artifact into a repository.

Remember that the lifecycle definition state has no relation to the states that are part of the lifecycle. The lifecycle definition state is stored as an integer in `dm_policy.r_definition_state`—0 for draft, 1 for validated, and 2 for installed. Information about states constituting the lifecycle are stored in attributes `i_state_no`, `state_*`, and other attributes on the `dm_policy` object. Note that `i_state_no` stores integers but the integer sequence (0, 1, 2) may not correspond to the sequence of states (NEW, REVIEW, CLOSED) within the lifecycle. So NEW may be represented as 2 and REVIEW may be represented as 1.

When a new lifecycle object is created it has *draft* definition state. It can be validated for any errors and its definition state changes to *validated* if there are no errors.

Validation of a lifecycle is performed by one of two system-defined validation programs, based on the implementation type of the lifecycle (Java or Docbasic). If a custom validation module has been configured, it runs after the system-defined validation program. Each validation run must succeed for the validation to succeed.

The system-defined validation programs check the following:

- The lifecycle has at least one attachable state.
- The attachable primary object type is dm_sysobject or one of its subtypes other than dm_policy. All secondary types are the subtypes of the primary type.
- Objects referred to by ID in the lifecycle exist in the repository.
- For Java-based lifecycles, SBOs referred to by service name exist in the repository.

A validated lifecycle can be installed into a repository to make it available to all users, whereby its definition state changes to *installed*. WRITE permission is required on the lifecycle to install it. Only installed lifecycles can be applied to objects.

Usage

A lifecycle in the installed definition state can be applied to objects of types supported by the lifecycle. In order to apply a lifecycle to an object, the user must have RELATE permission on the lifecycle, be the object owner or superuser, and have WRITE permission on the object. When a lifecycle is applied to an object, the object enters the initial state. An object can only be associated with one lifecycle at a time. Since two different versions of an object are two separate objects, they can be attached to different lifecycles.

 A **default lifecycle** can be specified for a custom type as discussed in *Chapter 11, Custom Types*. This default lifecycle could be applied to new objects of this type programmatically without requiring it to be identified by name.

Information regarding the lifecycle state of an object is captured on the object in the following attributes:

- dm_sysobject.r_policy_id identifies the lifecycle applied to the object
- dm_sysobject.r_current_state identifies the current state of the object in the associated lifecycle
- dm_sysobject.r_resume_state identifies the normal state to resume to, if the current state is an exception state

These relationships between sysobjects and lifecycles are illustrated for two objects with the same lifecycle in the following figure. Note that the two sysobjects share the same lifecycle but are in different states:

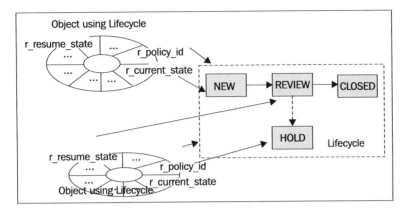

 Note that, unlike workflows, lifecycles don't have run-time instances. If an analogy *must* be made then the dm_policy object would be the lifecycle definition and the lifecycle-related attributes on a sysobject would reflect its run-time instantiation.

In Webtop, a lifecycle can be applied to an object from **Tools | Lifecycle | Apply** menu item or the context menu **Lifecycle | Apply** item. It can also be applied from the object properties screen by editing the lifecycle attribute. The shortcut for applying a lifecycle is **L**.

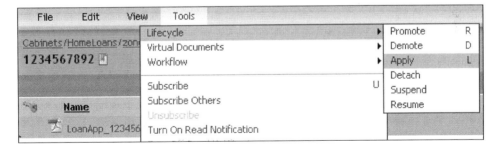

When the user attempts to apply a lifecycle to an object only the lifecycles applicable to its type and in installed definition states are shown. After the lifecycle has been applied the lifecycle and current state are shown on the properties screen for the object, as shown in the following screenshot:

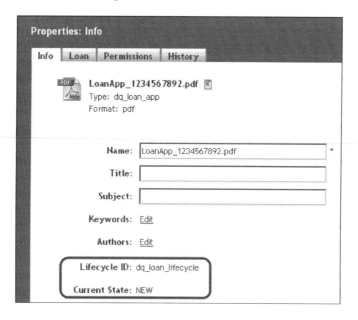

Once a lifecycle has been attached to an object, lifecycle operations can be performed on the object using the **Lifecycle** submenus mentioned earlier. The lifecycle state of an object can also be changed automatically. For example, an automatic workflow task can promote an object in its lifecycle.

> An object can be attached to a lifecycle and be processed by a workflow at the same time. In fact, this combination provides great flexibility in terms of implementing and enforcing business rules.
>
> Recall that an object to be processed by a workflow is wrapped in a package. A package can have multiple components and `dmi_package.r_component_id` stores the object IDs of its components.

As an object with lifecycle progresses through its lifecycle states, all the rules related to state transitions discussed earlier are enforced.

Modification

It is possible to modify a lifecycle after it has been installed and applied to objects. If the lifecycle needs to be edited, it is uninstalled (definition state changes to validated) and objects using this lifecycle can no longer change their states. Once the modifications are completed, the lifecycle needs to be validated and installed again. At this point existing objects using this lifecycle can change states and other objects can be attached to this lifecycle.

Normally, lifecycle changes are designed in the lifecycle artifact in Composer. During this time the lifecycle in the repository remains in the installed definition state. When the updated artifact is installed, the lifecycle goes through changes in the lifecycle definition state rapidly.

 It is recommended not to create multiple versions of a lifecycle because multiple versions of lifecycles often lead to confusion. The lifecycle artifact can be configured with Overwrite as the upgrade option in Composer, as shown in the following figure.

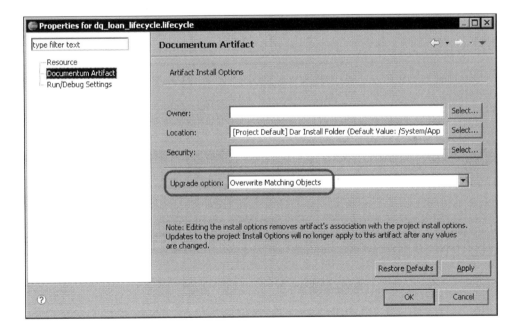

Help—some DQL queries

While Composer and Webtop can be used to interact with objects and lifecycles, the following queries can be used to obtain specific information directly.

The following DQL query identifies the lifecycle ID, current state, and the resume state (meaningful only if the current state is an exception state) for a document. Note, however, that all of this information is system data (internal) and not user-friendly. This information neither names the lifecycle nor the states; they are all numbers.

```
SELECT r_policy_id, r_current_state, r_resume_state
FROM dm_document
WHERE object_name like 'LoanApp_%'
```

The user-friendly information can be obtained from the lifecycle separately or by joining with the preceding query. The following query lists information about the states in a lifecycle dq_loan_lifecycle:

```
SELECT i_position, object_name, state_name, state_description, state_
class
FROM dm_policy
WHERE object_name = 'dq_loan_lifecycle'
ORDER BY i_position
```

Note that the state properties queried here are repeating properties and list all the states. Recall from *Chapter 3, Objects and Types* that i_position specifies the order of the repeating values. If all the values are desired in one record, r_object_id should be added to the list of selected attributes. Information about a particular state cannot be extracted using an index, such as state_name[0], in a DQL query. All the repeating values are retrieved when a repeating attribute is selected. However, DFC can retrieve values at specific indices.

Another helpful query can display the definition state of each lifecycle. For lifecycle definition state, 0 means draft, 1 means validated, and 2 means installed, as discussed earlier.

```
SELECT object_name, r_definition_state FROM dm_policy
```

Documentum product notes

Lifecycles are designed using Lifecycle Editor in Documentum Composer. Typically, lifecycles are bundled in Documentum projects along with workflows and other customization artifacts. Lifecycles provide powerful automation capabilities that can be used independently of or in conjunction with workflows.

The following internal methods support lifecycle actions:

- State transition is performed by `dm_bp_transition_java`/ `dm_bp_transition`.

- Objects can be promoted in batches using `dm_bp_batch_java`/`dm_bp_batch`.

- Jobs for scheduled state changes call `dm_bp_schedule_java`/ `dm_bp_schedule`. These methods call the corresponding transition methods to execute the actual state change.

- Lifecycle definitions are validated via `dm_bp_validate_java`/ `dm_bp_validation`.

When a state transition is scheduled, Content Server creates a job named `Bp_<object_id><scheduled_time>` where time is formatted as `yyyyMMDDhhmmss` (year month day hour minute second). The job runs as the user configured in `dm_docbase_config.a_bpaction_run_as`, if any. Otherwise, it runs as the user who scheduled the change.

Learn more

The topics discussed in this chapter can be further explored using the following resources:

- EMC Documentum Content Server 6.5 Fundamentals
- EMC Documentum Content Server 6.5 Administration Guide
- EMC Documentum Webtop 6.5 SP2 User Guide
- EMC Documentum System 6.5 Object Reference Manual
- EMC Documentum Documentum Composer 6.5 SP2 User Guide
- EMC Documentum Documentum Composer 6.5 SP2 Building a Documentum Application Tutorial

Checkpoint

At this point you should be able to answer the following key questions:

1. What is a lifecycle? What purpose does it serve? How is it different from a workflow?

2. What are states, state transitions, entry criteria, entry actions, post-entry actions?

3. How are lifecycles defined and modified? What are lifecycle definition states and how do they differ from lifecycle states?

4. How can one apply lifecycles to objects and check object states? How can the lifecycle operations be performed using Webtop?

Part 5

Advanced Concepts

Aliases

Virtual Documents

14
Aliases

In this chapter, we will explore the following concepts:

- Creating aliases and alias sets
- Referencing aliases
- Alias resolution

Customization—reusability and portability

Documentum customization involves multiple components at various architecture layers and these customizations can easily become fairly complex. This complexity can be compounded by the fact that developing and deploying customizations often involves multiple environments—development, QA, and production are typical. Further, multiple departments in an enterprise may have separate repositories of their own.

For example, two departments and three environments for each department lead to a total of six repositories if a clean separation is maintained. Ideally, customization developed in one repository should be easily ported to all these repositories if the customizations are intended to be reusable in this manner. This portability is achieved by parameterizing everything that can vary across these repositories such that the parameters specific to a repository can be specified/evaluated when the customization is deployed to that repository.

The customization artifacts are bundled together in Documentum projects and making customizations portable effectively means making Documentum projects and their contents portable. Documentum supports **aliases**, which act as placeholders for values that can be inserted at an appropriate time before they are needed. Thus, aliases can be used to handle the differences among repositories and they get replaced with values specific to the repository when they are deployed and used within a specific repository.

The portability benefits of aliases are not limited to handling differences across repositories. Aliases can also make customizations portable across areas or situations within the same repository. In our business scenario, different zones may have separate permissions and performers for workflow tasks. Using aliases the same lifecycle and workflow template can handle these differences.

 Handling differences within a repository is the more common application of aliases in customizations within organizations. On the other hand, products based on the Documentum platform are more likely to use aliases to handle differences across repositories.

Aliases

An **alias** is a placeholder name that needs to be replaced with a value before it can be used. In a way, an alias acts like a variable in a program where the variable is referred to by a name but its value is used when the program runs.

An alias can represent a user, a group, a folder location (path in a repository), or an ACL (permission set). However, when a particular alias is stored its specific intent is identified in terms of an **alias category**, which can be one of the following:

- Unknown (0)
- User (1)
- Group (2)
- User or Group (3)
- Cabinet path (4)
- Folder path (5)
- ACL name (6)

A completely specified alias includes its name, value, and category.

Alias sets

An **alias set** provides a list of aliases and, optionally, values for their replacement. It is stored as an object of type `dm_alias_set`. The information about each alias is stored in three repeating attributes of an alias set, which correspond to each other via identical indices.

Property	Description
alias_name	Name of the alias
alias_value	Value for the alias, may or may not be present
alias_category	Alias category, as discussed earlier

A simplistic, but fundamentally sound, view of an alias set is that of a lookup table containing key-value pairs. Each row in the table corresponds to an alias. In our example, an alias set suitable for zone 1 could look like the following table. As long as this alias set is used for zone 1, the references to these aliases will be replaced by the correct groups. In the table below, the alias category 2 means that the alias represents a group:

Alias name	Alias value	Category
processor	zone1_processor	2
underwriter	zone1_underwriter	2
closer	zone1_closer	2

It is possible to provide different values for an alias within the same repository. One alias may appear in multiple alias sets with different values. The value used for the alias depends on the alias set that is selected in a given situation. These concepts are discussed in detail later in this chapter.

The following figure illustrates a Documentum project with artifacts that use aliases named `processor` and `underwriter`. These aliases could be used for identifying performers for workflow tasks in our example scenario. They could also be used for defining different permissions on the loan application in various lifecycle states.

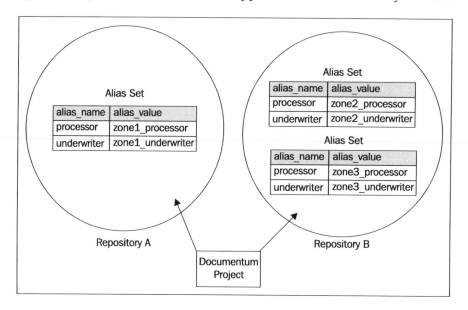

Referencing aliases

So far we have loosely mentioned "using aliases" where we needed to use a placeholder to be replaced with a value later. When an alias needs to be used instead of a literal value its **reference** is stored using a % prefix. This is a way to distinguish the alias reference from normal values. An alias is referenced using one of two formats—`%alias_set_name.alias_name` or just `%alias_name`. If the name of the alias set containing the alias is known at design time the first format can be used. However, the full potential of aliases can be realized only with the second format. When no alias set is specified in the reference, Content Server uses an algorithm based on the situation to identify an alias set to locate the alias value. This mechanism of searching alias sets is called **alias resolution** and is discussed later in the chapter.

The following figure shows an alias named `underwriter` being referenced in an activity object. If the shown alias set is used, this reference will be replaced with the group named `zone1_underwriter`.

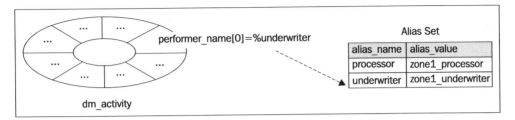

We now know how to reference an alias but can we use an alias reference in any string attribute? While it is possible to place an alias reference in any such attribute, Content Server only looks in certain attributes for alias references for resolving them (replacing the placeholder with a desired value) at an appropriate time. These attributes are listed below:

Type	Attribute	Description
`dm_sysobject`	`owner_name`	Owner of an object. Alias reference is resolved when the object is saved.
`dm_sysobject`	`acl_domain`	Owner of the ACL associated with an object. Alias reference is resolved when the object is saved.
`dm_sysobject`	`acl_name`	Name of the permission associated with an object. Alias reference is resolved when the object is saved.
`dm_acl`	`r_accessor_name`	User or group getting permission in this permission set template (PST). PSTs are discussed later in this chapter. Alias reference is resolved when the PST is applied to an object.
`dm_activity`	`performer_name`	Performer of a workflow activity. Alias reference is resolved when the activity is started in a workflow instance.

There is one other place where Content Server recognizes alias references—in the `folderSpec` argument of the `link` and `unlink` DFC methods. This argument specifies the folder path (or folder object ID) where an object is linked or unlinked. The signatures for these methods for sysobjects are as shown below:

```
public void link   (String folderSpec) throws DfException
public void unlink(String folderSpec) throws DfException
```

 No other place, including custom attributes, is examined by Content Server for alias references. However, applications (custom code) can examine other places and provide an alias resolution mechanism.

Permission set templates

An ACL that contains one or more alias references to users or groups in the `r_accessor_name` property is known as **permission set template (PST)** or **ACL template**. A PST is stored as a `dm_acl` object but is distinguished by the value of `dm_acl.acl_class`, which can have one of the following values:

ACL class	Description
0	Private (or regular) ACL
1	Permission set template
2	Instance of PST
3	Public ACL

Managing permission set templates

PSTs are managed via Composer and packaged in Documentum projects. The following screenshot shows a PST artifact in Composer:

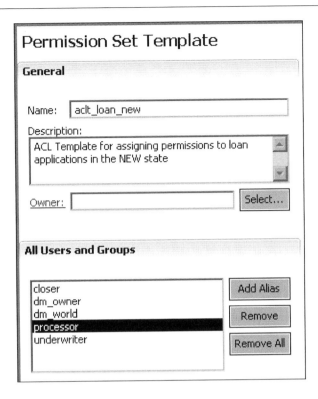

This PST defines permissions that could apply to a new loan application in our example. Going from zone to zone the permissions will look similar but the accessor groups are going to be different. This is a perfect requirement to be satisfied with PSTs. The accessors can refer to aliases (such as processor) that get replaced with real groups (such as zone1_processor) at run time.

At the outset, the previous figure looks like any other ACL. However, the accessor list consists of aliases in addition to dm_world and dm_owner. Selecting an accessor reveals the permissions via the **ACL Entry Details** section, as shown below:

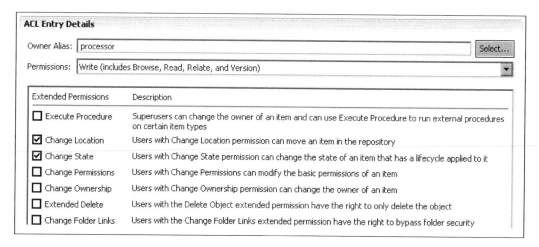

Using permission set templates

Unlike ACLs, a PST (dm_acl.acl_class=1) is not associated with an object directly. When a PST is assigned to an object, Content Server copies the PST into a custom ACL (dm_acl.acl_class=2 and named dm_45*) and replaces the alias references in accessor names with actual values in the custom ACL. The actual values are picked from one of the alias sets present in the repository using the process of alias resolution, which is discussed later in the chapter. This custom ACL is assigned to the object.

Even though the name of the custom ACL created from a PST starts with dm_45, it follows a different rule compared to the other custom ACLs. The name of such a custom ACL (with acl_class=2) does not contain the object ID of the ACL object. Rather it follows a naming pattern illustrated in the following figure:

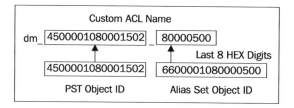

A custom ACL created from a PST is uniquely identified by the combination of the PST and the alias set used to resolve the aliases in the PST. This is also evident from the naming structure illustrated in the previous figure. Given the PST and the alias set, the permissions in the custom ACL can be completely determined.

It should also be obvious that the number of custom ACLs created from a PST cannot exceed the number of alias sets present in the repository. The following figure illustrates the relationship between a PST, alias sets, custom ACLs, and the objects to which the PST has been applied:

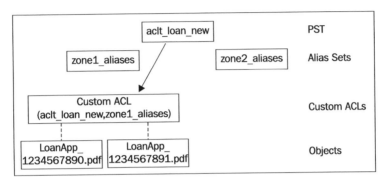

In our example, the PST can be applied automatically via lifecycle actions so that permissions get applied and changed appropriately as the loan application progresses through its lifecycle. The key consideration here is to provide the appropriate group name to replace the alias references when the PST is applied to a document. This design aspect deals with alias resolution, which is discussed shortly.

The objects secured using PSTs can be equivalently secured using normal ACLs. However, when similar permissions need to be granted across a well-defined organization with well-defined business roles for users, PSTs provide an advantage in terms of ease of administration of object security. The advantage is even better when there is a need for ongoing management of this security configuration across the organization because the permissions can be updated in one PST rather than in a number of ACLs (that the PST equivalently represents). The case for using PSTs becomes very strong when there is a need for implementing lifecycle-based security, where state changes also trigger permission changes.

Modifying permission set templates

When the permissions in an ACL are modified, they are immediately reflected on all objects that are secured by that ACL. Objects secured by a PST are not directly associated with it. Rather they are associated with a custom ACL that was created from the PST. What happens when permissions in a PST are modified?

Content Server keeps track of the relationship between a PST and each custom ACL created from it. As is evident from the naming pattern for them, such custom ACLs refer to the object ID of the PST and the object ID of the alias set used to resolve the alias references while creating the custom ACL. After the custom ACL has been created, any changes to the PST or the relevant alias set automatically update the custom ACL to reflect these changes.

Resolving aliases

Aliases provide placeholders for users, groups, locations, and ACLs. When a real value is substituted for a placeholder (alias reference), the alias is said to be **resolved**. Thus, **alias resolution** completes the missing information such that the objects and properties dependent on the aliases become usable.

Alias resolution looks up the appropriate value for an alias name from an alias set. If the alias set name is present in the reference, the lookup process is straightforward — pick up the value corresponding to the alias name from the specified alias set.

On the other hand, if the alias set name is omitted, Content Server tries to locate an appropriate alias set to look up the alias value. This lookup process utilizes a concept referred to as **alias scope**.

An alias scope specifies the alias sets that will be inspected for finding a value for the alias. If an alias set name is present in the alias reference, that alias set constitutes the scope. When the reference does not include an alias set name, a sequence of alias sets is searched. This sequence of alias sets (scopes) varies depending on the situation and the selection of these alias sets for resolution will be discussed shortly. The following figure shows how an alias is resolved after checking three alias sets in scope for the presence of an alias named `processor`.

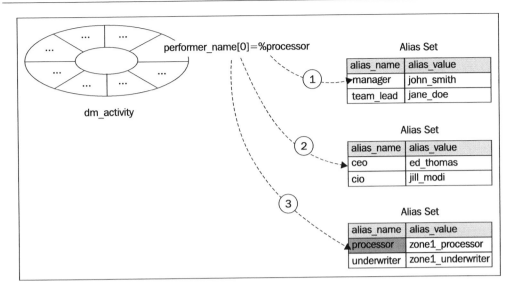

It is important to understand the alias resolution process because it provides key details for alias sets to be located when they are needed. An alias set is useless until it has been placed in an alias scope. An alias set can be attached to process definitions, users, groups, and server configuration objects, to name a few candidates for alias scopes. The alias resolution process can be used to identify suitable objects for attaching alias sets.

Content Server follows different approaches for alias resolution in the following situations:

- A workflow activity needs to be started and its performer refers to an alias
- A sysobject is saved and its `owner_name`, `acl_name`, or `acl_domain` refers to an alias
- The DFC link or unlink method is invoked and the `folderSpec` argument refers to an alias
- A PST is assigned to an object and one or more accessors refer to aliases

The alias resolution approaches for these situations are described in detail now.

Workfow alias resolution

A workflow activity (dm_activity) may contain an alias reference without an alias set name in the performer_name property. This alias is resolved when the activity is started in a workflow instance. The sequence of alias scopes searched for this purpose is dependent on the value of dm_activity.resolve_type, which can be one of the following:

Resolve type	Description
0	Default/normal sequence
1	Package sequence
2	User sequence

Default sequence

When dm_activity.resolve_type = 0 the following sequence of alias scopes is searched to resolve an alias reference in performer_name:

- The alias set specified on the workflow instance — dm_workflow.r_alias_set_id. The workflow instance gets a copy of the alias set specified in the corresponding process definition (dm_process. perf_alias_set_id).

- The alias set present in the session, that is, non-persistent session config object — alias_set.

- The alias set of the performer of the previous activity – dm_user.alias_ set_id.

- The alias set of the default group of the performer of the previous activity — dm_group.alias_set_id.

- The alias set of the server configuration — dm_server_config.alias_set_id.

Package sequence

When dm_activity.resolve_type = 1, the following sequence of alias scopes is searched to resolve an alias reference in performer_name. The alias sets of package components (dm_sysobject.r_alias_set_id) are examined in the order they are stored within the package. Packages are discussed in *Chapter 12, Workflows* .

If there are multiple packages, dm_activity.resolve_pkg_name is inspected. If this property has a name specified and a package with that name is present, the components of that package are searched. Otherwise, all packages are examined in the order of their storage with components within the packages being examined as described earlier.

User sequence

When `dm_activity.resolve_type = 2`, the following sequence of alias scopes is searched to resolve any alias reference in `performer_name`:

1. The alias set of the performer of the previous activity—`dm_user.alias_set_id`.

2. The alias set of the default group of the performer of the previous activity—`dm_group.alias_set_id`.

Resolution process

The resolution process for aliases in workflows consists of two key steps—the referenced alias is located using scopes as described earlier and then the resolved alias is validated to be of a suitable type.

The validation is carried out by matching `dm_activity.performer_type` against the `alias_category` for the alias on the selected alias set. The performer type can be any of the following:

*   Workflow supervisor (0)
*   Repository owner (1)
*   Last performer (2)
*   User (3)
*   All members in a group (4)
*   Any user in a group (5)
*   The member who has the least number of tasks (6)
*   Some members of a group, or some users in the repository (8)
*   Some members of a group, or some users in the repository *sequentially* (9)
*   A user from a work queue (10)

Valid alias categories to match the performer type are user (1), group (2), and user or group (3).

 Note that there is no valid performer type with value 7 in Documentum 6.5.

It is possible for the resolution process to be unsuccessful, that is, no suitable substitution is found for the alias reference. This can happen in three cases:

- The referenced alias name is not found in any of the scopes
- The alias name is found but there is no corresponding value
- The alias name is found but the alias type is not compatible with the performer type on the activity

When alias resolution fails for any reason, a warning is generated and the workflow supervisor is notified. The task corresponding to the activity is also assigned to the supervisor.

Sysobject alias resolution

When a sysobject is saved for the first time, its `owner_name`, `acl_name`, and `acl_domain` may contain alias references. In order to resolve these alias references the following sequence of scopes is examined:

- Alias set of the sysobject—`dm_sysobject.r_alias_set_id`
- Alias set present in the session—`alias_set`
- Alias set of the current user—`dm_user.alias_set_id`
- Alias set of the default group of the current user—`dm_group.alias_set_id`
- Alias set of the server configuration—`dm_server_config.alias_set_id`

 Alias resolution for the `folderSpec` argument of DFC `link` and `unlink` methods also examines the sequence listed above.

Alias resolution for a sysobject can fail if the alias is not found, if the alias is found without a value, or if the category of the found alias is incompatible with its reference.

Permission set template alias resolution

Recall that a PST is an ACL with alias references in accessor names. When a PST is assigned to an object, a copy of the PST is created and the alias references in the accessor names in the copy are replaced with actual values. Finally, this copy is assigned as a custom ACL to the object. The sequence of alias sets examined in the resolution process depends on whether a lifecycle has been applied to the object. These two cases are discussed below.

Object with lifecycle

When an object is associated with a lifecycle, its alias set has possibly been assigned by the lifecycle. Therefore, alias resolution only examines the alias set currently assigned to the object and identified by `dm_sysobject.r_alias_set_id`.

Object without lifecycle

When a PST is assigned to an object without a lifecycle, the following sequence of alias sets is examined:

1. Alias set present in the session — `alias_set`
2. Alias set of the current user — `dm_user.alias_set_id`
3. Alias set of the default group of the current user — `dm_group.alias_set_id`
4. Alias set of the server configuration — `dm_server_config.alias_set_id`

Alias resolution for PST can fail if the alias is not found, if the alias is found without a value, or if the category of the found alias is incompatible with its reference.

Lifecycle scope determination

Recall that a lifecycle can have multiple alias sets associated with it. When a lifecycle with multiple alias sets is applied to an object, it needs to be determined which *alias set* (alias scope) should be applied to the object. Note that this process is not resolving an alias, rather it is identifying an alias set to apply, which can later be used for alias resolution. As a result of the following process, `dm_sysobject.r_alias_set_id` will be set if an appropriate alias set is found:

- Check if `alias_set` in session config is present in `dm_policy.alias_set_ids` for the lifecycle. If found use this, otherwise continue.

- Check if `dm_user.alias_set_id` for the current user is present in `dm_policy.alias_set_ids` for the lifecycle. If found use this, otherwise continue.

- Check if `dm_group.alias_set_id` of the default group for the current user is present in `dm_policy.alias_set_ids` for the lifecycle. If found use this, otherwise continue.

- Check if `dm_server_config.alias_set_id` for the server configuration is present in `dm_policy.alias_set_ids` for the lifecycle. If found use this, otherwise continue.

- Use the alias set specified by `dm_policy.alias_set_ids[0]`, also known as the **default alias set** of the lifecycle. If there are no alias sets assigned to the lifecycle the sysobject's `r_alias_set_id` is not set.

Manual alias updates

The alias resolution discussion above pertained to automatic alias resolution. Workflows provide a flexible customization mechanism where users help resolve aliases. When a workflow is started it gets its alias set from the process definition. However, this alias set may have aliases listed without any values. The user initiating the workflow provides the missing values for the alias set. This alias set is used later when aliases need to be resolved for activities.

Documentum client applications prompt the user for missing alias values mentioned above when a workflow is started. The user-provided values are added to the alias set attached to the workflow object. If a custom client is providing this feature, it should mimic the above behavior to prevent activities from failing on alias resolution.

Managing alias sets

Alias sets are typically designed in Composer though they can also be managed in DA. In DA, alias sets can be created and modified under the **Administration | Alias Sets** node. The following screenshot shows an alias set in DA:

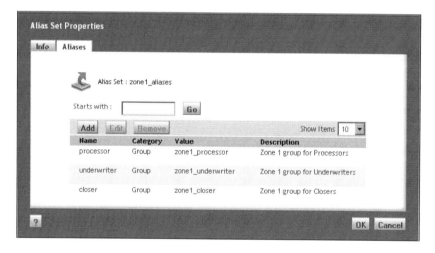

The Composer screen for defining an alias set consists of two sections—**General** and **Alias Details**. The **General** section shows information for the alias set as shown below:

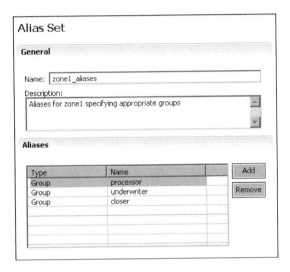

The screen above shows an alias set for zone1 in our example. It contains three aliases, each of type (category) group. Aliases can be added or removed by using the **Add** and **Remove** buttons. Selecting an alias displays the details for that alias in the **Alias Details** section as shown below:

The screen above shows details about the alias named `processor`. Note that the value for the alias can be left blank, specified explicitly, or deferred until project installation time when it can be populated using an installation parameter.

Attaching alias sets

Recall that an alias set provides values for aliases at resolution time and only the alias sets in the alias scope are inspected. Alias scopes are defined in terms of alias sets attached to various objects such as workflows, users, and groups. Thus, an alias set can be utilized only after being attached to another object. An alias set can be attached to one of the following:

Object Type	Attribute	Description
dm_server_config	alias_set_id	System-level (Content Server level) default alias set.
Session config (non-persistent)	alias_set	Session-level default alias set.
dm_user	alias_set_id	User-level default alias set.
dm_group	alias_set_id	Group-level default alias set.
dm_sysobject	r_alias_set_id	Alias set for a sysobject
dm_policy	alias_set_ids	Alias sets for a lifecycle.
dm_process	perf_alias_set_id	Alias set copied to workflows created from this process definition. Note that this alias set doesn't participate in alias resolution until it has been assigned to a workflow.
dm_workflow	r_alias_set_id	Object ID of the alias set used to resolve performer aliases when the workflow is created.

 An alias set not attached to any object can be included in an alias scope by explicitly including it in the alias reference such as %zone1_aliases.underwriter.

Summary

Aliases provide a customization feature that sounds simple—placeholders to be replaced with actual values at run time. However, the foregoing details of its implementation can appear intricate and confusing. It is worthwhile to take a step back and review how aliases are designed and used.

An alias set defines a list of alias name-value pairs, where values are optional. Multiple alias sets can be created in a repository and one alias name may appear in multiple alias sets. The alias sets are attached to various objects so that they can be found in the alias resolution process.

Content Server supports certain places (certain object attributes and method parameters) where placeholders can be used instead of literal values. A placeholder is specified as a reference to an alias using % as prefix. At design time, alias references can be inserted in supported places.

At run time, when an alias reference is encountered it needs to be resolved and replaced with a literal value. Depending on where the alias reference is found, Content Server searches a well-known sequence of objects for their attached alias sets. In each alias set found, it looks for the alias being referenced. This search may fail if the alias name is not found, if it is found without a value, or if it is found to be of an incompatible category. Otherwise, the resolved value is used to replace the alias reference.

Outside the process described above, custom code is needed to provide an alias resolution mechanism.

Help—some DQL queries

Some helpful queries related to alias sets are described here. These queries are based on the information provided in this chapter.

The following query retrieves aliases (names, values, and types) present in an alias set:

```
SELECT alias_name, alias_value, alias_category
FROM dm_alias_set
WHERE object_name = 'zone1_aliases'
```

The following query assigns an alias set (using its object ID) to a sysobject explicitly:

```
UPDATE dq_loan_app OBJECTS
SET r_alias_set_id = '6600001080000500'
WHERE object_name = 'LoanApp_1234567890.txt'
```

Note that r_alias_set_id can be modified like this even though its name starts with r_.

The following query retrieves the performer names for an activity:

```
SELECT performer_name
FROM dm_activity
WHERE object_name = 'Prep App File'
```

The following query retrieves the accessor names for PSTs:

```
SELECT r_object_id, object_name, r_accessor_name
FROM dm_acl
WHERE acl_class=1
```

Documentum product notes

PSTs can only be created in Composer.

In addition to the scenarios discussed in the chapter, alias sets can also be associated with objects of types dm_application and dm_audittrail_group. However, these associations do not participate in alias resolution directly.

dm_application.def_alias_set_id holds the reference for the default alias for a DocApp. Note that this is for backward compatibility with Documentum versions prior to 6.0. See appendix *DocApps* for details about DocApps.

dm_audittrail_group captures audit information for events related to groups. dm_audittrail_group.alias_set_id captures the alias set associated with the group being audited.

Learn more

The topics discussed in this chapter can be further explored using the following resources:

- EMC Documentum Content Server 6.5 Fundamentals
- EMC Documentum Content Server 6.5 Administration Guide
- EMC Documentum System 6.5 Object Reference Manual
- EMC Documentum Documentum Administrator 6.5 SP2 User Guide
- (White Paper) Designing a Documentum Access Control Model— https://community.emc.com
- Permission Set Templates—Friend or Foe? Part 1—http://johnnygee. wordpress.com/2006/09/12/permission-set-templates-friend-or-foe-part-1/
- Permission Set Templates—Friend or Foe? Part 2—http://johnnygee. wordpress.com/2006/09/14/permission-set-templates-friend-or-foe-part-2/

Checkpoint

At this point you should be able to answer the following key questions:

What are aliases and alias sets? What purpose do they serve?

1. How are alias references used and resolved in various scenarios?
2. What is alias scope? How does an alias set get included in an alias scope?
3. How are alias sets designed and managed?

15
Virtual Documents

In this chapter, we will explore the following concepts:

- Structure of virtual documents
- Assembling virtual documents
- Using virtual documents

Managing content hierarchically

Hierarchical content is fairly common in everyday life. A book is an excellent example of hierarchical content. Books are usually organized into chapters, chapters into sections, and sections into sub-sections, and there can be more layers in such a hierarchy. This hierarchical structure is shown in the following figure:

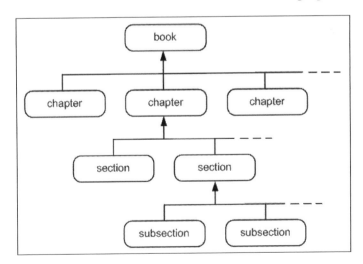

In addition to our example scenario of loan application processing, this chapter uses the example of a book for illustrating virtual document concepts, because it is a perfect example for that purpose.

Documentum enables hierarchical content management through **virtual documents**. Virtual documents allow parts of a document to be treated as independent documents. From another perspective, a set of independent documents can be combined and treated as one virtual document. In our example scenario, a loan application file can be represented by a virtual document that contains the loan application and its associated documents. The following figure shows a possible hierarchical structure for the application file:

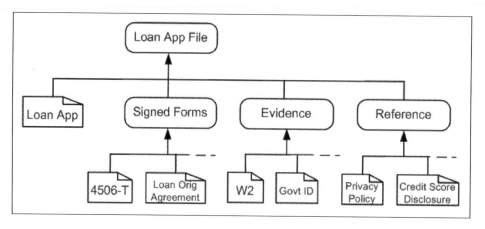

Note that the supporting documents for the application are further grouped under nodes named Signed Forms, Evidence, and Reference. Some supporting documents are shown under each node.

 We will refer to this *loan application file virtual document* as *loan file* for brevity.

Virtual documents offer various benefits. One document can be *reused* in multiple virtual documents. In the loan file example, Privacy Policy and other reference documents are not loan-specific and they could be reused across multiple loan files.

Collaboration is another great capability where multiple users can own various components of a virtual document. This capability enables each contributor to create and update the individually owned content while allowing a reviewer to look at the combined document as a whole. Suppose that a team working on creation of a book consists of two authors, two subject matter reviewers, and one editor. It is highly desirable for all these participants to be able to work on various portions (sometimes even the same portions) of the book in order to complete their tasks efficiently and effectively. In our loan processing example, a processor may update a supporting document under `Evidence` in the loan file that an underwriter is reviewing.

A virtual document *facilitates interaction* with its components in one place irrespective of the repository locations of these components. In the loan file example, the reference documents are likely to be present in some common folders separate from the loan account folder. Virtual documents also help in overcoming some technical challenges associated with electronic format. Usually a document (or its rendition) has one format—`doc` for MS Word, `pdf` for Adobe Acrobat, `ppt` for Microsoft PowerPoint, and so on. A virtual document allows documents in *multiple formats* to be combined into one virtual document. In the loan file example, scanned documents are expected to be images, standard documents in `pdf` format, while custom documents are likely to be in `doc` format.

Based on what we have discussed so far, it may appear that a well-designed folder structure should offer the same benefits as virtual documents for managing hierarchical content. However, virtual documents offer features such as *assembly* and *snapshot*, which are not available via folders. These features are discussed later in the chapter.

Webtop provides a special interface called **Virtual Document Manager** (VDM) for working with virtual documents. The usual document management functions in Webtop such as copy and delete are also aware of virtual documents. DFC provides programmatic support for working with virtual documents and DQL has keywords for working with virtual documents. This chapter discusses the rich features of virtual documents and the underlying details.

Virtual documents

A **virtual document** is a container for **component** documents, which are either simple non-folder sysobjects (objects of type dm_sysobject or a subtype excluding dm_folder and its subtypes) or virtual documents. The virtual document is also a non-folder sysobject. This definition is illustrated in the following figure:

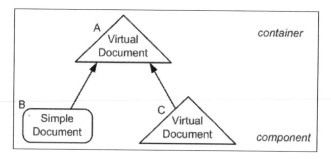

Note that it is a *recursive* definition—the definition of virtual document, in turn, uses the term virtual document. In computer science, recursive definitions facilitate description of tree-like structures. In a virtual document hierarchy, objects are generically referred to as **nodes** and the object corresponding to the virtual document in question as the **root node**. For an introduction to tree terminology, see *Chapter 2, Working with Content*.

In the preceding figure, component C is a virtual document so it can be a container for its own components. The containment relationship between a virtual document and its component virtual document is known as **nesting**. Repeated nesting gives rise to a tree structure, which was also seen in version trees and folder trees. Therefore, much of the tree terminology also applies to virtual documents.

Even though its primary purpose is to act as a container, a virtual document object can have content of its own because it is a non-folder sysobject.

Webtop supports virtual document operations through menu items, the browser-tree component, and the VDM interface. The menu options related to virtual documents can be accessed via **Tools | Virtual Documents,** as shown in the next screenshot. Note that the menu items are enabled based on the selection (selected objects in the list when the menu was displayed) and the actions allowed on the selection.

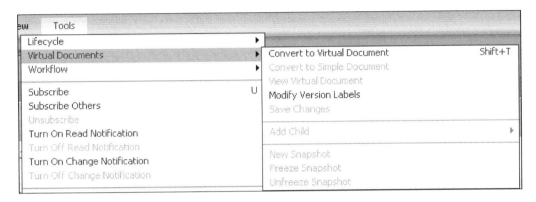

A virtual document is created by converting a simple document to a virtual document. This operation can be performed via Webtop using the **Convert to Virtual Document** action shown here or using the *Shift+T* shortcut. This operation sets the sysobject attribute `r_is_virtual_doc=1`.

For a loan file, we want the virtual document to be a just a container so we can create a contentless `dm_document` object named `File_1234567892` using **File | New Document** or *Shift+N*. When this document is converted to a virtual document it has no components but its icon changes to reflect that it is a virtual document. Further, the virtual document is also shown at the folder level in the browser tree within Webtop, as shown here:

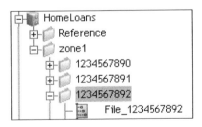

Selecting the virtual document in the browser tree, or double-clicking/viewing the object in the right pane opens it in VDM, as shown in the following screenshot:

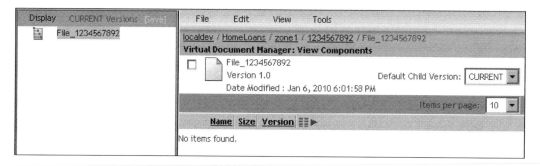

VDM shows the root node at the top on the left. Components are shown on the right for the selected node on left. Since there are no components for loan file at this time, no components are shown.

Parent-child relationship

A virtual document and its components have a *parent-child relationship*. One virtual document can have many components (children). At the same time, one document can be a component (child) of multiple virtual documents. The information about a document being a component (child) of a virtual document (parent) is stored in an object of type `dmr_containment`. The following figure shows the containment relationship after the loan application has been added as a component to the loan file virtual document we created earlier:

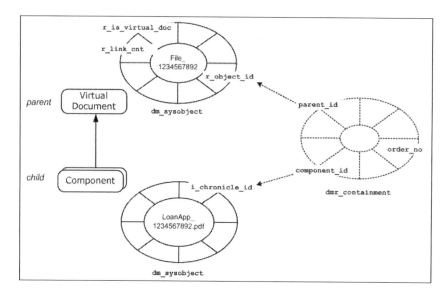

The parent-child relationship exists only in the `dmr_containment` objects. The virtual document and its component don't point to each other directly. The containment object points to the parent's `r_object_id` via its `parent_id` attribute. This means that a specific version of the parent is identified in this relationship. On the other hand, the containment object points to the child's `i_chronicle_id` via its `component_id` attribute. This means that any version in the version tree of the child object could participate in this relationship.

What happens if a virtual document is versioned? Since the existing containment objects (prior to versioning of the virtual document) for its children point to the object ID of the parent, they cannot point to the new version as well. One copy of each of the containment objects is created where the copy points to the new version as the parent. The `component_id` property continues to point to the same child chronicle ID as shown in the following figure:

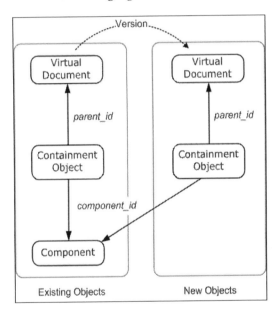

 DQL only supports querying of virtual documents. Virtual documents and containment objects can be created and modified using DFC.

Let's add the loan application as a component (child) to the loan file created earlier. A document existing in the repository can be added as a component to a virtual document. A file existing outside the repository needs to be imported into the repository before it can be added as a component. There are three ways for adding components to a virtual document:

- One or more existing documents can be added to *clipboard* and then added as components to a virtual document. Clipboard usage was discussed in *Chapter 2, Working with Content*.

- One or more existing documents can be added as components by using the file selector interface. The file-selector interface enables users to browse the repository and select multiple objects from different locations.

- A n*ew document* can be created and added as a component of a virtual document in one interaction. This option is particularly convenient for adding component nodes, which will also be virtual documents.

Components can be added in VDM using the **Tools | Virtual Documents | Add Child** submenu, which shows the three options described above.

Using the **File Selector** interface, the loan application can be added to the loan file as shown in the following screenshot. Note that the interface allows for browsing objects in the repository, filtering by initial letters in object name, and paginating when a large number of objects need to be displayed on the left. The selected objects are shown on the right.

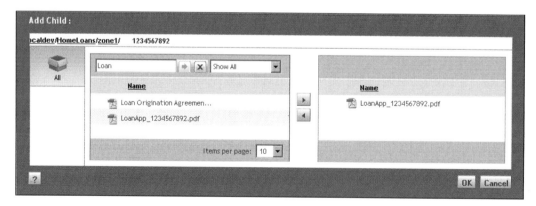

Clicking **OK** adds the selected documents as components and VDM appears as shown in the following screenshot:

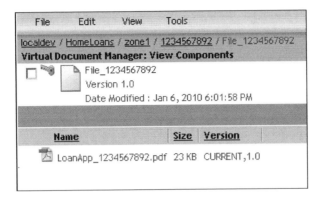

In VDM, when a virtual document structure is modified by adding or removing components the parent virtual document is checked out automatically. The parent virtual document needs to be checked in or saved as the same version to commit these changes. However, multiple changes could be performed on one virtual document before it is saved or checked in. The following figure shows the loan file structure after several nodes have been added to the virtual document:

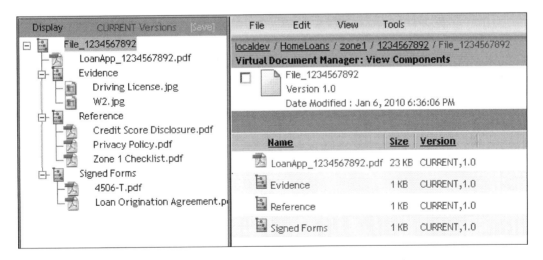

A virtual document records the number of its children in `dm_sysobject.r_link_cnt` attribute. This attribute is updated whenever children are added or removed from the virtual document.

A child of a virtual document can be selected and removed using **Tools | Virtual Documents | Remove Child** menu option. This operation only deletes the containment object (link to the parent object) and does not delete the component object. Any attempt to delete a component object is blocked by Content Server, by default. This ensures that containment objects don't point to missing objects. This behavior can be changed by setting `dm_server_config.compound_integrity` (which is TRUE by default) to FALSE. In this case, components of *unfrozen* virtual documents can be deleted. Freezing virtual documents overrides the `compound_integrity` setting and is discussed later in the chapter.

> Note that `dm_server_config.compound_integrity` controls the behavior of Content Server. Clients may still block attempts to delete components of a virtual document when Content Server may have allowed it.

Recognizing virtual documents

In Webtop, a virtual document is easily recognizable due to its distinctive icon. How can we tell a virtual document apart from other sysobjects in the repository when Webtop is not being used?

Recall that virtual documents are non-folder sysobjects. Documentum client applications treat a non-folder sysobject as a virtual document if *at least one* of the following conditions on sysobject attributes is true:

- `r_is_virtual_doc` = 1
- `r_link_cnt` > 0

We have already seen that `r_is_virtual_doc` is set to 1 when a document is converted to virtual document and that `r_link_cnt` holds the number of children of the virtual document. It is possible for `r_is_virtual_doc` to be reset to 0 but the object will be treated as a virtual document while `r_link_cnt` remains greater than 0.

In summary, a non-folder sysobject is not a virtual document if its `r_is_virtual_doc` = 0 AND `r_link_cnt` = 0. Otherwise, it is a virtual document.

Component ordering

Content Server uses `dmr_containment.order_no` (shown in the parent-child relationship figure earlier) to store a sequence number that orders the children of the virtual document. Since the children of each virtual document are ordered, a sequence can be obtained among all the nodes in a virtual document hierarchy.

The ordering may or may not be relevant from the business perspective but it is always available internally. For example, the ordering may not have an obvious relevance for the loan file but it is critical for the book example. The chapters and sections need to be in proper order. In fact, even underwriting organizations usually prescribe a document ordering for paper-based loan files.

Let's look at the node ordering for the book virtual document. The top level is just the book and the level below has chapters, which are ordered as 1, 2, 3, and so on. The level below chapters consists of sections, which may be ordered as 2.1, 2.2, 2.3, and so on for *Chapter 2* and similarly for others. There can also be subsections such as 2.2.1, 2.2.2, and so on. The natural ordering of all the components in this example is the order in which the headings for these components are expected to appear in the book. This ordering in the hierarchy is shown in the following diagram:

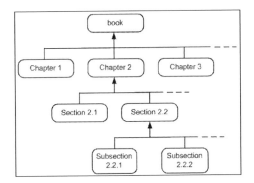

Children of a virtual document can be **reordered** in Webtop in two ways—using *drag-and-drop* or using the *reorder interface*. The drag-and-drop feature allows two options on dropping the dragged item, as shown in the following screenshot. The **Reposition** option moves a component to its new position. The **Add here** option creates a copy of the dragged component in the new position.

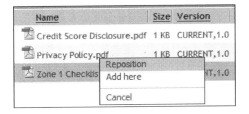

Selecting a virtual document and using **Tools | Virtual Documents | Reorder Children** provides an interface to move components up or down in the order shown here:

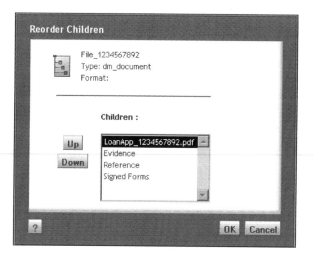

Using DFC, it is possible to programmatically bypass the automatic numbering provided by Content Server via a custom ordering scheme. However, once custom ordering has been used for a virtual document Content Server does not manage ordering for it anymore. Custom logic also needs to manage ordering for the virtual document operations that affect ordering.

Permissions for modifying virtual documents

The modified virtual document can be checked in as a new version using VERSION permission. However, WRITE permission is required for saving the changes as the current version. If folder security is enabled, WRITE permission is needed on the primary folder of the virtual document. Folder security is discussed in *Chapter 7, Object Security*.

Copying virtual documents

Virtual documents can be copied just like simple documents but what happens to its components? Copy behavior for a component of a virtual document is controlled by the copy_child property on the containment object corresponding to the component. This attribute can have the following values:

Value	Description
0	Behavior specified at copy time by the user or application requesting copy. The behavior can be specified as one of the following two options.
1	Create a pointer to the source component
2	Create a copy of the source component

In each of these options, a new containment object is created for each component in the new virtual document. The only difference is whether the new containment object points to the source component or its copy.

Deleting virtual documents

A virtual document object can be deleted just like simple objects. However, a virtual document has associated containment objects (and possibly assembly objects, as discussed later). What happens to these additional objects when the virtual object is deleted? When a virtual document is deleted the associated containment and assembly objects are also deleted.

Virtual documents and versions

Each component of a virtual document can be independently managed and versioned. While this feature provides flexibility, it also leads to some challenges regarding component versions and versions of the virtual document as a whole. These concerns are discussed in this section.

Assembling a virtual document

Recall that a containment object points to the object ID of the parent but to the *chronicle ID* of the child. This means that the parent object is a known version but the child is a version tree until it is restricted to a particular version. Multiple combinations are possible when trying to identify the exact objects that are part of the virtual document hierarchy. The process of selecting specific components from these combinations to produce a complete virtual document is called **assembling** the virtual document. *The essence of the assembly process is to select a version at each node in the virtual document hierarchy.*

A virtual document can be assembled on retrieval or for creating a persistent record of the exact virtual document structure at a particular time. A client may retrieve the virtual document for viewing or copying and each node in the hierarchy needs to resolve to a particular object (as opposed to a version tree). A persistent record of a virtual document is called a **snapshot**, which also records exactly one object at each node of the hierarchy.

When a client needs to assemble a virtual document it can issue a DQL query with the IN DOCUMENT clause. This clause can be used to assemble the virtual document or to identify the component object IDs in the virtual document. The query can include additional conditions and this kind of assembly is known as **conditional assembly**. For example, the following query assembles a virtual document with an additional condition on version label. DQL support for virtual documents is discussed later in the chapter:

```
SELECT r_object_id, object_name
FROM dm_sysobject
IN DOCUMENT ID('090000108001193a')
WITH ANY r_version_label = 'CURRENT'
```

Content Server uses an algorithm guided by the metadata on containment objects for assembling a virtual document. The algorithm for resolving a node to a specific component version is discussed below.

A specific version of an object is said to be **bound** to a virtual document if that version is selected in the virtual document assembly. A **binding rule** for a node specifies how to select a component version when resolving that node during virtual document assembly. A node in the virtual document is **early-bound** or **late-bound** depending upon the value of version_label in its containment object, as explained in the following table:

Value	Description
Some label	Early-bound to the specified label. This label will be used during assembly.
Empty	Late-bound. Version selected during assembly based on an explicitly specified version or the preferred version for the virtual document.

In VDM, a child can be selected and the menu option **Tools | Virtual Documents | Fix to Version** can be used to specify a binding rule for a component, as shown in the following screenshot:

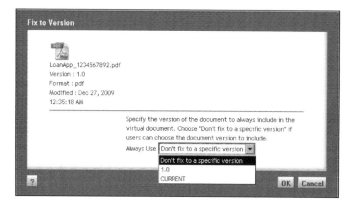

The binding rule can be set to one of the following:

- Use the CURRENT version of the component document.

- Use a specific version number of the component document.

- Use a specific version label of the component document.

- Do not fix a specific version and allow the component version to be determined at assembly time. This option is typically useful for applications that can take user input or preferences into account to make this decision. This option makes the node late-bound.

During virtual document assembly, early-bound nodes are already resolved but the late-bound ones need to be resolved to specific versions. This process is affected by some additional parameters, including standard binding rule, dmr_containment. use_node_vers_label, and includeBrokenBindings.

At the virtual document level, a **standard binding rule** (default version label) can be specified for its components. This setting uses CURRENT by default, and applies to all components that don't have a more specific binding rule specified (are not fixed to a specific version). Thus, this value becomes the preferred version label for the late-bound components whose binding cannot be resolved by other means. The standard binding rule is displayed as **Default Child Version** in VDM. The default version label is stored in dm_sysobject.resolution_label.

If a node in the virtual document hierarchy is early-bound (dmr_containment. version_label is not empty) and is a virtual document, it can affect the binding resolution for its late-bound descendants. When the containment object for this node has use_node_vers_label=TRUE, its version_label is used to select late-bound descendants of the node during assembly. Since multiple such nodes may be present in the virtual document we need a rule to pick one such document when we need it. When a late-bound node has multiple such ancestor nodes, its closest such ancestor is picked. This rule will become clearer in the resolution algorithm, which will be summarized shortly.

After processing the late binding rules for a component, a binding version label will be resolved for it. At this time, the component version with this version label needs to be included in the assembly. What happens if there is no version of the component with this version label? When no version for the node can be found with the resolved late-binding version label it is referred to as a **broken binding**. The assembly behavior for broken bindings is controlled by the run-time argument includeBrokenBindings. If this parameter is set to TRUE, the CURRENT version is used. Otherwise, a broken binding results in an error.

In summary, the following logic is used for resolving a node A to a particular version:

1. If the containment object for node A has `version_label` set (early-bound), use this version label and exit.

2. Scan nodes on the ancestor path from A up to the root node.

   a. If a node with `use_node_vers_label=TRUE` and non-empty `version_label` on containment object found, stop at first such node, say X.

      i. Resolve A to this version label

   b. Otherwise, resolve to the default version label from the standard binding rule.

3. If the resolved version label exists in the component version tree at node A, use this version and exit.

4. If `includeBrokenBindings=TRUE`, use CURRENT version and exit.

5. Raise error for broken binding.

Snapshots

A virtual document is usually an evolving document while its components are being versioned. For example, consider a book being managed as a virtual document for which no specific binding rules have been set. This means that the virtual document always considers the current versions of descendants to be participating in the hierarchy. If a chapter document is versioned, the new current version of the chapter becomes a part of the book. Each time this virtual document is assembled it will include the current versions of the chapters.

An assembled virtual document can be saved as a **snapshot**, which captures the included component versions at that point in time. VDM in Webtop can also be used for working with snapshots, as shown in the following figure:

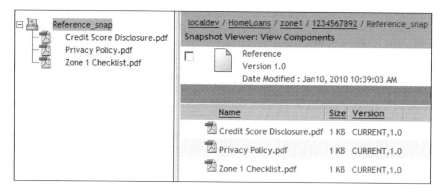

At most one snapshot can be assigned to each version of a virtual document. If additional snapshots are needed they can be associated with copies of that virtual document made specifically for this purpose.

In the book example, a snapshot may reflect an edition of the book. When the first edition of the book is published, a snapshot may be created for it. The authors may continue to work towards the second edition but the exact contents of the first edition may be retrieved using the snapshot.

A snapshot is a persistent record of a virtual document assembly and it identifies the exact object version representing each node in the virtual document. Snapshots use assembly objects (type `dm_assembly`) in a manner analogous to the containment objects in a virtual document. The key difference is that an assembly object connects a *specific version of the child* to a specific version of the parent document. The following figure illustrates the use of a `dm_assembly` object in a snapshot. Note that only one version of the child is shown and that `dm_assembly.component_id` points to `r_object_id` of the child.

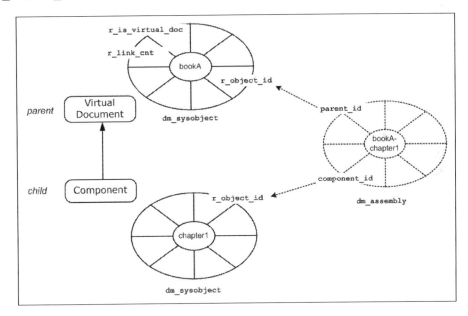

There are some additional relevant details that are stored in a snapshot as illustrated in the following figure. The hierarchy in the middle shows a virtual document named book. Note the version trees at various nodes shown as stacked boxes. Creating a snapshot for this virtual document results in new objects, which are shown in addition to the virtual document but with varying detail. The dotted shapes represent dm_assembly objects and the rest represent non-folder sysobjects.

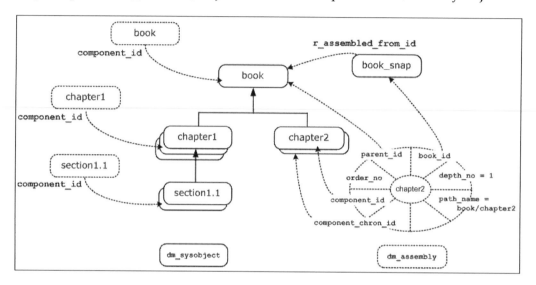

Suppose that a snapshot named book_snap was created from the virtual document named book. Later, Chapter1 and Section1.1 were versioned. The snapshot is represented by a dm_document (or another non-folder sysobject type) object named book_snap and each of the components is represented by a dm_assembly object in the snapshot. All the dm_assembly objects in this snapshot point to book_snap.r_object_id via their book_id attribute. The snapshot object book_snap points to the virtual document it was created from via dm_sysobject.r_assembled_from_id.

The dm_assembly object corresponding to Chapter2 illustrates some key attributes. We have already discussed the usage of parent_id and component_id. The chronicle ID of the component is stored in component_chron_id. The level in the virtual document is represented by depth_no, where the depth of the root document is 0. The path down to the component, starting from the root document, is stored in path_name. The path consists of object names delimited by forward slashes, as shown in the figure. If the path is too long for the attribute's length, the path is truncated at the right end. There is also an order_no attribute, which represents the order among all the nodes in this hierarchy.

Follow assembly

The earlier discussion about resolving nodes during virtual document assembly omitted one detail since it preceded the discussion of snapshots.

Consider the loan file example again and look at the supporting documents under the Reference node. These are documents such as privacy policy that don't change frequently. Whenever a loan file is assembled Content Server resolves all the nodes in it even though the tree below Reference is known not to change. In this case, we can create a snapshot of Reference (which includes all the nodes under it) and tell Content Server to use the saved snapshot (recall that at most one snapshot can be assigned to a virtual document version) rather than resolving the sub-tree rooted at Reference each time. This can be achieved by setting dmr_containment.follow_assembly to TRUE on the containment object corresponding to Reference. The follow_assembly setting will have no effect if no snapshot is found for Reference.

Freezing snapshots

It is obvious that virtual documents can be modified in various ways. What may not be obvious is that a snapshot does not have fixed structure or contents. For example, consider the state illustrated by the figure showing the snapshot named book_snap. Now Chapter2 is modified and saved as the same version. In this case, the contents retrieved using the snapshot will be different from the contents at the time the snapshot was created. Similarly, the structure of a snapshot may be modified by deleting an assembly object that is part of the snapshot, for example.

A snapshot can be **frozen**, which prevents components from being added, removed, or modified. Freezing a snapshot sets r_immutable_flag on the snapshot to TRUE and increments r_frzn_assembly_cnt on each component in the snapshot. The r_frzn_assembly_cnt represents the number of frozen snapshots containing this component.

Recall that the compound_integrity setting controls deletion of objects that belong to a virtual document hierarchy. However, freezing a snapshot overrides the compound_integrity setting. This means that the constraints imposed by freezing apply irrespective of the compound_integrity setting.

Finally, frozen virtual documents and snapshots can also be **unfrozen,** which reverses the effects of freezing.

Snapshot operations and permissions

Creating a snapshot, modifying it, or destroying it requires VERSION or higher permission on the virtual document from which it was created.

An assembly object may be deleted from a snapshot with VERSION or higher permission on the snapshot (referenced by dm_assembly.book_id). It does not remove the corresponding component from the virtual document.

Help—some DQL queries

DQL provides the keyword IN DOCUMENT for checking direct membership of a component in a virtual document. Suppose that the virtual document in the book example has the object ID 090000108001193a. The following query retrieves information about all the chapters and the virtual document itself:

```
SELECT r_object_id, object_name
FROM dm_sysobject
IN DOCUMENT ID('090000108001193a')
WITH ANY r_version_label = 'CURRENT'
```

If all the descendants in the hierarchy are desired, the keyword DESCEND can be used after ID(). Similarly, the IN ASSMEBLY keyword can be used to examine the snapshot for the virtual document rather than the virtual document itself.

Further, suppose that books are being represented as a custom type book_doc and stored somewhere in the folder tree under a cabinet named books. The following query retrieves the names of all such books:

```
SELECT object_name
FROM book_doc
WHERE r_is_virtual_doc = 1 or r_link_cnt > 0
AND FOLDER('/books', DESCEND)
```

DQL supports some additional keywords related to virtual documents. The CONTAIN_ID keyword returns the object IDs of the containment objects corresponding to the components of a virtual document. The following query illustrates the use of this keyword:

```
SELECT r_object_id, object_name, CONTAIN_ID
FROM dm_sysobject
IN DOCUMENT ID('090000108001193a')
```

The DEPTH keyword returns a component's level within a virtual document when IN DOCUMENT and DESCEND are used in a SELECT query. The following query illustrates the use of this keyword.

```
SELECT r_object_id, object_name, DEPTH
FROM dm_sysobject
IN DOCUMENT ID('090000108001193a') DESCEND
```

The PARENT keyword returns the object ID of the object that directly contains a component in a virtual document hierarchy. The following query illustrates the use of this keyword:

```
SELECT r_object_id, object_name, PARENT
FROM dm_sysobject
IN DOCUMENT ID('090000108001193a') DESCEND
```

Documentum product notes

If a virtual document is subject to a retention policy, its components cannot be added, removed, or rearranged. The effect of retention policies on object immutability was discussed in *Chapter 3, Objects and Types*.

Webtop supports virtual document preferences for users, as shown in the following screenshot:

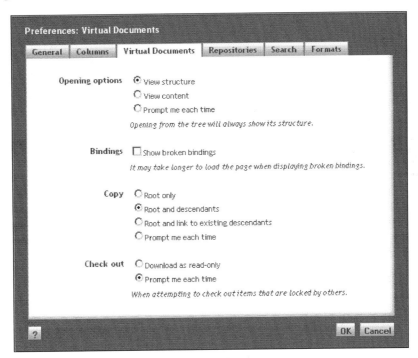

These preferences specify the default behavior on opening, copying, or checking out a virtual document. Opening a document can mean opening the structure of the document or opening the content of the root virtual document object, if it does have any content. A user may choose one of these alternatives or to be prompted when opening a virtual document.

Similarly, copying a virtual document may mean any of the following:

- Only the root document is to be copied
- The root document is to be copied along with the links to the existing components
- All the descendants are also to be copied

The user may choose one of these alternatives or to be prompted when copying a virtual document.

If the user attempts to check out an item as a part of the virtual document and it is locked by another user, the only options for the user are to cancel the operation or to obtain a read-only copy. The user may specify a preference to get a read-only copy or to be prompted each time.

The user may also specify a preference to show **broken bindings**, which shows the descendants linked from the virtual document hierarchy that are no longer present in the repository.

XML content is hierarchical by nature and Documentum provides rich XML management capabilities via **XML applications**, which make extensive use of virtual documents. The capabilities of XML applications include:

- Chunking out content and granting different permissions to different groups for accessing content chunks
- Reusing content chunks in multiple documents and publishing them to multiple locations
- Using XML chunks as wrappers for non-XML documents
- Constructing Web pages dynamically with XML content chunks

XML applications can automatically recognize various types of XML documents and rules can be set up for concerns such as storage locations, the need to create chunks, extraction and assignment of metadata, security configuration, and so on. On import or checkin, the XML content is automatically processed according to these rules, facilitating efficiency and robustness in XML content management.

XML management was discussed in other chapters including *Chapter 4, Architecture* and *Chapter 10, Documentum Projects*.

Learn more

The topics discussed in this chapter can be further explored using the following resources:

- EMC Documentum Content Server 6.5 Fundamentals
- EMC Documentum Content Server 6.5 Administration Guide
- EMC Documentum System 6.5 Object Reference Manual
- EMC Documentum Documentum Administrator 6.5 SP2 DQL Reference Manual

Checkpoint

At this point you should be able to answer the following key questions:

1. What are virtual documents? What purpose do they serve?
2. How are virtual documents created and managed? What are containment objects?
3. How are virtual documents assembled? What are assembly objects?
4. What are snapshots? What effect does freezing a snapshot have?

Index

Symbols

$value 265

A

Access Control Lists. *See* **ACLs**
accessor
  about 166
  categories 167
ACLs
  about 167
  and folders 179-181
  assigning 176
  assignments 176
  categories 178
  creating 175
  custom ACLs 175
  default ACL 176
  external ACLs 175
  individual permissions 177
  internal ACLs 175
  key attributes 173
  managing 172
  public category 179
  special groups 170
  special users 168
  system ACLs 175
  template ACL 178
  user ACLs, private 175
  user ACLs, public 175
acl_class attribute 173
ACLs 25
ActiveX Data Objects. *See* **ADO.NET**
activity
  about 288

activity definition 288, 296
  automatic activity 289
  configuring, in Work Manager 289, 290
  connecting, in parallel 288
  connecting, in serial 288
  definition tab 294
  example 288
  manual activity 289
  performer 290
  priority 294
  transitions 294
ad hoc relation types 234
ADO.NET 111
ADTS
  product notes 62
Advanced DTS. *See* **ADTS**
advanced search
  about 193
  specific search criteria, enabling 193, 194
AIS 116
alias_category property 335
aliases
  about 178, 334
  alias sets 335
  category 334
  permission set template 340, 346
  PST 340, 341
  references 336, 337
  resolution 343
  resolving 342
  using 340, 341
alias_name property 335
alias_set_id property 153
alias sets
  about 335
  attaching 350

B

BAM 109
binding rule 366
BOF
  about 119
  Service-based Business Object 119
  Type-based Business Object 119
branch 50, 54
broken binding 367
browser tree, Webtop GUI
  nodes 30
  use 29
Business Activity Monitor. *See* **BAM**
Business Object Framework. *See* **BOF**
business process
  about 279
  activity 288
  analysis 285
  automating, Documentum used 280-285
  content management 309
  customizing, workflow used 284
  defining, in repository 283
  definition 286
  example 279, 280
  modeling 286

C

CAS
  about 21, 102
  EMC Centera 102
CDS
  IDS 109
  IDSx 109
check constraint 255
checkpoint 122
checkpoint interval 122
child node 49
CIS 30, 109
class loading 229
client infrastructure, experience layer
  application connectors, SDK 111
  portlets 111
  UCF 110
  WDK 110
clipboard 41

CMIS 112
  about 112
  URL 130
CMS 20
comma-separated Values. *See* **CSV**
communication pattern
  Connection Broker 121
  DFS 125, 126
  DocBroker 121
  key components 120, 121
  Primary Interop Assembly 121
  projection 122, 123
  WDK application pattern 127
component_id attribute 359
component_id property 359
compound_integrity setting 371
conditional assembly 366
constraints
  check 272
  foreign key 272
  primary key 272
  unique key 272
content
  branching 54, 56
  cancel checkout action 45
  checking in 46-48
  checking in, options 48
  checking out 43-45
  concurrency control 43
  content file 20
  deep export functionality 43
  Documentum product notes 62
  exporting 42, 43
  formats 59
  importing 39, 40
  interacting with 38
  locking 43
  lock owner 43
  renditions 60
  version tree 51
  working with 37
Content-Addressed Storage. *See* **CAS**
content application 101
Content Delivery Services. *See* **CDS**
content files, locating
  about 81, 82
  content object 80

T

Task Manager
 performer, specifying 302
 task 300
 task, comment adding 301
 task, progress tab 302
tasks 282
TBO 230
TCM
 about 84, 114
 business process management 114, 115
 capture, capabilities 114
TCS 26, 105
tools layer
 about 118
 administration features 120
 configuration features 120
 Design/Development components 118
 purpose 101
transactional content 84
Transactional Content Management. *See*
  TCM
tree
 about 49
 branch 50
 child node 49
 descendant 50
 edges 49
 leaf nodes 50
 link 49
 parent node 49
 path 50
 root 50
 subtree 50
 trunk 50
trunk 50
Trusted Content Services. *See* **TCS**
type
 managing, DQL used 272
 object type, queries 275, 276
type-based objects. *See* **TBO**
type hierarchy, custom type
 dm_document 251
 dq_document 251
 dq_loan_app 252
 dq_loan_doc 252

 dq_loan_evidence 252
type managing, DQL used
 ALTER TYPE 273
 ALTER TYPE, superusers modification 273
 CREATE TYPE 272
 DROP TYPE 274
type UI information
 Application Interface Display section 266
 Display Configuration section 266

U

UCF 110
UDDI 126
Unified Client Facilities. *See* **UCF**
Uniform Resource Locator. *See* **URL**
Uniform Resource Name. *See* **URN**
Universal Description Discovery and
  Integration. *See* **UDDI**
URL 201
URN 242
user management
 about 142, 143
 DA, using 144
 users, creating 144
user management, DA used
 existing users, managing 145
 features 144
 users, creating 146
users
 about 135
 authentication 136
 DQL queries 146, 147
 global users 148
 installation owner, special users 138
 local users 148
 repository owner, special users 139
 special users 138, 168
 superusers 170
 user management 142
users_names property 153

V

value assistance
 about 262
 conditional list 264
 default list 264

Thank you for buying
Documentum 6.5 Content Management Foundations

About Packt Publishing

Packt, pronounced 'packed', published its first book "Mastering phpMyAdmin for Effective MySQL Management" in April 2004 and subsequently continued to specialize in publishing highly focused books on specific technologies and solutions.

Our books and publications share the experiences of your fellow IT professionals in adapting and customizing today's systems, applications, and frameworks. Our solution based books give you the knowledge and power to customize the software and technologies you're using to get the job done. Packt books are more specific and less general than the IT books you have seen in the past. Our unique business model allows us to bring you more focused information, giving you more of what you need to know, and less of what you don't.

Packt is a modern, yet unique publishing company, which focuses on producing quality, cutting-edge books for communities of developers, administrators, and newbies alike. For more information, please visit our website: www.packtpub.com.

About Packt Enterprise

In 2010, Packt launched two new brands, Packt Enterprise and Packt Open Source, in order to continue its focus on specialization. This book is part of the Packt Enterprise brand, home to books published on enterprise software – software created by major vendors, including (but not limited to) IBM, Microsoft and Oracle, often for use in other corporations. Its titles will offer information relevant to a range of users of this software, including administrators, developers, architects, and end users.

Writing for Packt

We welcome all inquiries from people who are interested in authoring. Book proposals should be sent to author@packtpub.com. If your book idea is still at an early stage and you would like to discuss it first before writing a formal book proposal, contact us; one of our commissioning editors will get in touch with you.

We're not just looking for published authors; if you have strong technical skills but no writing experience, our experienced editors can help you develop a writing career, or simply get some additional reward for your expertise.

Web Content Management with Documentum

ISBN: 978-1-904811-09-1   Paperback: 484 pages

Setup, Design, Develop, and Deploy Documentum Applications

1. Design and implement Documentum applications

2. Practical examples to help you get the most from Documentum

3. Tips and tricks to ease everyday working with the system

Alfresco 3 Enterprise Content Management Implementation

ISBN: 978-1-847197-36-8   Paperback: 600 pages

How to customize, use, and administer this powerful, Open Source Java-based Enterprise CMS

1. Manage your business documents with version control, library services, content organization, and advanced search

2. Create collaborative web sites using document libraries, wikis, blogs, forums, calendars, discussions, and social tagging

3. Integrate with external applications such as Liferay Portal, Adobe Flex, iPhone, iGoogle, and Facebook

4. Automate your business process with the advanced workflow concepts of Alfresco 3

5. Fully revised and updated for version 3.0, covering Alfresco Surf and more

Please check **www.PacktPub.com** for information on our titles

TYPO3 Extension Development

ISBN: 978-1-847192-12-7   Paperback: 232 pages

Developer's guide to creating feature rich extensions using the TYPO3 API

1. Covers the complete extension development process from planning and extension generation through development to writing documentation

2. Includes both front-end and back-end development

3. Describes TYPO3 areas not covered in the official documentation (such as using AJAX and eID)

4. Hands on style, lots of examples, and detailed walkthroughs

5. Written by Dmitry Dulepov, TYPO3 core developer and developer of TYPO3 extensions such as RealURL and TemplaVoila

TYPO3: Enterprise Content Management

ISBN: 978-1-904811-41-1   Paperback: 624 pages

The Official TYPO3 Book, written and endorsed by the core TYPO3 Team

1. Easy-to-use introduction to TYPO3

2. Design and build content rich extranets and intranets

3. Learn how to manage content and administrate and extend TYPO3

Please check **www.PacktPub.com** for information on our titles

5803269R0

Made in the USA
Lexington, KY
15 June 2010